D1128469

WILMETTE PUBLIC LIBRARY
1242 WILMETTE AVENUE
WILMETTE, IL 60091
847-256-5025

THE FALL OF
CONSTANTINOPLE

The Ottoman Conquest of Byzantium

OSPREY
PUBLISHING

WILMETTE PUBLIC LIBRARY

WITHDRAWN
Wilmette Public Library

THE FALL OF
CONSTANTINOPLE

The Ottoman Conquest of Byzantium

D. NICOLLE • J. HALDON • S. TURNBULL

First published in Great Britain in 2007 by Osprey Publishing,
Midland House, West Way, Botley, Oxford OX2 0PH, United Kingdom.
443 Park Avenue South, New York, NY 10016, USA.
Email: info@ospreypublishing.com

Previously published as John Haldon, Essential Histories 33: *Byzantium at War: AD 600–1453*,
Stephen Turnbull, Fortress 25: *The Walls of Constantinople AD 324–1453*,
David Nicolle, Campaign 78: *Constantinople 1453: The end of Byzantium.*

© 2007 Osprey Publishing Ltd

All rights reserved. Apart from any fair dealing for the purpose of private study, research, criticism or review, as
permitted under the Copyright, Designs and Patents Act, 1988, no part of this publication may be reproduced,
stored in a retrieval system, or transmitted in any form or by any means, electronic, electrical, chemical, mechanical,
optical, photocopying, recording or otherwise, without the prior written permission of the copyright owner.
Enquiries should be addressed to the Publishers.

Every attempt has been made by the publisher to secure the appropriate permissions for materials reproduced in
this book. If there has been any oversight we will be happy to rectify the situation and written submission should
be made to the Publishers.

A CIP catalogue record for this book is available from the British Library

ISBN 978 1 84603 200 4

Stephen Turnbull has asserted his right under the Copyright, Designs and Patents Act, 1988,
to be identified as the author of *The Walls of Constantinople AD 324–1453.*

Page layout by Ken Vail Graphic Design, Cambridge, UK
Index by Margaret Vaudrey
Typeset in ITC Stone Serif, Centaur MT, Monotype Gill Sans and Truesdell
Maps by The Map Studio Ltd
Originated by United Graphics Pte Ltd, Singapore
Printed and bound in China through Bookbuilders

07 08 09 10 11   10 9 8 7 6 5 4 3 2 1

For a catalogue of all books published by Osprey please contact:

NORTH AMERICA
Osprey Direct c/o Random House Distribution Center
400 Hahn Road, Westminster, MD 21157, USA
E-mail: info@ospreydirect.com

ALL OTHER REGIONS
Osprey Direct UK, P.O. Box 140, Wellingborough, Northants, NN8 2FA, UK
E-mail: info@ospreydirect.co.uk

www.ospreypublishing.com

Front cover: Conquest of Constantinople by Panagiotis. (akg-images)
Spine: *Solidus* of Constantine VII. (Werner Forman Archive/Barber Institute of Fine Arts, University of Birmingham)
Back cover: The death of Emperor Constantine XI. (Christa Hook © Osprey Publishing Ltd)
Title page: The painted front of the Trebizond Cassone, made in 15th-century Florence, includes a stylized
representation of Constantinople with a number of ships in the Golden Horn. (Metropolitan Museum, New York)
Endpapers: *The History of John Scylitzes*, folio 234v. (Werner Forman Archive/ Biblioteca Nacional, Madrid)

949.61
HA

Contents

CHRONOLOGY

655	Sea battle of Phoenix, Byzantines defeated by Muslim fleet	792	Byzantines under Constantine VI defeated by Bulgars at Markellai
662	Constans II leads expedition through Balkans into Italy, takes up residence in Sicily	797	Constantine VI deposed by mother Eirene; blinded and dies
668	Constans assassinated; Mizizios proclaimed emperor in Sicily, but defeated by forces loyal to Constantine IV	800	Coronation of Charlemagne by Pope in St Peters, Rome
		802	Eirene deposed by chief finance minister Nikephoros (Nikephoros I)
674–678	Arab blockade and yearly sieges of Constantinople. First recorded use of Greek fire, to destroy Arab fleet	811	Nikephoros defeated and killed by forces under Khan Krum after initially successful campaign in Bulgaria
679–680	Arrival of Bulgars on Danube; defeat of Byzantine forces under Constantine IV	813	Bulgar victories over Byzantine forces
680–681	Third council of Constantinople (sixth ecumenical council)	815	Leo V convenes synod at Constantinople; iconoclasm reintroduced as official policy
685–692	Truce between caliphate and Byzantium (Arab civil war)	821–823	Rebellion of Thomas 'the Slav'
691–692	Quinisext or Trullan council at Constantinople	824	Beginning of Arab conquest of Sicily and of Crete
693	Byzantine defeat at Sebastoupolis	838	Arab invasion of Asia Minor; siege and sack of Amorion
698	Carthage falls to Arabs; final loss of Africa	843	Council held in Constantinople to reaffirm acts of seventh ecumenical council; empress regent Theodora and chief courtiers restore images; end of official iconoclasm
717–718	Siege of Constantinople; Leo, general of Anatolikon, seizes power and crowned as Leo III		
726–730	Leo III condones iconoclastic views of some bishops. Beginnings of iconoclast controversy	850s	Missionary activity in Bulgaria
		860	Rus' (Viking) attack on Constantinople; mission to Chazars of St Cyril
739–740	Leo III and Constantine V defeat Arab column at Akroinon	863	Major Byzantine victory over Arabs at Poson in Anatolia
739	Earthquake hits Constantinople	864	Conversion of Bulgar Khan and leaders. Council convoked by Basil I at Constantinople to settle Photian schism: Photios deposed, Ignatios, his predecessor, reinstated. Bulgaria placed under Constantinopolitan ecclesiastical jurisdiction
741	Artabasdos, Leo's son-in-law, rebels against Constantine V and seizes Constantinople		
743–744	Artabasdos defeated		
746	Plague begins in Constantinople		
750	Abbasid revolution, removal of Umayyads from power, capital of Caliphate moved to Baghdad	900	Final loss of Sicily; Start of Bulgar expansionism under Tsar Symeon; war with Byzantines
750s–770s	Constantine V launches major expeditions against Bulgars and Arabs	917	Bulgar victory at river Achelo

922	Peace with Bulgars
923–944	Byzantine conquests and eastward expansion led by general John Kourkouas
960–961	Recovery of Crete under general Nikephoros Phokas
c.963	Major Byzantine offensives in east followed by the creation of new frontier regions
965	Nikephoros II captures Tarsus and Cyprus
969	Nikephoros II captures Aleppo and Antioch
969–976	Reign of John I Tzimiskes. Continuation of eastern expansion; defeat of Bulgars with help of Rus' allies under Svyatoslav; defeat of Rus' at Silistra in 971
975	John I invades Palestine, takes several towns and fortresses, but withdraws
985	Beginning of Bulgar resistance in western Balkans which leads to growth of Bulgarian empire under Tsar Samuel
989	Conversion of Vladimir of Kiev to Christianity
990–1019	Basil II crushes Bulgar resistance; Bulgaria reincorporated into empire, Danube new frontier in north
1022	Armenian territories annexed to empire
1034–1041	Michael IV takes first steps in debasement of gold currency
1047	Siege of Constantinople by Leo Tornices
1054	The schism between the papacy and Byzantium
1055	Seljuks take Baghdad; Norman power in southern Italy expanding
1071	Romanos IV defeated and captured at Mantzikert by Seljuks; beginning of Turk occupation of central Anatolia; Normans take Bari
1070+	Major Petcheneg advances into Balkans; civil war within empire
1081	Alexios Komnenos rebels and defeats Nikephoros III and is crowned emperor
1082–1084	Norman invasion of western Balkan provinces
1091	Seljuk-Petcheneg siege of Constantinople; defeat of Petchenegs
1097–99	First Crusade; Jerusalem captured; Latin principalities and Kingdom of Jerusalem established in Palestine and Syria
1108	Alexios defeats Normans under Bohemund
1111	Commercial privileges granted to Pisa
1130s	Alliance with German empire against Normans of southern Italy
1138–1142	Byzantine confrontation with Crusader principality of Antioch
1143–1180	Manuel I Komnenos: pro-western politics become major factor in Byzantine foreign policy
1146–1148	Second Crusade
1153	Treaty of Constanz between Frederick I (Barbarossa) and papacy against Byzantium
1155–1157	Successful imperial campaign in Italy; commercial and political negotiations with Genoa
1158–1159	Imperial forces march against Antioch
1160–c.1168	Successful imperial political involvement in Italy against German imperial interests; Manuel defeats Hungarians and Serbs in Balkans and reaffirms imperial pre-eminence
1169–1170	Commercial treaties with Pisa and Genoa
1171	Byzantine–Venetian hostilities begin to increase
1175–1176	Manuel plans crusade in east
1176	Defeat of imperial forces under Manuel by Seljuk Sultan Kilidj Aslan at Myriokephalon
1180	Manuel dies; strong anti-western sentiments in Constantinople
1182	Massacre of westerners, especially Italian merchants and their dependents, in Constantinople

1185	Normans sack Thessaloniki; Andronikos Komnenos deposed
1186+	Rebellion in Bulgaria, defeat of local Byzantine troops, establishment of second Bulgarian empire
1187	Defeat of Third Crusade at battle of Horns of Hattin; Jerusalem retaken by Saladin
1192	Treaties with Genoa and Pisa
1203–1204	Fourth Crusade, with Venetian financial and naval support, marches against Constantinople; after the capture and sack of the city the Latin empire is established, along with several principalities and other territories under Latin or Venetian rule
1204–1205	Successor states in Nicaea, Epiros and Trebizond established
1205	Latin emperor Baldwin I defeated by Bulgars
1259	Michael VIII succeeds to throne in empire of Nicaea; Nicaean army defeats combined Latin and Epirot army at battle of Pelagonia; fortress town of Mistra handed over to Byzantines (Nicaea)
1261	During absence of main Latin army Nicaean forces enter and seize Constantinople
1265	Pope invites Charles of Anjou, brother of Louis IX of France, to support him militarily against Manfred of Sicily and the Hohenstaufen power in Italy
1266	Manfred of Sicily defeated at battle of Benevento by Charles of Anjou; Angevin plans, supported by papacy, evolve to invade and conquer the Byzantine empire
1274	Gregory X summons second council of Lyons; representatives of Byzantine Church present; union of the Churches agreed, under threat of papally approved invasion led by Charles of Anjou; union not accepted in the Byzantine empire
1280–1337	Ottomans take nearly all remaining Byzantine possessions in Asia Minor
1282	'Sicilian vespers'; death of Charles of Anjou and end of his plans to invade Byzantium
1285	Council of Constantinople ('second synod of Blachernae'): discussed and rejected pro-western interpretation of the Trinity as enunciated by the patriarch John XI Bekkos. Also rejected decisions of Council of Lyons
1303	Andronikos II hires Catalan company as mercenary troop
1321–1328	Civil war between Andronikos II and Andronikos III
1329	Turks take Nicaea
1331–1355	Stefan Dushan Kral (King) of Serbia
1337	Turks take Nicomedia
c.1340	Serbian empire under Stefan Dushan at height of power
1341–1347	Civil war between John V (supported by Serbs) and John VI Kantakouzenos (with Turkish help)
1346	Stefan Dushan crowned emperor of the Serbs and Greeks
1347	Black death reaches Constantinople
1354–1355	Civil war between John VI and John V (backed by Genoa); Ottomans employed as allies establish themselves in Gallipoli and Thrace
1345	Extensive repairs carried out to the walls of Constantinople
1351	Repairs to sea walls of Constantinople
1355	John VI abdicates and enters a monastery; John V proposes union of Churches to Pope
1365	Ottomans take Adrianople, which becomes their capital
1366	John V visits Hungary seeking support against Ottoman threat
1371	Ottomans defeat Serbs in battle

1373	John V forced to submit to Ottoman Sultan Murat I; John's son Andronikos IV rebels, but is defeated
1376–1379	Civil war in Byzantium: Andronikos IV rebels against John V, who is supported by his younger son Manuel
1379	John V restored with Turkish and Venetian support
1388	Bulgarians defeated by Ottomans
1389	Battle of Kosovo: Serbs forced to withdraw by Ottomans, Serb empire ends; accession of Bayezid I
1390	First use of gunpowder at Constantinople
1393	Turks capture Thessaly; battle of Trnovo, Bulgarian empire destroyed
1396	Sigismund of Hungary organizes crusade against Ottoman threat, but is utterly defeated at Nicopolis
1397–1402	Bayezid I besieges Constantinople, but army withdrawn when Turks defeated by Timur at battle of Ankyra
1399–1402	Manuel II tours Europe to elicit military and financial support
1422	Murat II lays siege to Constantinople
1423	The governor of Thessaloniki hands the city over to the Venetians
1430	Thessaloniki retaken by Ottomans; populace and Venetian garrison massacred
1437	John VIII seeks support in Italy
1439	Çandarli Halil Pasha made Grand Vizier, Ishak Pasha Second Vizier, Zaganos Pasha Third Vizier. Council of Ferrara moves to Florence; Union of Churches formally agreed by Emperor John VIII, present at council
1442	Janos Hunyadi, the Hungarian voyvode of Transylvania, defeats Ottomans in Wallachia

1443	11-year-old Prince Mehmet made governor of Amasya; Janos Hunyadi leads crusading army into Balkans; Sultan Murad II campaigns against Karaman but makes peace and returns to face Hunyadi
1444	Karaman invades Ottoman provinces in Anatolia; revolt against Ottoman rule spreads in Albania
	12 June Peace between Murad II and Janos Hunyadi
	August Murad II abdicates in favour of Mehmet II and retires to Bursa to ensure Mehmet's succession against the pretender Prince Orhan in Constantinople
	September Byzantine despots of Morea invades central Greece; Crusader army breaks peace agreement and invades Ottoman territory; Islamic rising against Mehmet II in Edirne
	October Murad II reassumes military leadership
	10 November Ottomans defeat Hunyadi and crusaders at battle of Varna
1446	Murad II returns to throne; Mehmet II retains title of sultan but only acts as governor of Manisa; Ottoman campaigns re-establish Ottoman authority in Balkans and force Byzantine despots of Morea to accept Ottoman suzerainty
1448	John VIII dies; his brother Constantine, Despot of Morea, succeeds as Constantine XI; Ottomans defeat Hungarian crusaders at second battle of Kosovo and reimpose suzerainty on Wallachia
1449	Heraclea on Marmora taken by Ottomans
1451	Death of Murad II; Mehmet II becomes sultan for second time; Heraclea on Marmora probably returned to Byzantines; Ibrahim Bey of Karaman invades disputed area and instigates various revolts against Ottoman rule; Mehmet II conducts first campaign against Ibrahim of Karaman;

Byzantines threaten to release Ottoman claimant Orhan

1452

14 February Venice agrees to send gunpowder and armour to Constantinople

15 April–31 August Ottomans build Rumeli Hisar; this encourages the Venetian Senate to prepare ships and send an embassy to discover the sultan's intentions

28 August Mehmet II examines the walls of Constantinople then returns to Edirne

Autumn Mehmet II start assembling troops at Edirne; Byzantine emperor gathers grain and people into Constantinople

1 September Mehmet II arrives at Edirne; Hungarian gunfounder Urban transfers from Byzantine to Ottoman service and starts making giant cannon in Edirne

6 September Ottoman fleet returns to Gallipoli from Bosphorus

October Mehmet II sends troops to raid Byzantine Morea; Cardinal Isidore arrives in Constantinople with 200 archers

November Concern about Rumeli Hisar leads Genoa to send Giovanni Giustiniani Longo with men and ships to Constantinople

10 November Two Venetian merchant ships from the Black Sea pass Rumeli Hisar under fire

25 November Venetian ship from the Black Sea is sunk by gunfire from Rumeli Hisar

December Venetian galley from Trebizond under command of Giacomo Coco sails through the Bosphorus under fire; Venetian council in Constantinople agrees that no Venetian ships should leave without permission

12 December Joint Orthodox-Latin religious service in Hagia Sophia cathedral and agreement to a Union of the Churches

1452–53

Winter Byzantine emperor sends ships to purchase food and military equipment in the Aegean; Byzantine galleys pillage Turkish coastal villages in the Sea of Marmara; defences of Constantinople repaired; roads strengthened from Edirne to Constantinople; Mehmet plans siege of Constantinople

1453

January Mehmet returns to Edirne from Didimotikon; Genoese galleys with 700 soldiers under Giovanni Giustiniani Longo arrive in Constantinople; Giustiniani made commander of land defences

February Ottoman advance guard under Karaca Bey storms Byzantine forts of Studius and Therapia

26 February Six ships escape from Golden Horn carrying 700 people

Spring Ottoman heavy guns brought from Edirne to face Constantinople; Karaca Bey captures several towns on Black Sea and Marmara coast

March Ottoman fleet assembles off Gallipoli and sails into Marmara; Anatolian troops cross Bosphorus via Rumeli Hisar

23 March Mehmet II leaves Edirne with palace regiments

Late March–early April Pope sends three Genoese ships to Constantinople with arms and provisions but these are storm-bound at Chios

2 April Chain drawn across Golden Horn; Mehmet II arrives in front of Constantinople

6 April Ottomans moves forward from assembly positions to within a mile of the walls of Constantinople; Byzantine defenders take up positions around walls

9 April First Ottoman naval attack on boom unsuccessful. Around this time, Ottoman troops take Therapia and Studios

11 April Erection of large mangonels in front of walls; giant Ottoman gun called Basiliske fires first shot

12 April Second Ottoman naval attack on boom unsuccessful

15 April Large Byzantine vessel and the three Genoese-Papal warships delayed by contrary winds, sail from Chios

16 April Ottoman fleet reinforced by large ships from northern Anatolia

17–18 April Ottoman surprise night attack driven back

18 April Ottoman attack on mesoteichion area; Ottoman fleet occupies Princes Islands

19 April Alvise Longo sails from Venice with one galley instead of proposed fleet of 16; possibly five others sail after 7 May

20 April Large Byzantine vessel and three Genoese-Papal warships break through Ottoman blockade into Constantinople

21 April Baltaoglu replaced as commander of the Ottoman fleet; cannon placed on northern side of Golden Horn; council of war near Diplokionion decides to continue the siege; large tower near St Romanos Gate collapses

22 April Ottomans complete slipway from Bosphorus and launch smaller warships into the Golden Horn

25–27 April Ottoman guns make further breaches in the walls

29 April Byzantines behead 260 Ottoman prisoners

30 April Ottoman guns make a breach at the St Romanos Gate

May Emperor collects more funds from churches to buy food for troops

2 May Great gun Basiliske returned to its original position

3 May Byzantines place guns on wall to attack Ottoman ships in Golden Horn; Emperor Constantine sends small ship beyond the Dardanelles to seek news of the Venetian relief fleet

5 May Ottoman high-angle mortar fires over Galata and sinks 'neutral' Genoese ship in Golden Horn

6 May Ottoman giant gun repaired; additional guns added to the St Romanos battery make another breach

7–8 May Ottoman night assault on breach at St Romanos Gate fails

9–13 May Venetian ships unload in Golden Horn

10 May Alvise Diedo given command of ships in harbour; Gabriele Trevisan takes spare crews to help defend Blachernae

11 May Loredan's ship leaves Venice

12–13 May Ottoman night assault penetrates Blachernae Palace, but is driven out

14 May Ottomans win full control of Golden Horn then move guns from Valley of the Springs to reinforce those bombarding Blachernae

16 May Guns from Valley of the Springs not effective against Blachernae so moved to main batteries in the Lycus Valley; Ottoman mines beneath Blachernae wall are discovered and defeated

16–17 May Ottoman fleet makes demonstration against boom, no shots fired

18–19 May Ottoman wooden towers are destroyed by kegs of gunpowder by night, others are then dismantled

19 May Ottomans complete construction of pontoon bridge across upper part of Golden Horn

21 May Ottoman ships unsuccessfully attack boom

23 May Small boat returns from reconnaissance with news that no relief fleet is in sight

24 May Lunar eclipse; Constantine refuses final surrender terms, Mehmet announces final assault within five days

25 May Byzantines destroy last of Ottoman mines

26 May Ottomans hear rumours of approaching European relief army; Mehmet II holds council with senior men

27 May Mehmet II tours the army and heralds announce final attack

27–28 May Celebration fires lit at night in Ottoman camp because of forthcoming attack

28 May Day of prayer and rest in Ottoman camp; Mehmet tours fronts; late afternoon Ottoman troops start filling in the fosse and bring cannon to close range

28–29 May Ottoman ships brought as close as possible to the sea walls at night

29 May Final Ottoman assault; Mehmet enters Constantinople early afternoon

30 May Çandarli Halil replaced as Grand Vizier by Zaganos Pasha

1 June Mehmet II stops looting; Ottoman army is ordered back to camp Byzantine garrisons at Silivri and Epibatos surrender peacefully; Galata surrenders to Ottoman rule

3 June Start of demolition of Galata's land-walls; execution of Loukas Notaras

9 June Cretan ships reach home with first news of the fall of Constantinople

1460 Mistra falls to the Turks

1461 Trebizond falls to the Turks

Part I   Byzantium at War

INTRODUCTION

The Byzantine empire was not called by that name in its own time, and indeed the term 'Byzantine' was used only to describe inhabitants of Constantinople, ancient Byzantion on the Bosphorus. The subjects of the emperor at Constantinople referred to themselves as *Rhomaioi*, Romans, because as far as they were concerned Constantinople, the city of Constantine I, the first Christian ruler of the Roman empire, had become the capital of the Roman empire once Rome had lost its own pre-eminent position, and it was the Christian Roman empire that carried on the traditions of Roman civilization. In turn, the latter was identified with civilized society as such, and Orthodox Christianity was both the guiding religious and spiritual force which defended and protected that world, and the guarantor of God's continuing support. Orthodoxy means, literally, correct belief, and this was what the Byzantines believed was essential to their own survival. Thus, from the modern historian's perspective, 'Byzantine' might be paraphrased by the more long-winded 'medieval eastern Roman' empire, for that is, in historical terms, what 'Byzantium' really meant.

In its long history, from the later 5th century, when the last vestiges of the western half of the Roman empire were absorbed into barbarian successor kingdoms, until the fall in battle of the last eastern Roman emperor, Constantine XI (r. 1448–53), the empire was almost constantly at war. Its strategic situation in the southern Balkans and Asia Minor made this inevitable. It was constantly challenged by its more or its less powerful neighbours – at first, the Persian empire in the east, later the various Islamic powers that arose in that region – and by its northern neighbours, the Slavs, the Avars (a Turkic people) in the 6th and 7th centuries, the Bulgars from the end of the 7th to early 11th centuries and, in the later 11th and 12th centuries, the Hungarians, later the Serbs and finally, after their conquests in Greece and the southern Balkans, the Ottoman Turks. Relations with the western

PREVIOUS PAGE

A portrait of c.1017 of Basil II, called Bulgaroctonos, or the Bulgar-slayer. A superb soldier, contemporaries reported that at the very sight of his banner the enemy used to flee, screaming 'Run! Run! It is the emperor!' He totally subjugated Bulgaria, and also scored victories over Armenians, Georgians, Arabs and Normans. His own reign followed on from those of two other brilliant generals, Nikephoros II Phokas, and John I Tzimiskes. (akg-images/Erich Lessing)

powers which arose from what remained of the western Roman empire during the 5th century were complicated and tense, not least because of the political competition between the papacy and the Constantinopolitan patriarchate, the two major sees – Alexandria, Antioch and Jerusalem were far less powerful after the 7th-century Islamic conquests – in the Christian world. Byzantium survived so long partly because internally it was well-organized, with an efficient fiscal and military system; and partly because these advantages, rooted in its late Roman past, lasted well into the 11th century. But as its western and northern neighbours grew in resources and political stability they were able to challenge the empire for pre-eminence, reducing it by the early 13th century to a second- or even third-rate rump of its former self, subordinated to the politics of the west and the commercial interests of Venice, Pisa and Genoa, among others, the greatest of the Italian merchant republics. In this part, we will look at some of the ways in which the medieval east Roman empire secured its long existence.

THE BYZANTINE LANDS

The Byzantine, or medieval eastern Roman, empire was restricted for most of its existence to the southern Balkans and Asia Minor – very roughly modern Greece and modern Turkey. In the middle of the 6th century, after the success of the emperor Justinian's reconquests in the west, the empire was much more extensive, including all of the north African coastal regions from the Atlantic to Egypt, along with south-eastern Spain, Italy and the Balkans up to the Danube. But by the later 6th century the Italian lands were already contested by the Lombards, while the Visigoths of Spain soon expelled the imperial administration from their lands. The near eastern provinces in Syria, Iraq and the Transjordan region along with Egypt were all lost to Islam by the early 640s, and north Africa followed suit by the 690s. In a half century of warfare, therefore, the empire lost some of its wealthiest regions and much of the revenue to support the government, the ruling élite and vital needs such as the army.

Much of the territory that remained to the empire was mountainous or arid, so that the exploitable zones were really quite limited in extent. Nevertheless, an efficient (for medieval times) fiscal administration and tax regime extracted the maximum in manpower and agricultural resources, while a heavy reliance on well-planned diplomacy, an extensive network of ambassadors, emissaries and spies, a willingness to play off neighbours and enemies against one another, and to spend substantial sums on 'subsidies' to ward off attack, all contributed to the longevity of the state. And these measures were essential to its survival, for although Constantinople was itself well defended and strategically well placed to resist attack, the empire was surrounded on all sides by enemies, real or potential, and was generally at war on two, if not three, fronts at once throughout much

THE EAST ROMAN EMPIRE IN THE MID-6TH CENTURY

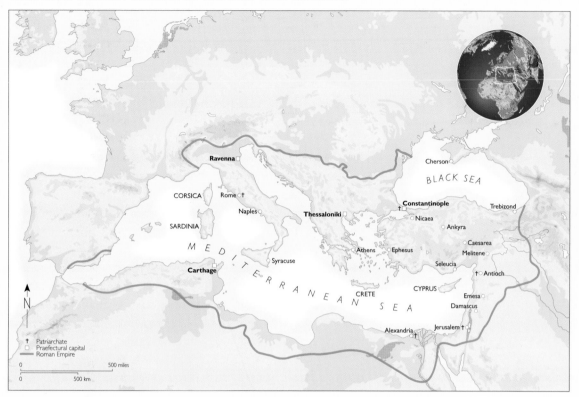

of its long history. The 10th-century Italian diplomat Liutprand of Cremona expressed this situation well when he described the empire as being surrounded by the fiercest of barbarians – Hungarians, Pechenegs, Khazars, Rus' and so forth.

Asia Minor was the focus of much of the empire's military activity from the 7th until the 13th century. There are three separate climatic and geographical zones in Asia Minor: the coastal plains, the central plateau regions, and the mountains which separate them. While hot, dry summers and extreme cold in winter characterize the central plateau, and where, except for some sheltered river valleys, the economy was mainly pastoral – sheep, cattle and horses – the coastlands, where most productive agricultural activity and the highest density of settlement was located, offered a friendlier, 'Mediterranean'-type climate, and were also the most important source of revenues for the government. The pattern of settlement was similarly strongly differentiated – most towns and cities were concentrated in the coastal regions, while the mountains and plateaux were much more sparsely settled. Similar considerations applied to the Balkans, too, and in both cases this geography affected road systems and communications. The empire needed to take these factors into account in strategic planning and campaign organization, of course, for logistical considerations – the sources of manpower, food and shelter, livestock and weapons, how to move these around, and how they were consumed – played a key role in the empire's ability to survive in the difficult strategic situation in which it found itself.

Armies, whether large or small, and whether Byzantine or hostile forces, faced many problems when campaigning in or across Asia Minor, in particular the long stretches of road through relatively waterless and exposed country, and the rough mountainous terrain separating coastal regions from central plateaux. The complex Roman and Hellenistic road system was partly retained during the Byzantine period, but the empire after the 6th century developed a range of military routes together with a series of fortified posts and military bases – for these same routes also served as means of access and egress for Arab forces. Strategic needs changed, of course, and so did the road system, with routes falling in to and out of use.

The Balkans present a rugged and fragmented landscape falling broadly into two zones: the coastal and riverine plains (of Thrace, of Thessaly and of the south Danubian area), which are productive and fairly densely occupied; and the mountain ranges that dominate the whole region and represent about two-thirds of its area – the Dinaric Alps in the west, stretching from north-east to south-west; the southerly Pindus range with which they merge, and which together dominate western and central Greece; and the Balkan chain itself, stretching from the Morava river as far as the Black Sea coast, with the Rhodope range forming an arc to the south, through Macedonia towards the plain of Thrace. The fragmented terrain has given rise to a series of distinct geopolitical units separated by ridges of highlands, fanning out along river valleys towards the coastal areas.

A number of major routes served from ancient times to give access to the interior of the Balkan region or to pass through it from north to south or west to east. The Balkans are characterized by relatively narrow and often quite high, easily controlled passes, and this terrain was ideally suited to guerrilla strategy – tough campaigning conditions, and difficult access to some regions during the winter. The structure of communications and the effectiveness of Byzantine political authority demonstrate this, for there were no obvious focal points in the ancient and medieval period in the south Balkan region apart from Thessaloniki and Constantinople, both on the edge of the peninsula and its fragmented landscape.

Geography affected land use in the Balkans as it did in Asia Minor. The uplands and mountains, dominated by forest and woodland, and the lower foothills by woodland, scrub and rough pasturage, were suited to pastoral activity only. Agriculture was limited to the plains, river valleys and coastlands of Thessaly, Macedonia and the Danube. The sea played an important role, since it surrounds the Balkan peninsula apart from along the northern boundary, and acted, as it still does today, as an efficient means of communication along the heavily indented coastline

en cellui champ. pour il
aunat ses grec qui te.r
noient la cite oantiode
furet mit espouetes et re

aumier les mirs quip
as fideimes ne onqs puic
ne fu habitee cele cite. Et
la separtirt et umorent

and with more distant regions. The disadvantage of relatively easy seaborne access, however, was that it opened up the southern Balkan peninsula to invasion.

One of the factors that made the Roman army so successful and efficient was the military road system, established for the most part between the end of the 2nd century BC and the middle of the 2nd century AD. The network also facilitated commerce, civilian traffic and the movement of information. But in the later 4th and 5th centuries the roads went into decline – a reflection of economic and social changes across the empire and the consequences of these for local governors and town councils. One result was a decline in the use of wheeled vehicles, which could not use roads that were not properly maintained, and a corresponding increase in dependence on beasts of burden.

After the 6th century a limited number of key routes were kept up by means of compulsory burdens imposed on local communities. The fast post, consisting of pack-animals, relay horses and light carts, and the slow post, which provided ox-carts and heavy vehicles, were amalgamated into a single system in the 6th or 7th century, and continued to operate until the last years of the empire. The imperial road systems in both the Balkans and Anatolia were less extensive than hitherto, but remained nevertheless effective. But the costs of maintenance and the problem of supervising upkeep meant that many routes were hardly more than tracks or paths

This illumination shows the battle of Antioch in 632, where the Saracens drove out the army of Heraclius. From Hayton, La fleur des histoires de la terre d'Orient, Cod. 2623, fol. 15 r, mid-14th century, Austrian National Library. (akg-images/Erich Lessing)

Mosaic in the dome of the monastery church of Daphni showing Christ Pantokrator. (akg-images/Rainer Hackenberg)

usable only by pack-animals, with paved or hard surfaces only near towns and fortresses. Travel and transport by water was usually faster and much cheaper. This was especially so in the case of the long-distance movement of bulk goods, such as grain. The expense of feeding draught-oxen, drovers and carters, paying tolls, together with the slow rate of movement of ox-carts, added very considerably to the price of the goods being transported, generally well beyond the price of ordinary subjects of the emperors. It was really only the government and the army, and to a certain extent the Church and a few wealthy individuals, who could pay for this. In contrast, shipping was much more cost effective, since large quantities of goods could be transported in a single vessel, handled by a small crew, relatively inexpensively, once the capital investment in vessel and cargo had been made.

This was the physical world of the later Roman and medieval eastern Roman, or Byzantine, empire, and this was the context within which the politics, diplomacy, warfare and social evolution of Byzantine culture are to be understood. Geography and physical context were not the only factors: cultural assumptions – the 'thought world' of Byzantium, also partly determined the complex network of causes and effects, the results of which we call 'history'. But means of communication, speed of movement of people and information were key aspects on which the effectiveness of armies or the availability of resources to support a campaign might depend. Geography affected how the government worked, the amount of agricultural wealth that it could make available for specific purposes, the distribution and well-being of the population, rates of production and consumption, the availability of livestock, and so forth. And geographical factors were, of course, fundamental to warfare and the strategic organization of the empire.

A BRIEF SURVEY OF BYZANTINE HISTORY

By the later 5th century the western part of the Roman empire had been transformed into a patchwork of barbarian successor states. Emperors at Constantinople continued to view all the lost territories as part of their realm, however, and in some cases to treat the kings of the successor kingdoms as their legitimate representatives, governing Roman affairs in the provinces in question until Constantinople could re-establish a full administrative and military presence. This is most obviously the case with the Ostrogothic leader Theoderic who, although he ruled nominally in the name of the emperor, established a powerful state in Italy. The leader of the Salian Franks in northern Gaul, Clovis, had quite deliberately adopted Orthodox Christianity in the last years of the 5th century in order to gain papal and imperial recognition and support for his rule, where he also claimed, at least nominally, to represent Roman rule. Roman emperors considered the west not as 'lost', but rather as temporarily outside direct imperial authority.

Michael I proclaims Leo V the Armenian as co-emperor in 813, in the 11th-century illuminated manuscript of The History of John Scylitzes. Both step onto the shield which was raised aloft and saluted by trumpeters and high officials. The ceremony of raising the shield dated from the Roman Empire. Cod.gr.S-3, fol. 10v. (Werner Forman Archive/Biblioteca Nacional, Madrid)

The emperor Justinian (527–65) used this as the justification for a series of remarkable reconquests, aimed at restoring Rome's power as it had been at its height – north Africa from the Vandals by 534, Italy from the Ostrogoths by 552. But the plan was too ambitious to have had any chance of permanent success. And while the emperor nevertheless came very close to achieving a major part of his original aims, the problems that arose after his death illustrated the problems his policies brought with them. Warfare with the Persian empire in the east meant that resources were always stretched to the limit and there were never enough soldiers for all fronts. Upon his death in 565 Justinian left a vastly expanded but perilously overstretched empire, in both financial and military terms. His successors were faced with the reality of dealing with new enemies, a lack of ready cash, and internal discontent over high taxation and constant demands for soldiers and the necessities to support them. The Persian war was renewed, while in 568 the Germanic Lombards crossed from their homeland along the western Danube and Drava region into Italy, in their efforts to flee the approaching Avars, a Turkic nomadic power which was establishing a vast steppe empire. The Lombards soon overran Roman defensive positions in the north of the peninsula, founding a number of independent chiefdoms in the centre and south, while the Avars established themselves as a major challenge to imperial power in the northern Balkan region. Between the mid-570s and the end of the reign of the emperor Maurice (582–602), the empire was able to re-establish a precarious balance in the east and along the Danube.

Maurice was deposed in 602 following a mutiny of the Danube forces, and the centurion Phokas was raised to the throne. Phokas (602–10), popularly regarded in later Byzantine sources as a tyrant, ruled until he was overthrown in 610, when he was in turn replaced by Heraclius, the son of the military governor of Africa. Heraclius was crowned emperor and ruled until 641.

But the empire was unable to maintain its defences against external pressure. Within a few years the Avars and Slavs had overrun much of the Balkans, while the Persians occupied and set up their own provincial governments in Syria and Egypt between 614 and 618, and continued to push into Asia Minor. Italy was left to its own devices and became increasingly autonomous. In spite of a great siege of Constantinople by a Persian and an Avaro–Slav army in 626, Heraclius proved an able strategist and by 628 had utterly destroyed the Persian armies in the east, restoring the situation at the end of Maurice's reign. The regional dominance of the Roman empire seemed assured. But while the Danube remained nominally the frontier, much of the Balkan region was no longer under imperial authority, except when an army appeared. The financial situation of the empire, whose resources were quite exhausted by the long wars, was desperate.

The origins of Islam lie in the northern Arabian peninsula, where different forms of Christianity, Judaism and indigenous beliefs coexisted, in particular in the

BYZANTINE RULERS

Justinian I	527–65	Constantine IX Monomachos	1042–55
Justin II	565–578	Theodora (second reign)	1055–56
Tiberius II Constantine	578–82	Michael VI Stratiotikos	1056–57
Maurice	582–602	Isaac I Komnenos	1057–59
Phokas	602–10	Constantine X Doukas	1059–67
Heraclius	610–41	Eudokia	1067
Constantine III and Heraclonas	641	Romanos IV Diogenes	1068–71
Constans II	641–68	Eudokia (second reign)	1071
Constantine IV	668–85	Michael VII Doukas	1071–78
Justinian II	685–95	Nikephoros III Botaneiates	1078–81
Leontios	695–98	Alexios I Komnenos	1081–1118
Tiberios III	698–705	John II Komnenos	1118–43
Justinian II (restored)	705–11	Manuel I Komnenos	1143–80
Philippikos Bardanes	711–13	Alexios II Komnenos	1180–83
Anastasios II	713–15	Andronikos I Komnenos	1183–85
Theodosios III	715–17	Isaac II Angelos	1185–95
Leo III	717–41	Alexios III Angelos	1195–1203
Constantine V	741–75	Isaac II (restored) and	
Artabasdos	741–42	Alexios IV Angelos	1203–1204
Leo IV	775–80	Alexios V Mourtzouphlos	1204
Constantine VI	780–97	Constantine (XI) Laskaris	1204 (Nicaea)
Eirene	797–802	Theodore I Laskaris	1204–22 (Nicaea)
Nikephoros I	802–11	John III Doukas Vatatzes	1222–54 (Nicaea)
Staurakios	811	Theodore II Laskaris	1254–58 (Nicaea)
Michael I	811–13	John IV Laskaris	1258–61 (Nicaea)
Leo V	813–20	Michael VIII Palaiologos	1259–82
Michael II	820–29	Andronikos II Palaiologos	1282–28
Theophilos	829–42	Michael IX Palaiologos	1294–1320
Michael III	842–67	Andronikos III Palaiologos	1328–41
Basil I	867–86	John V Palaiologos	1341–91
Leo VI	886–912	John VI Kantakouzenos	1341–54
Alexander	912–13	Andronikos IV Palaiologos	1376–79
Constantine VII	913–59	John VII Palaiologos	1390
Romanos II	959–63	Manuel II Palaiologos	1391–1425
Nikephoros II Phokas	963–69	John VIII Palaiologos	1425–48
John I Tzimiskes	969–76	Constantine XI (XII) Palaiologos	1448–53
Basil II	976–1025		
Constantine VIII	1025–28		
Romanos III Argyros	1028–34		
Michael IV the Paphlagonian	1034–41	The Grand Komnenoi of Trebizond	
Michael V Kalaphates	1041–42	(1203–1461) or the semi-autonomous rulers	
Zoe and Theodora	1042	of the Despotate of Epiros (1205–1318) are	
		not included.	

Major Byzantine routes in Asia Minor

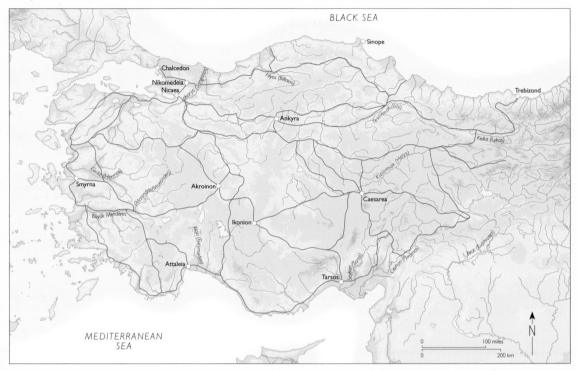

much-travelled trading and caravan communities of Mecca and Medina. Mohammed was himself a respected and established merchant who had several times accompanied the trade caravans north to Roman Syria. Syria and Palestine already had substantial populations of Arabs, both farmers and herdsmen, as well as mercenary soldiers serving the empire as a buffer against the Persians. Although Mohammed's preaching – a synthesis of his own beliefs with Judaic and Christian ideas – met initially with stiff resistance from his own clan, by 628–29 he had established his authority over much of the peninsula and begun to consider the future direction of the new Islamic community. On his death (traditionally placed in 632) there followed a brief period of warfare during which his immediate successors had to fight hard to reassert Islamic authority. The raids mounted against both Roman and Persian territories were in part a response to the political demands generated by this internal conflict. A combination of incompetence and apathy, disaffected soldiers and inadequate defensive arrangements resulted in a series of disastrous Roman defeats and the loss of Syria, Palestine, Mesopotamia and Egypt within the short span of 10 years, so that by 642 the empire was reduced to a rump of its former self. The Persian empire was completely overrun and destroyed by the 650s. The Arab Islamic empire was born.

Justinian's army,
6th century. Centre, a
Thracian cavalryman of
the Leones Klibanarii, late
6th century. Right, a
Guards infantryman, of
Justinian's bodyguard,
mid-6th century. This
irregular (left) of the
Numerus Felicium
Theodosiacus, 6th century,
represents the bulk of
6th-century Byzantine
armies. (Angus McBride
© Osprey Publishing Ltd)

The defeats and territorial contraction which resulted from the expansion of Islam from the 640s in the east, on the one hand, and the arrival of the Bulgars and establishment of a permanent Bulgar Khanate in the Balkans from the 680s, on the other, radically altered the political conditions of existence of the east Roman state. The Balkans up to the Danube were claimed by the empire, and when imperial armies appeared, the local, predominantly Slav, chieftains and leaders acknowledged Roman authority. But this lasted only as long as the army was present. The Bulgars were a new element whose nomadic military organization and technology enabled them quickly to establish a political hegemony over the region south of the Danube delta, from which their Khans rapidly expanded their power, so that by the end of the 7th century they were a substantial threat to imperial claims in the region.

The resulting transformation of state administrative structures produced an army that was based almost entirely on defensive principles, for which offensive warfare became a rarity until the middle of the 8th century, and which was encouraged by the imperial government to avoid pitched battles and open confrontation with enemy forces wherever possible. The field armies of the late Roman state were transformed in effect into provincial militias, although a central core of full-time 'professional' soldiers seems always to have been maintained by each regional military commander. A strategy of guerilla warfare evolved in which enemy forces were allowed to penetrate the borderlands before being cut off from their bases and harried and worried until they broke up or were forced to return to their own lands. Byzantine officers conducted a 'scorched earth' policy in many regions, and local populations in endangered regions were encouraged to keep lookouts posted, so that they could gather their livestock and other movable possessions and take refuge in mountain fortresses, thereby depriving enemy units of forage and booty. Although individual emperors did launch offensive expeditions in the period c.660–730, these were generally designed to forestall a major enemy attack into Roman territory in Asia Minor, or had a punitive nature, designed more as ideologically motivated revenge attacks on important enemy targets, and with no lasting strategic value (although they did have implications for military morale). Although a few notable successes were recorded, many of them failed and resulted in substantial defeats and loss of men and materials. The differentiation between different arms at the tactical level – between light and heavy cavalry or infantry, archers, lancers or spearmen – appears to have lessened, surviving only in a few contexts, associated with imperially maintained élite units. Byzantine armies and Arab armies looked very much the same.

Only from the 730s on, during the reign of Leo III (717–41), an emperor from a military background who seized the throne in 717, and more particularly that of his son and successor Constantine V (741–75), a campaigning emperor who introduced a number of administrative reforms in the army and established an élite field army at Constantinople in the 760s, does this situation begin to change. Political stability internally, the beginnings of economic recovery in the later 8th century and dissension among their enemies enabled the Byzantines to re-establish a certain equilibrium by the year 800. In spite of occasional major defeats (for example, the annihilation of a Byzantine force following a Bulgar surprise attack in 811, and the death in battle of the emperor Nikephoros I) and an often unfavourable international political situation, the Byzantines were able to begin a more offensive policy with regard to the Islamic power to the east and the Bulgars in the north – in the latter case, combining diplomacy and missionary activity with military threats. By the early 10th century, and as the Caliphate was weakened by internal strife, the Byzantines were beginning to establish a certain advantage; and in spite of the fierce and sometimes successful opposition of local Muslim warlords (such as the emirs of Aleppo in the 940s and 950s), there followed a series of brilliant reconquests of huge swathes of territory in north Syria and Iraq, the annihilation of the second Bulgarian empire, and the beginnings of the reconquest of Sicily and southern Italy. By the death in 1025 of the soldier–emperor Basil II 'the Bulgar-slayer' (976–1025) the empire was once again the paramount political and military power in the eastern Mediterranean basin, rivalled only by the Fatimid Caliphate in Egypt and Syria.

But the offensive warfare that developed from the middle of the 9th century had important effects upon the organization of the armies. The provincial militias became less suited to the requirements of such campaigning, tied as they had become to their localities and to the seasonal campaigning dictated by Arab or Bulgar raiders. Instead, regular field armies with a more complex tactical structure and more offensive élan developed, partly under the auspices of a new social élite of military commanders who were also great landowners, partly encouraged and financed by the state. Mercenary troops played an increasingly important role as the state began to commute military service in the provincial armies for cash with which to pay them. By the middle of the 11th century, a large portion of the imperial armies was made up of indigenously recruited mercenary units together with Norman, Russian, Turkic and Frankish mercenaries. The successes achieved between c.900 and 1030 were thus based on effective organization and better resources than in the preceding period. Morale and ideology also played a key role, while the increase in the tactical complexity of Byzantine field armies played a significant part, with the various different types of arms familiar from the late Roman period, which had all but vanished in the period of crisis of the 7th and 8th centuries, reappearing once more. Arab commentators remark on the effectiveness of the Byzantine heavy cavalry 'wedge', employed with, literally, crushing effect in the Byzantine wars with both Muslims and northern foes such as the Bulgars and the Rus' of Kiev.

This expansionism had its negative results, however. Increasing state demands clashed with greater aristocratic resistance to tax-paying; political factionalism at court led to policy failures, the overestimation of imperial military strength, and neglect of defensive structures. When Seljuk Turkish raiding parties were able to defeat piecemeal a major imperial force in 1071 and capture the emperor Romanos IV, the empire could offer no organized counter-attack, with the result that central Asia Minor was lost permanently to the empire. Major military and fiscal reforms under the emperors of the Komnenos dynasty (a military aristocratic clan) from 1081 re-established stability and, to a degree, the international position of the empire. While foreign mercenary units continued to play a prominent role, the recruitment of indigenous Byzantine units specializing in a variety of arms restored the ability of the imperial armies to fight external enemies on their own terms. This was partly based on a reformed fiscal administration, on the one hand, and the raising and maintenance of troops on the basis of grants of revenue to certain individuals in return for the provision of trained soldiers, both infantry and cavalry. Increasing western influence, in the form of the introduction of weapons such as the crossbow and the adoption of western heavy cavalry tactics, differentiate this period from the preceding century. But the successes of the new dynasty were relatively short-lived: overexpansion, the loss of Bulgaria and much of the Balkans to what might be called 'nationalist' rebellions, and the collapse of the empire into renewed factional strife in the 1180s and 1190s, laid it open to external threat. This materialized in the form of the Fourth Crusade. The capture and sack of Constantinople in 1204 and the subsequent partition of the empire among the Venetian and western victors ended the empire's role as a major

MAJOR BYZANTINE ROUTES IN THE BALKANS

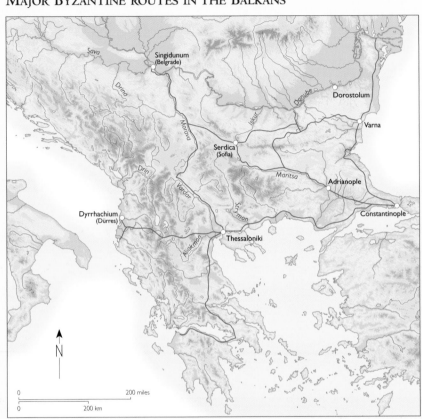

political and military power, although it survived after the recovery of Constantinople in 1261 and re-establishment of an imperial regime, on an ever smaller territorial scale, until only Constantinople and a few Aegean islands remained. And in 1453 the Ottoman Sultan Mehmet II extinguished even this remnant.

There are, very roughly, five phases of military development in the history of the Byzantine empire: reconquest and expansion under Justinian in the 6th century; contraction, localization and a primarily defensive character in the 7th and 8th centuries; consolidation, recovery and a more offensive approach in the period from the 9th to the early 11th century; the breakdown and reform of the structures inherited from the late ancient period during the 11th and 12th centuries, with a brief expansion back into Asia Minor under the emperors Alexios I, John II and Manuel until the 1170s; and a final, slow decline as the empire shrank under the effects of, first, the partition which followed the Fourth Crusade; second, the growth of the power of Serbia in the 14th century; and third, of that of the Ottomans in the 14th and 15th centuries.

THE POLITICAL WORLD OF BYZANTIUM

The Christian Roman state was structured as a hierarchy of administrative levels: at the top was the emperor, understood to be God's representative, surrounded by a palace and household apparatus, the centre of imperial government and administration. Civil and fiscal government was delegated from the emperor to the praetorian prefects, whose prefectures were the largest territorial circumscriptions in the state; each prefecture was further divided into *dioecesae* (dioceses), which had a predominantly fiscal aspect; and each diocese was divided into *provinciae* (provinces), territorial units of fiscal and judicial administration. These were further divided into self-governing *poleis* or *civitates*, the cities, each with its *territorium* or hinterland (which might be more or less extensive, according to geographical, demographic and other factors).

Rural production dominated the economy, but the cities were the homes of a literate élite of landowners. Social status was largely determined by one's relationship to the system of imperial titles and precedence, whether one had held an active post in the imperial bureaucracy, and at what level, and so forth, although regional variations were marked. The Church and the theological system it represented (from the late 4th century the official religion of the Roman state) played a central role in the economy of the Roman world – it was a major landowner – as well as in imperial politics, in influencing the moral and ethical system of the Roman world, and in directing imperial religious policy. The prevailing view was that the emperor was chosen by God, that he had to be Orthodox, and that his role was to defend the interests of Orthodoxy and the Roman i.e. Christian *oikoumenê* (the inhabited, civilized – Roman – world). The political implications were such that heresy was construed as treason, and opposition to the (Orthodox) emperor could effectively be treated as heresy. The late Roman state was thus a complex bureaucracy, rooted in and imposed upon a series of overlapping social formations structured by local variations on essentially the same social relations of production across the whole central and east Mediterranean and Balkan world. Social and political tensions were exacerbated by religious divisions, local economic conditions, imperial politics, and the burden placed upon the tax-paying population as a result of the state's needs in respect of its administrative apparatus and, in particular, its armies.

These structures were radically transformed between the later 6th and early 9th centuries, and as the result of a number of factors, the single most important being the Islamic conquests. By 642 all of Egypt and the middle-eastern provinces had been lost, Arab forces had penetrated deep into Asia Minor and Libya, and imperial forces had been withdrawn into Asia Minor, to be settled across the provinces of the region as the only available means of supporting them. Within a period of some 12 years, therefore, the empire lost over half its area and three-quarters of its resources – a drastic loss for an imperial state which still had to maintain and equip a considerable army and an effective administrative bureaucracy if it was to survive at all. While many of the developments which led to this transformation were in train long before the 7th-century crisis, it was this conjuncture that served to bring things to a head and promote the structural responses that followed.

The changes that accompanied the developments of the 7th century affected all areas of social, cultural and economic life. There occurred a 'ruralization' of society, a result of the devastation, abandonment, shrinkage or displacement of many cities in Asia Minor as a result of invasions and raids. The defensive properties of 'urban' sites, their direct relevance to military, administrative or ecclesiastical needs, and so on, played the key role in whether a city survived or not. Constantinople became the pre-eminent city of the empire.

The social élite was transformed as 'new men' selected by the emperors on a more obviously meritocratic basis increased in number, and who were initially heavily dependent on the emperor and on imperially sponsored positions. Yet as a result of its increasing grip on state positions and the lands it accrued through the rewards attached to such service, this élite soon turned into an aristocracy, during the 8th and 9th centuries still very dependent on the state, during the 10th and especially the 11th increasingly independent. The state had to compete directly with a social group whose enormous landed wealth and entrenched position in the apparatuses of the state meant that it posed a real threat to central control of fiscal resources.

The events of the 7th century also produced a reassertion of central state power over late Roman tendencies to decentralization. The state was both limited, and in its turn partly defined, by the nature of key economic relationships. This is exemplified in the issue and circulation of coin, the basic mechanism through which the state converted agricultural produce into transferable fiscal resources. Coin was issued chiefly to oil the wheels of the state machinery, and wealth was appropriated and consumed through a redistributive fiscal mechanism: the state issued gold in the form of salaries and largesse to its bureaucracy and armies, who exchanged a substantial portion thereof for goods and services in maintaining themselves. The state could thus collect much of the coin it put into circulation through tax, the more so since fiscal policy generally demanded tax in gold and offered change in bronze. There were periods when this system was constrained by circumstances, resulting in the ad hoc arrangements for supplying soldiers and raising tax in kind, for example (as in the 7th century), and it also varied by region. But in a society in which social status and advancement (including the self-identity of the aristocracy) were connected with the state, these arrangements considerably hindered economic activity not directly connected with the state's activities. For the continued power and attraction of the imperial establishment at Constantinople, with its court and hierarchical system of precedence, as well as the highly centralized fiscal administrative structure, consumed the whole attention of the Byzantine élite, hindering the evolution of a more localized aristocracy which might otherwise have invested in the economy and society of its own localities and towns, rather than in the imperial system.

The growth in the power of the élite was stimulated by two developments. In the first place, there took place an increasing subordination of the peasantry to both private landlords and to holders of grants of state revenue. In the second place the state conceded from the later 11th century the right to receive the revenues from certain public (i.e. fiscal, or taxed) districts or of certain imperial estates with their tenants, encouraging a process of very gradual alienation of the state's fiscal and juridical rights. By exploiting the award by the emperors of fiscal exemptions of varying sorts, landlords – both secular and monastic – were able to keep a larger proportion of the revenues extracted from their peasant producers for themselves, as rent, while the government's hold on the remaining fiscal land of the empire was constantly challenged by the provincial élite. This had important consequences, for it meant that the overall burden placed on the peasant producers grew considerably. Tenants of landlords with access to imperial patronage attempted to free themselves from many of these impositions through obtaining grants of exemption of one sort or another, although the needs and demands of the local military meant that privileges were often entirely ignored. The amount of resources lost to the state through grants of exemption from additional taxes cannot have been negligible, while the burden of landlords' demands on peasant tenants is hinted at by an 11th-century writer who notes that cancelling fiscal privileges freed the rural communities from the burdens which they owed in rents and services.

The split between the interests of the landed and office-holding élite and the interests of the government, evident during the later 10th and 11th centuries, was papered over from the time of Alexios I and until the end of the 12th century by virtue of the transformation of the empire under the Komnenos dynasty into what was, in effect, a gigantic family estate, ruled through a network of magnates,

This miniature depicts an episode of the siege of Thessaloniki by the Bulgars. Byzantine forces are making a sortie from the gates of the city and putting the Bulgar horsemen to flight. Trumpeters on the walls signal the attack. The History of John Scylitzes, folio 217.r. (Werner Forman Archive/ Biblioteca Nacional, Madrid)

relatives and patronage that expanded rapidly during the 12th century and that, in uniting the vested interests of the dominant social-economic élite with those of a ruling family, reunited also the interests of the former with those of a centralized empire. The factional politics that resulted from these developments, in particular over who would control Constantinople and sit on the throne, become apparent in the squabbles and civil wars which followed the defeat of Romanos IV by the Seljuks in 1071, a situation resolved only by the seizure of power by Alexios I in 1081. By the end of the 12th century, if not already a century earlier, the vast majority of peasant producers in the empire had become tenants, in one form or another, of a landlord. The élite had meanwhile crystallized into a multifactional

aristocracy, led by a few very powerful families, with a number of dependent subordinate and collateral clans. Under the Komnenoi, the imperial family and its immediate associates monopolized military and higher civil offices, while the older families who had been its former rivals dominated the bureaucratic machinery of the state. In the provinces local élites tended to dominate. It was these social relations that facilitated the internecine strife and factionalism that marks the 14th and 15th centuries in particular.

The 11th-century monastery church at Daphni, Greece. (R. Sheridan, The Ancient Art and Architecture Collection)

WARRING SIDES: NEIGHBOURS AND ENEMIES

We have already referred to the strategically very awkward situation of the Byzantine state, with enemies or potential enemies on virtually every front and with a constant need to fight wars on more than one front at a time. In the north and west the situation was especially complex as a result of the variety of neighbouring states and political powers. From its establishment in the 680s, the Bulgar Khanate rapidly grew in power, and until its extinction at the hands of the emperor Basil II, known as the 'Bulgar-slayer' (976–1025), represented a constant threat to the security of imperial territory in the Balkans. Throughout the 8th and 9th centuries and into the early 10th century, Bulgar power and influence grew, in spite of successful counter-attacks under the emperor Constantine V in the 760s and 770s. The nadir of Byzantine fortunes was probably the year 811, when the Khan Krum defeated and destroyed an imperial army, killing the emperor Nikephoros I. Conversion to Christianity of elements of the ruling élite in the 860s was intended to stabilize the situation in favour of Byzantium; but the gradual Byzantinization of this élite only contributed to the growth of an imperialistic Bulgar politics which hoped to bring the two states together under a Bulgar dynasty. But Bulgar successes under the Christian Tsar Symeon in the first 15 years of the 10th century were as dangerous; while the reassertion of Bulgar imperial ideology under Tsar Samuel inaugurated a conflict – after a relatively peaceful period in the middle of the 10th century – and led finally to the eradication of Bulgar independence and the recovery of much of the Balkans up to the Danube in the early 11th century. In spite of occasional rebellions, the region remained firmly in Byzantine hands until just before the Fourth Crusade in 1203–1204. The Latin division of the empire after 1204 resulted in the rapid growth of local Balkan cultural independence and the evolution of new states – the Serbian empire of Stefan Dushan being perhaps the most remarkable. Only the arrival of the Ottomans in the 14th century put an end to this development.

Relations with Italy and the west were similarly complicated. Italy, north Africa and the south-eastern corner of the Iberian peninsula were reconquered under Justinian, at enormous cost, from the Ostrogoths, Vandals and Visigoths respectively. But the appearance of the Lombards in Italy (pursued by the Avars, at Byzantine request) soon resulted in the fragmentation of imperial possessions into a number of distinct regions under military commanders or duces. Imperial territory in the north-east and central regions was represented by the exarch, an officer with military and civil authority. But distance from Constantinople, local cultural differentiation and political conditions, together with the spiritual and political power of the popes in Rome soon led to the gradual but inevitable diminution of imperial power. The extinction of the exarchate with the capture of Ravenna, its capital, at the hands of the Lombards in 751; increased papal dependence on the Franks for support against the Lombards, and increasingly autonomous and mutually competing local polities in the Italian peninsula had led to the reduction of imperial power to the regions of Calabria, Bruttium and Sicily by the early 9th century. Other political centres such as Naples remained technically Byzantine, but were in practice quite independent. Venice, which grew in importance from the early 9th century, likewise remained nominally an imperial territory.

The coronation by the pope of Charles the Great – Charlemagne – as (western) Roman emperor in Rome in 800 set the seal on the political and cultural separation of east Rome and the west. Cultural differences, expressed in particular through ecclesiastical politics and the struggle between Franks, Byzantines and the papacy for dominance in the central and western Balkans, became increasingly apparent, complicated by rivalry within the eastern Church. Despite various attempts at marriage alliances between the Byzantine and various western courts, the growing political, cultural and military strength of the western world precluded any serious reassertion of east Roman imperial power in the central Mediterranean basin.

Byzantine influence was struck a further blow by the loss of Sicily to Islamic forces during the 9th century. The weakening of the empire in the civil wars of the middle and later 11th century and the growth of the Crusading movement

A naval battle in which the crews of two ships are about to meet in hand to hand combat, a detail from the 11th-century Cynegetica *of Pseudo-Oppian, Venice, folio 24 r. (Werner Forman Archive/Biblioteca Nazionale Marciana, Venice)*

THE BYZANTINE EMPIRE *c.*600

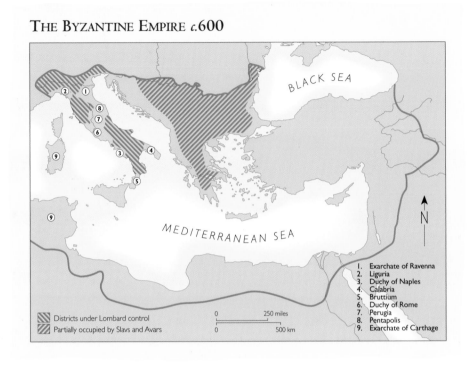

BLACK SEA

MEDITERRANEAN SEA

N

1. Exarchate of Ravenna
2. Liguria
3. Duchy of Naples
4. Calabria
5. Bruttium
6. Duchy of Rome
7. Perugia
8. Pentapolis
9. Exarchate of Carthage

Districts under Lombard control
Partially occupied by Slavs and Avars

| 0 | 250 miles |
| 0 | 500 km |

further complicated matters: caricatures of western arrogance and ignorance on one side were matched by equally inaccurate caricatures of Byzantine treachery and effeteness on the other. Although the imperial revival under the Komnenos dynasty during the late 11th and 12th centuries made a rapprochement possible, including the development of a strong pro-western faction at Constantinople (promoted by the emperor Manuel I (1143–80)), the conflict between imperial interests in controlling trade and commerce and Italian merchant expansionism, coupled with cultural suspicion and Venetian political intrigue and opportunism, resulted in the launching of the Fourth Crusade, the sack of Constantinople, and the partition of the eastern empire into a number of Latin kingdoms and principalities.

A somewhat different tone existed in relations between Byzantium and the Rus', Norse settlers from the central Russian river belt who entered the Black Sea to trade and raid for booty, but who soon became close trading partners with the empire, certainly by the 920s, and provided mercenary household troops for the emperors – from the 980s, the famous Varangian guard. Acceptance of Christianity under Vladimir in the 980s and a marriage alliance between the latter and Basil II inaugurated a long period of Byzantine cultural and spiritual influence on the Rus', fundamentally inflecting the evolution of Russian culture, the Church and tsarist ideology. The enduring influence of Byzantine methods of cultural

penetration in the Balkans was expressed most clearly in the structure, organization and ideology of the Orthodox Church of the region.

The empire's main neighbours in the north and west until the 10th century were thus the Bulgars – with the various Serb and other Slav chiefdoms and principalities in the western Balkans supporting or being directly controlled by now one side, now the other; the Rus' beyond them, along with the various steppe peoples – Chazars from the 8th century, then during the 9th the Magyars (who went on to establish the Christianized kingdom of Hungary), the Pechenegs in the 10th and 11th centuries, and thereafter the Cumans, relations of the Seljuks in the east. In Italy and western and central Europe foreign relations were dominated by the papacy and the neighbouring Lombard Kingdom and duchies in the former region until the later 8th century, and thereafter by the Frankish empire in its various forms. In particular the 'German' empire of the Ottonian dynasty dominated central Europe and Italy from the 10th century, and its rulers had a keen interest in eastern Europe and the Balkans. During the 11th century the rising power of the young kingdom of Hungary introduced a new element into this equation. Eastern Roman relations with the kingdom of Hungary were particularly strained during the 1150s and 1160s, for Hungary played an important role on the international political stage, in particular in relation to Byzantine policy with regard to the German empire. Hungarian interest in the north-western Balkans was perceived by Constantinople as a destabilizing element and a threat to imperial interests. The emperor Manuel tried to address the issue by both military and diplomatic pressure, sending frequent expeditions to threaten dissident rulers in the region to follow the imperial line, and interfering in the dynastic politics of the Hungarian court. The rise of the Italian maritime cities, especially

The foot soldiers of Emperor Basil I, distinguished by their long shields, deserting their general in the face of hostile Arab forces who carry round shields. The Byzantine general, Procopius, is killed. The History of John Scylitzes, folio 99. (Werner Forman Archive/Biblioteca Nacional, Madrid)

Byzantine soldiers of the 7th century. From left, armoured infantryman, noble commander from the late 7th century, armoured cavalryman from the early 7th century. (Angus McBride © Osprey Publishing Ltd)

Venice, Pisa and Genoa with their powerful fleets and mercantile interests, was to play a key role in both the political and economic life of the empire from this time onward.

Perhaps the most dangerous foe the Byzantines had to face in the west were the Normans of southern Italy, who had served originally as mercenaries in the Byzantine armies, but who by the last decades of the century had established an independent state of their own, and who invaded the Balkans from Italy during the reign of Alexios I in the 1090s and early 12th century. Eventually defeated on this front, they nevertheless went on to establish one of the most powerful states in the central Mediterranean, the Norman kingdom of Sicily, and presented a major threat to Byzantine interests throughout the century. Yet it was not the Normans who played the key role in diverting the Fourth Crusade in 1203–1204 from its original targets in the Muslim east to Byzantium, but rather the republic of Venice, and it was Venetian interests that dictated the form taken by the political fragmentation of the empire in the period immediately thereafter.

Until the extinction of the Sassanid empire by the Islamic armies in the 630s and early 640s, the Persian state had been the main opponent of the Roman empire in the east. Thereafter, the Umayyad (661–750) and then Abbasid (751–1258) caliphates posed a constant threat to the empire. But this complex history falls into several phases: 650s–720s, when Arab–Islamic invasions were a regular phenomenon aimed at the destruction of the east Roman state; 720s–750s, when a *modus vivendi* had been established, but in which Muslim attacks remained a constant source of economic and political dislocation; and thereafter until the middle of the 11th century, when the collapse and fragmentation of Abbasid authority made it possible for the empire to re-establish a military and political pre-eminence in the region. The increasingly important role of Turkic slave and mercenary soldiers in the Caliphate from the 840s, and the eventual arrival of the Seljuk Turks in the 1050s, was to alter this picture drastically. A combination of internal political dissension and a relatively minor military defeat at the hands of the Seljuk Sultan Alp Aslan in eastern Anatolia in 1071 (battle of Mantzikert, mod. Malazgirt) resulted in the imperial loss of central Asia Minor, which henceforth became dominated by groups of Turkic nomadic pastoralists (known as Türkmen) who presented a constant threat to all forms of sedentary occupation. The growth of a series of Turkic emirates in the region thereafter made recovery of the region impossible; and the rise of the dynasty of Osman – the Ottomans – from the later 13th century was eventually to prove fatal to the east Roman empire.

The political world of Byzantium was thus complex and multifaceted. The government at Constantinople needed to run an efficient, intelligent and above all watchful diplomatic system, for it was on diplomacy, alliances, gifts and the careful use of intelligence that the empire depended. But when these failed, as they often did, it needed an army, and it is the imperial armies, the way they were maintained and how they fought, that is the main theme of this part.

WHY AND HOW DID BYZANTIUM FIGHT WARS?

Byzantine generals and rulers were generally fully aware of the relationship between the allocation and redistribution of resources – soldiers, supplies, equipment, livestock and so forth – and the ability of the empire to ward off hostile military action or to strike back at its enemies. Military handbooks and treatises dating from the 6th to the 11th centuries make it apparent that the imbalance in resources between Byzantium and its enemies was recognized. Generals were exhorted not to give battle in unfavourable conditions, because this might lead to waste of life and resources; indeed the dominant motif in these works is that it was the Byzantines who were compelled to manoeuvre, to use delaying tactics, to employ ambushes and other strategems to even the odds stacked against them; but that it was quite clearly a main war aim to win without having to fight a decisive battle. Victory could be achieved through a combination of delaying tactics, intelligent exploitation of enemy weaknesses, the landscape, seasonal factors, and diplomacy. Wars were costly, and for a state whose basic income derived from agricultural production, and which remained relatively stable as well as being vulnerable to both natural and man-made disasters, they were to be avoided if at all possible.

Another, closely related, factor in imperial strategic thinking was manpower: from a Byzantine perspective, they were always outnumbered, and strategy as well as diplomacy needed to take this factor into account in dealing with enemies. One way of evening the balance was to reduce enemy numbers: delay the enemy forces until they could no longer stay in the field, destroying or removing any possible sources of provisions and supplies, for example, misleading them with false information about Byzantine intentions, these are all methods which the military treatises recommend. Avoiding battle, which was a keystone of Byzantine strategy, would also increase the possibility that the enemy host might be struck by illness, run out of water and supplies, and so on.

Defence thus had to be the primary concern of Byzantine rulers and generals. Byzantine military dispositions were administered upon a consistent and logistically well-considered basis, and their main purpose was to secure the survival of the empire by deploying the limited resources available to the best effect. They were, necessarily, defensive in orientation, a point noted quite clearly by the mid-10th-century visitor from Italy, the ambassador Liutprand of Cremona, with regard to the precautions taken to secure Constantinople at night, in case of an unexpected enemy attack. The emphasis placed by Byzantine writers and governments on effective and intelligent diplomacy is not just a question of cultural preference informed by a Christian distaste for the shedding of blood: to the contrary, the continued existence of the state depended upon the deployment of a sophisticated diplomatic arsenal. The whole history of Byzantine foreign relations and both the theory and practice of Byzantine diplomacy reflect this. Diplomacy had its military edge, of course: good relations with the various peoples of the steppe were essential to Byzantine interests in the Balkans and Caucasus, because a weapon might thereby be created that could be turned on the enemies of the empire. Such contacts were also an essential source of information, of course, and much effort was expended in gathering information that might be relevant to the empire's defence.

Going to war was thus rarely the result of a planned choice made by emperors or their advisers, for the empire was perpetually threatened from one quarter or another, and was thus in a constant state of military preparedness. The difference

A battle that took place in 842 between the cavalry of the Byzantines and the Arabs. The History of John Scylitzes, folio 54v. (Werner Forman Archive/Biblioteca Nacional, Madrid)

between war and peace in the frontier areas became a matter, not of the state of the empire as a whole in relation to a particular neighbouring power, but rather of the part of the empire in which one found oneself. While recovery of former territories was permanently on the ideological agenda, efforts to implement it reflected an ad hoc reaction to an unforeseen advantage gained through victories in battle and the exploitation of favourable circumstances. In real terms, the potential for the reconquest and restoration of lost territories was severely limited. Strategy was determined by the interplay between resources and political beliefs, tempered by ideological pragmatism: most Byzantine warfare was fought not on the basis of delivering a knock-out blow to the enemy, but on that of attempting to reach or maintain a state of parity or equilibrium, through attrition, raid and counter-raid, and destruction of the enemy's short-term potential. Members of the government and imperial court may have shared common ideals in respect of their relations with the outside world; but the strategic dispositions of the armies of the later Roman and Byzantine empire were not necessarily arranged with these concerns as a priority.

Mid-6th-century mosaic of the Emperor Justinian I and his entourage, from right two deacons, Archbishop Maximian, two patricians and guards. North wall of the apse of San Vitale, Ravenna. (akg-images/ Nimatallah)

Resources were a key element in strategic thinking, for obvious reasons – armies cannot fight without adequate supplies, equipment, training and shelter. But warfare was not necessarily conducted with a purely material advantage in mind, since ideological superiority played an important role in Byzantine notions of their own identity and role in the order of things; nor was it conducted with any longer-term strategic objective in mind. Any damage to the enemy was a good thing, but some ways of hitting the enemy also carried an ideological value – strategically wasteful attacks against symbolically important enemy fortresses or towns were carried out by all medieval rulers at one time or another, since the short-term propaganda value, associated perhaps also with a raising of morale, was often considered as valuable as any real material gains. By the same token, some theatres were ideologically more important than others. Fighting the barbarians in the Balkans and north of the Danube was regarded as much less prestigious and glorious than combating the religious foe, the Muslims in the east: an 11th-century writer remarks: 'There seemed nothing grand (in fighting) the barbarians in the West ... but were he (the emperor Romanos III) to turn to those living in the east, he thought that he could perform nobly ...'

There is little evidence that warfare was conducted to gain resources that could then be deployed in a coherent way to further a given strategy, except in the sense that more territory and the wealth that usually accompanied it were desirable in themselves. Warfare was conducted on the basis of inflicting maximum damage to the enemy's economy and material infrastructure – enslavement or killing of populations, destruction of fortifications and urban installations, devastation of the countryside. Equally, measures to protect one's own side had to be taken, and by the middle of the 10th century the Byzantines had developed both aspects of such warfare to a fine art. Both in the war against the Arabs in the east from the 7th to 10th centuries, and against Slavs and Bulgars in the west, Byzantine warfare was conducted effectively on the basis of a struggle of attrition. This is not to suggest that there was never a longer-term strategic aim or ulterior motive at issue – in the case of the accelerated eastward expansion in the 10th century and in the slightly later, but closely related, conquest of Bulgaria under Basil II, it is possible to suggest that this was the case, for example. In the first case, through an aggressive imperialism towards the minor Muslim powers in Syria and Jazîra, the extension and consolidation of the empire's territorial strength in the area was clearly an important consideration; in the second case, and partly stimulated by the first development, the creation of a new resource-base for the emperors and Constantinopolitan government, independent of the power and influence of the eastern magnates, was a significant consideration; but it was also in the context of an equally practical decision to eradicate the threat from an independent Bulgaria and reassert imperial dominance throughout the Balkan regions. Both facets of these processes mirror very particular structural tensions within Byzantine state and society, and at the same time they also demonstrate particularly clearly the extent to which the foreign policies and military strategy of a state can reflect power relations within the society as a whole.

Warfare for ideological reasons alone was very rare. Clearly, all defensive warfare could be justified on a range of such grounds – the threat to the empire's territory and population; the challenge to Orthodox rule and God's appointed ruler, the emperor at Constantinople; challenges to Roman sovereignty; and so forth. Offensive or aggressive warfare was, in the Christian Roman empire, a little more difficult to justify, but it was readily accomplished. But there is no doubt that the dominant element in Byzantine military thinking throughout the long history of the empire was defensive, and necessarily so in view of its strategic situation. Byzantium survived as long as it did because it was able to defend itself, intelligently exploit natural frontiers or boundaries in the crisis years of the 7th and 8th centuries, and manage diplomatic and political relationships thereafter. And whatever the specific details of the process of its political–historical withering

Church of the monastery at Daphni, Greece. (akg-images/ Erich Lessing)

away after 1204, the gradual demise of the Byzantine empire went hand-in-hand with its declining ability to muster the resources necessary to defend itself. Strategy was, in practical terms, a matter of pragmatic reaction to events in the world around the empire, only loosely informed by the political-ideological imperatives of the Christian Roman empire. In this respect, the political and strategic conditions of existence of the east Roman or Byzantine state rendered a grand strategy in the narrower sense irrelevant – the strategy of the empire was based on maintaining the conditions appropriate to political, cultural and ideological survival.

DEFENSIVE WARFARE

Wars can, crudely speaking, thus be divided into two broad categories, defensive and offensive, although it must be said at the outset that pre-emptive attacks could count as both, and were frequently so justified. Defensive fighting took several forms: guerrilla tactics against enemy invaders; major confrontations between field armies, often following a protracted period of manoeuvring in which each side tried to outwit the other; or a combination of the two. The defensive campaigns fought against the first Islamic armies took this form, with the imperial forces struggling to match the mobility and speed of the Arab raiders, who were able to deprive the Roman commanders of the initiative not simply by virtue of their fast-moving, hard-hitting tactics, but also because the type of warfare they practised made any notion of a regular front untenable.

This miniature depicts the Muslims besieging the Byzantine city of Messina in Sicily which they captured in 842–3. The History of John Scylitzes. (Werner Forman Archive/Biblioteca Nacional, Madrid)

The Arab Islamic conquests radically altered the strategic and political geography of the whole east Mediterranean region. The complete failure of attempts to meet and drive back the invaders in open battle induced a major shift in strategy whereby open confrontations with the Muslim armies were avoided. The field armies were withdrawn first to north Syria and Mesopotamia, and shortly thereafter back to the line of the Taurus and Anti-Taurus ranges. By the mid-640s the armies which had operated in Syria, Palestine and Mesopotamia had been withdrawn into Anatolia. The regions across which they were based were determined by the ability of these districts to provide for the soldiers in terms of supplies and other requirements. The field forces thus came to be quartered across Asia Minor and Thrace, where they were now referred to by the Greek term for these districts, *themata* or 'themes'.

This distribution was intended both to meet logistical demands by providing each army with an adequate hinterland from which it could be supported and to meet the strategic needs of defence. But it was a very defensive strategy, and it meant that the economic hinterland of the frontier incurred substantial damage, subject as it was to regular devastation. There resulted the appearance by the 700s of a 'no-man's land' between the settled and economically safer regions on both sides. The new arrangements did prevent the establishment by the Arabs of permanent bases in Asia Minor itself.

The themes were at first merely groupings of provinces across which different armies were based. By 730 or thereabouts they had acquired a clear geographical identity; and by the later 8th century some elements of fiscal as well as military administration were set up on a thematic basis, although the late Roman provinces continued to subsist. The number of themata expanded as the empire's economic and political situation improved, partly through the original large military divisions being split up into different 'provincial' armies, and partly through the recovery in the last years of the 8th century and the reimposition of imperial authority over lands once held in the southern Balkans.

The localization of recruitment and military identities which resulted from these arrangements led to a distinction between the regular elements – full-time soldiers – and the less competent or well-supplied militia-like elements in each theme region. In the 760s a small élite force, known as the *tagmata* ('the regiments') was established under Constantine V (741–75), which quickly evolved into the élite field division for campaign purposes. It had better pay and discipline than both the regular and the part-time provincial units, and this was the first step in a tendency to recruit mercenary forces, both foreign and indigenous, to form special units and to serve for the duration of a particular campaign or group of campaigns. As imperial power recovered in the 9th and 10th centuries, the empire reasserted its military strength in the east, and the role and the proportion of such full-time units became ever more important.

Defensive strategy was determined by several elements. To begin with, raiding forces were to be held and turned back at the Taurus and Anti-Taurus passes, wherever possible. Where this policy of meeting and repulsing hostile attacks at the frontier did not work, local forces would harass the invaders, keeping track of every movement and the location of each party or group. Numerous small forts and fortresses along the major routes, located at crossroads or locations where supplies might be stored as well as by the frontier passes through which enemy forces had to pass, reinforced the local troops. Although exposed to enemy action, these posts were a constant threat to any invading force. In addition, a series of frontier districts was set up in the 8th and 9th centuries as independent commands along the frontier, complementing the armies of the themes. Known as kleisourarchies (*kleisourarchiai*), they emphasized the highly localized pattern of defence.

The empire suffered many defeats, especially in the earlier period, but it also witnessed some major successes, particularly where the invaders could be shadowed and the imperial armies brought together at the right time and place. These encounters showed that the strategy operated by the imperial forces could succeed, when the armies were well led and adequate intelligence of enemy movements was available. But the war in the east was largely a struggle between two equal powers, with the imperial side having the advantage of geography and communications to offset the superior numbers on the side of the Caliphate. Only in the 10th century, when the empire went over fully to the offensive, does this picture change. These defensive arrangements were progressively allowed to fall into disuse as the empire went onto the offensive after the middle of the 10th century. And when the empire's situation changed for the worse, as a result of the appearance from the 1040s and afterwards of a host of new enemies, the lack of an effective, deep defensive structure permitted the Seljuk Turks to conquer and permanently occupy central Asia Minor after the battle of Mantzikert in 1071 with virtually no opposition. The empire was never again able to re-establish its power in the region.

PRE-EMPTIVE ATTACKS

Part of the imperial defensive strategy entailed launching pre-emptive strikes against the enemy, partly aimed at containment, partly at the reassertion of Roman ideological power. Some of these attacks were successful, some less so. Among the bleakest episodes in the history of the empire is the attack launched against the Bulgars by the emperor Nikephoros I in 811, which ended in both the death of the emperor and a crushing defeat. Nikephoros, who had been the chief finance officer of the empress Eirene, came to the throne in 802 and appears to have wished to defeat the Bulgars so comprehensively that the Bulgar Khanate could be recovered for the empire. An expedition in 809 had reached the Bulgar capital at Pliska in north-east Bulgaria, and sacked it. The expedition of 811 was intended to establish a more permanent Roman

THE BYZANTINE EMPIRE c.700–950

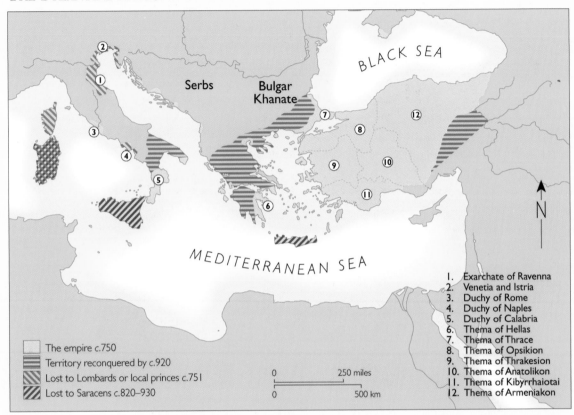

Legend:
- The empire c.750
- Territory reconquered by c.920
- Lost to Lombards or local princes c.751
- Lost to Saracens c.820–930

0   250 miles
0   500 km

1. Exarchate of Ravenna
2. Venetia and Istria
3. Duchy of Rome
4. Duchy of Naples
5. Duchy of Calabria
6. Thema of Hellas
7. Thema of Thrace
8. Thema of Opsikion
9. Thema of Thrakesion
10. Thema of Anatolikon
11. Thema of Kibyrrhaiotai
12. Thema of Armeniakon

presence in the region. Nikephoros ordered the assembly of a large force made up from contingents from the Asia Minor armies supplemented by troops from the European themata and the imperial guards units, the tagmata. There was a ceremonial aspect to the whole affair, since the emperor took victory for granted after the easy win in 809, and as well as the soldiers a large number of courtiers and palace officials accompanied the expedition. But the imperial troops were eventually drawn into an ambush, where during a night attack they were utterly routed. The defeat was one of the blackest days of imperial history, no less of a catastrophe than the battle of Adrianople in 378 at which the emperor Valens had died fighting the Goths. The Bulgar khan became the most dangerous enemy the empire had to face for the next few years, and was able to lay siege to Constantinople itself in 813.

OFFENSIVE WARFARE

Given the empire's strategic problems noted already, most fighting could be justified in some way or other as 'defensive', even where it was clearly aggressively motivated.

Such were the wars waged in the later 10th and early 11th centuries against the Bulgars and the Rus', for example, when the justification for war was both the rejection of previously agreed arrangements which were seen by the emperor as dishonourable, the threat which ensued from the Bulgars to the imperial territories in Thrace, and the involvement of the Rus'. In the autumn of 965, and following the conquest by Byzantine armies of the islands of Crete and Cyprus, as well as of Cilicia in southern Asia Minor and its incorporation into the empire, Bulgarian envoys arrived at the court of the emperor. Their purpose was to request the payment of the 'tribute' paid by Constantinople to the Bulgar tsar as part of the guarantee for the long-lasting peace which had been established after the death of the Tsar Symeon in 927. But the empire was in a very different position since the time that the original agreement had been made. The emperor Nikephoros II Phokas (963–69), reflecting the outrage represented by the presumptive demand of the Bulgarians, had the envoys sent home in disgrace. Instead of paying, he despatched a small force to demolish a number of Bulgarian frontier posts, and then called in his allies to the north, the Kiev Rus', to attack the Bulgars in the rear.

The steppe region stretching from the plain of Hungary eastwards through south Russia and north of the Caspian was very important in imperial diplomacy. The home of many nomadic peoples, mostly of Turkic stock, it was always important to keep these peoples well disposed towards the empire. Constantinople had been able to establish good relations with the Chazars from the 630s, whose khans remained faithful allies of most Byzantine emperors. Their strategic

Mosaic depicting the washing of the feet in the main church of the 11th-century monastery of Hosios Loukas, Greece. (akg-images/Erich Lessing)

49

significance was great: they were frequently invited to attack the Bulgars from the north, for example, and exerted crucial pressure on the latter at key moments. They also kept the empire informed of developments to the east, in central Asia. But the Chazar empire contracted during the later 9th century, as various peoples to the east were set in motion by the expansion of the Turkic Pechenegs, who established themselves in the steppe region between the Danube and Don. The empire continued to follow the same policy, of course, now with the Pechenegs, whose value as a check on both the Rus' and the Magyars was obvious. Yet they were a dangerous ally.

The Rus' were an amalgamation of Scandinavian settlers and warriors with indigenous Slavic peoples along the rivers of central and western Russia. During the 9th century they had grown to be an important political power, and by the 850s and 860s their longships were regularly entering the Black Sea. In the early 10th century, and following some hostilities, trading agreements were concluded with the empire. This developed into an alliance from the middle of the 10th century, so that when Nikephoros II asked for their support in 966, their ambitious and warlike prince Svyatoslav was only too willing to agree. In 968 Svyatoslav arrived on the Danube and easily defeated the Bulgarian forces sent against him. In 969 he had to return to Kiev to repulse an attack from the Pechenegs, but returned later in the year and, rapidly occupying northern and eastern Bulgaria, he deposed the tsar, Boris II, and incorporated Bulgaria into his own domain.

This was not a part of the emperor's original plan. In vain he attempted to establish an alliance with the defeated Bulgars, but towards the end of 969 the emperor was assassinated, and his successor, John I Tzimiskes, had to confront the difficult task of removing this potentially far more dangerous foe. Some of the Bulgar nobility saw a chance to recover their independence of the Byzantine state and its culture by working with the Rus'. Svyatoslav sent the new emperor an ultimatum to evacuate all the European provinces and confine the empire to Asia alone. In the spring of 970 a large Rus' force invaded Thrace, sacking the fortress of Philippoupolis (mod. Plovdiv) and moving on down the road to Constantinople.

The war that followed involved the assembling of a major imperial army, delaying tactics to distract and divert enemy resources and, eventually, the complete defeat of the Rus' force and the return of Svyatoslav to his own territories (although he was killed by Pecheneg raiders on the way home). It was a war fought initially as a result of a rejection of what the empire's rulers saw as an outdated and humiliating agreement with an inferior neighbour, but which quickly turned into a major offensive. The result was, on the one hand, the reincorporation of substantial parts of eastern Bulgaria up to the Danube into imperial territory. On the other, the Byzantine victory encouraged the development of a new independence movement and the rise, during the 970s and 980s, of a new Bulgarian empire which, under its tsar Samuel, was the major foreign threat to imperial power until the beginning of the 11th century. Only as a result of the tireless campaigning of Emperor Basil II, culminating in a final victory in 1014 and the total recovery of all the territory once held by the empire in the Balkans up to the Danube, was peace re-established, and the Balkans became once more an entirely Roman – from the point of view of political and military control – territory.

A major shift in strategy followed these successes as well as successes against Islamic powers in the east. The establishment of a system of alliances or buffer states made the maintenance of expensive standing forces, which constituted a great drain on the treasury, less necessary. Economic and cultural influence could be employed in addition to the threat of military action to maintain peace along the Danube, and similar policies were applied in the east. The emperors pursued a foreign policy which placed greater reliance on vassals and neighbouring powers supplying troops, thus limiting the demand on the empire's own resources. But in the 1040s and afterwards this strategy broke down, largely because the balance between diplomacy and military strength was damaged by civil war and provincial rebellion, in turn a reflection of important shifts in the social and political structure of the empire. The provincial or thematic militias had been neglected in favour of full-time, regionally recruited tagmata, better suited to the sort of offensive warfare the empire had been waging since the 950s; while reductions in the military budget encouraged a greater dependence on foreign mercenary troops, especially of western knights – Franks, Germans and Normans. In 1071 such an army of mixed Byzantine and foreign troops under the emperor Romanos IV suffered a defeat at the hands of the invading Seljuk Turks near the fortress of Mantzikert in eastern Asia Minor – not a great disaster from a purely military perspective. Yet the civil war and internal disruption that followed gave the invading Turks a free hand in central Asia Minor, which was never again fully recovered. Emperors from Alexios I onward spent the period from the 1080s until the 1180s attempting to recover the situation but, in the end, without success. The wars of the period were fought increasingly using western tactics and panoply, but with elements of a still clearly Byzantine or east Roman tactical organization – contemporaries continue to remark on the order, cohesion and discipline with which the multi-ethnic and colourful Byzantine armies still fought.

Byzantium went to war for many reasons in practical terms – perceived military threats to the frontier, responses to actual invasion and raiding from hostile neighbours, as well as ideologically motivated wars in which justification depended on notions of what territories used to be Roman and could be legitimately recovered, and on ideas about ideological challenges to the Christian Roman world view. The wars of reconquest in the later 10th century were in part motivated and justified on the latter grounds, for example, even though in Byzantium no notion of 'holy war' as such ever really evolved.

αὐτοῦ ἐπηρήσας φραγήου· οἱ ὁρμῆσας ἀπο δρόμου ἐξ· συρομμένου· καὶ κατ αὐτον ἀναφαμὲν πορτουῖραν
πνοσ ὠφελμων εἶναι κρίνας τὰς προσβολὰς· ἀπισχεῖν ὁλωσ μὴ δυνη θεῖς τὸ εἰ
τι κῶι καὶ πεζικῶν διὰ μέσων· ἐν τῷ προσ βλαχεμνα κόλπω· ἀπισχεῖν ὁλωσ μὴ δυνη θεῖς τὸ εἰ
ρι τ αυτῆς ἐκ τε ταμεμε νος ἡκρασάμπ εσο· προσβολῆ τοῖς τείχεσι παντα ὁ θεν ἐγένοντο· ἐπ

Λ—πα ἦτε δε μεθ ὀλίγον καὶ τῶ κᾶσ· Καὶ ἐργος παψ το θε ἐπι μετον ἀπολιορκίας· ὁ ὑδὲν ὑδὲ ἐπ κάμοι
Ἀξίον δ ε πραῆτ ἐτο· τῶν ἐν δ ὁμ εὑρεω προσαμμο μένων καὶ ταπελε πολε ἐκ πραομ μένον· ὡς ὁ
μεγ γρ ρ τὸ ἦμας· ἅμα πε ἐπ φ αῆνα τῇ βασιλικ ἔι· καὶ ἅμα γου πολιτας ἄμα πε ἐασα μαν τα τὰς πυλας,
ἅλα το προσ τομ κι χαλκ μῖ ος· Καὶ ε πα τῶν το τον περ τ η ρι γ ο ρ λον ἀπ ε πομεν π ρο τ ε ρον ε τ ει μᾳ
Καὶ α αυτος παψ ου ἀι μετ κα ου λ ε ο θε τι θε υπο ται τῶ ἀπαδασ τον· ἀρ ἡ το ὑμ ε ρα χ κον ἀ δ ρι π ο σα μ εν ου ὡ ι ος
καὶ προσ τον τουρ κος μι κον ἀπο κλιραυψοσ· Κα τ ο π τῆ ἐ π ι κολουθ ῆ σ εν· ὡ ς ὑ δὲ ὑ δὲν π ω κα τ ε λ ω ι ὁ ι λα
αὐτ ωι υπ ημν ησεν· ἀλλα καὶ ῖ β ε ο η μαλλον ῦ π ο π ι μ ε γ εδε ω λ ι ε τ ο· τ ο π ε μ ερ. π αρ εμβολ ην εν τοῖς
παλιν ου ἐργα το τε ω φα καὶ ου ρε π η ρ αμ α ρ γ ι σ α π ε τ ε μ ε νο ς ἡ β υ ται· ὁ χ υ ρα μ εν η π ξ α το· οι δα

η πα ρεμ β ο λη τ ο υ θε ο φ ι λ ο υ

ORGANIZING FOR WAR

THE EVOLUTION OF TACTICAL ADMINISTRATION

There were important changes in tactical structures over the period from the 6th to the 11th century, and again from the later 11th to the 12th centuries and beyond.

Units of the middle of the 6th century varied considerably in their regimental organization. The older legions and auxiliary forces continued to exist through the 3rd and 4th centuries, divided into *alae* of cavalry and *cohortes* of infantry, nominally of 500 and 1,000 men respectively; although under Constantine I (324–37), new infantry units called *auxilia* often replaced these *cohortes*. Newer legions, numbering 1,000–1,500, had also been created during the 2nd and 3rd centuries, and this number seems also to have applied to the original legions by the 4th century. Apart from these were units called *vexillationes*, originally detachments from various units formed for a particular reason during the period c.150–250, which had been turned into permanent units in their own right. This term, *vexillation*, was applied in the 4th century to most of the new cavalry units recruited at that time. Although some of these technical differences survived into the 6th century, the general term for most units was by then the word *numerus* or its Greek equivalent, *arithmos* or *tagma*, which simply meant 'unit' or 'number' (of soldiers).

Byzantine tactics and strategy had to adapt quickly to the situation following the Arab conquests in the middle of the 7th century. Armies along the frontiers are often referred to as *kaballarika themata* – 'cavalry armies' – showing that light cavalry had come to dominate the warfare of the period, much of which involved skirmishing and hit-and-run raids. But while infantry continued to be needed, and played an important part in many campaigns, their value appears slowly to have declined, to some extent reflecting social factors, since they were drawn mostly from the poorest of the provincial soldiery. The development of infantry tactics after the period of the first Islamic conquests, along with the higher profile of mounted warfare, therefore, reflected the strategic situation in which the empire found itself. During the period from the later 7th to the 9th or early 10th centuries, the differences which once existed between the different types of infantry and cavalry were subject to a general levelling out of the different arms, into light cavalry and infantry. Only the tagmata at

OPPOSITE
A miniature illustrating a siege of Constantinople, 9th–11th century. The History of John Scylitzes, folio 32v. (Werner Forman Archive/ Biblioteca Nacional, Madrid)

53

Gold Byzantine coin.
(Werner Forman Archive/
Barber Institute of Fine Arts,
University of Birmingham)

Constantinople seem to have provided a heavy cavalry force. It seems to have been the responsibility of local officers in the provinces to establish field units and to arm them as each specific occasion required. The sizes of units on the battlefield varied according to tactical need: there seems to have been no fixed number for the different formations, with figures recommended for the smallest infantry units, the banda, for example, ranging from as few as 150 to as many as 400. Several *tourmai* could appear on campaign as a single large division, for example, or vice versa. Most themes had two or three divisions or tourmai, but this does not mean that they were the same size or could muster the same number of soldiers.

The provincial armies were organized into what we would refer to as divisions, brigades and regiments – tourmai, *drouggoi* and *banda*. The first and last were also districts of their thema, or military region. Each *tourma* had a headquarters or base in a fortified town or fortress. Each *bandon* was identified with a particular locality from which its soldiers were recruited. Each *tourmarchês*, or commander of a tourma, was an important figure in the military administration of his theme, responsible for the fortresses and strongpoints in his district, as well as for the safety of the local population and their goods and chattels. His most important responsibility before the middle of the 10th century, however, was dealing with raids into his territory and informing his superiors of enemy movements.

During the course of the 10th century the army evolved a much more offensive tactical structure, the main causes being the need to recruit more professional soldiers, and the need to operate effectively on campaigns which demanded more than the seasonally available theme armies. The main changes were the introduction of a corps of heavy cavalry armed with lances and maces, which could operate effectively alongside infantry, and which substantially enhanced the aggressive power of the Byzantine cavalry, together with the revival of a corps of disciplined, effective heavy infantry, able to stand firm in the line of battle, confront enemy infantry and cavalry, march long distances and function as garrison troops away from their home territory on a permanent basis. At the same time, the army leadership developed new battlefield tactics, so that commanders had a flexible yet hard-hitting force at their disposal that could respond appropriately to a range of different situations.

The remarkable successes achieved by Byzantine armies in the second half of the 10th century in particular, under a series of very able commanders, and described in the historical accounts of the period, corroborate the evidence of the tactical treatises. In one tract a new formation of infantry soldiers is described, consisting of troops wielding thick-stocked, long-necked javelins or pikes, whose task it was to face and turn back enemy heavy cavalry attacks. Twenty years later the tactic had evolved further, so that there were in each major infantry unit of 1,000 men 100 soldiers so equipped, integrated with 400 ordinary spearmen, 300 archers and 200 light infantry (with slings and javelins). This important change in the role of infantry was reflected in the changed political and military situation of the 10th century. In the late 6th century cavalry began to achieve a certain pre-eminence in military organization and tactics, whereas the 10th-century texts give infantry formations equal or even preferential treatment. Infantry became once more a key element in the army, in terms of numbers as well as of tactics, a clear contrast to the situation in the preceding centuries. The new tactics were embodied in a new formation, in which infantry and cavalry worked together, essentially a hollow square or rectangle, depending on the terrain, designed to cope with encircling movements from hostile cavalry, as a refuge for Byzantine mounted units when forced to retreat, and as a means of strengthening infantry cohesiveness and morale. Infantry were no longer drawn up in a deep line with a largely defensive role, but actively integrated into the offensive heavy cavalry tactics of the period. And a very important aspect of the change was a focus on the recruitment of good infantry from war-like peoples within the empire, especially Armenians. The demand for uniformity in tactical function and

THE BYZANTINE EMPIRE c.1000–1180

The empire at its height c.1025–1030
Lost to the Normans by 1100
Territory lost c.1071–1100
Territory recovered under John II/Manuel I

| 0 | 250 miles |
| 0 | 500 km |

therefore equipment and weaponry meant that the Byzantine infantry of this period were more like their classical Roman predecessors than anything in the intervening period.

New formations of cavalry appear, heavily armoured troops armed from head to foot in lamellar, mail and quilting, whose horses were likewise protected. Face, neck, flanks and forequarters were all to be covered with armour to prevent enemy missiles and blows from injuring the cavalryman's mount. Known as *kataphraktoi* or *klibanophoroi*, they were relatively few in number due to the expense of maintaining them, and were the elite strike force in each field army, drawn up in a broad-nosed wedge with their only function to smash through the enemy heavy cavalry or infantry line, disrupt his formation, and open it up to permit supporting horse- and foot-soldiers to exploit the situation. Contemporary writers, both Byzantine and Arab, comment on the effects of this formation on their foes. The imperial armies achieved a powerful reputation, to the extent that by the 1030s the mere threat of an imperial

KLIBANOPHOROS, c.970

The *klibanophoroi* were a revival by Nikephoros II of the true cataphract, which had not been seen since late Roman times. The *Nikephoroi Praecepta Militaria* describes the armour of these super-heavy cavalry as a lamellar *klibanion* with elbow-length sleeves, and over it a thick, padded *epilorikion*. The head was protected by an iron helmet over a mail hood. The limbs were covered with splint-armour vambraces and greaves. Their horses were also armoured. They drew up in a wedge formation on the battlefield, with 20 men in the first rank, 24 in the second, and four more in each consecutive rank; the last rank (the twelfth) could comprise as many as 64 men, so making 504 in the whole unit. Apparently a unit of 384 was more common (i.e. only 10 ranks) The front four ranks carried *marzobarboula* in addition to the usual sword and *kontarion*. Some men, more lightly equipped than the lancers, were armed instead with bows; if there were 300 lancers there could be 80 archers. Because of their cost klibanophoroi were probably limited to the tagmata regiments, and it seems likely that Mantzikert saw the end of them. (Angus McBride © Osprey Publishing Ltd)

army marching into northern Syria was enough to keep the local Muslim emirs in check. Yet while these successes were the result of a combination of good organization and logistics, intelligent tactics, well-armed, trained and disciplined soldiers, and good morale, the key always remained the competence and effectiveness of the general in command. An army is only as good as its leadership, however, and although tactical order and training certainly gave Byzantine armies through much of the empire's history an obvious advantage, incompetent officers were the bane of the system:

dependence on the charisma and intelligence of its leaders was one of the most significant in-built weaknesses of the imperial military system at the tactical level. During the middle of the 11th century, and in a context of short-sighted strategic planning and internal political conflict, this produced serious problems and led to the erosion of the effectiveness of both the field armies and the provincial defences.

As the demands of offensive warfare required the employment of ever greater numbers of professional, mercenary soldiers, both indigenous and foreign, so many of the provincial, thematic units of the imperial armies were neglected, especially in the period after the death of Basil II in 1025. Michael Attaleiates, a contemporary of the Mantzikert campaign who travelled with the imperial entourage, paints a sad picture of the state of the thematic levy raised for the campaign of 1071, remarking that the provincial troops were entirely unfitted for warfare – they had been neither mustered nor paid or supplied with their traditional provisions for many years. Yet his account of the campaigns of the dynamic emperor Romanos IV in the years 1068–71 shows that the imperial armies still possessed an order, discipline and cohesion when properly led.

Byzantine armies in the middle and later 11th century were a mixture of regular mercenary units from the different parts of the empire, the older thematic soldiers, and foreign units. The growing political and cultural influence of the world around Byzantium, which had been held at bay for so long, meant that the empire was becoming more and more integrated into the tactical world of the lands around it. Byzantine order and discipline remained a significant element in the empire's armies, but the latter were a polyglot and multi-ethnic mixture of Seljuk, Pecheneg or Cuman horse archers, Norman, German and Frankish knights, Bulgarian and Anatolian light infantry, Georgians and Alans from the Caucasus, imperial guards recruited from outside the empire (Varangians, for example, were from the 1070s chiefly made up of Anglo-Saxons who had left recently conquered Norman England). The Byzantine army was no longer, strictly speaking, Byzantine.

One of the tactical innovations of the period with which Byzantine soldiers and generals had to contend was the massed heavy cavalry charge favoured by the Normans. Although they were quite familiar with Norman tactics (Norman mercenaries had served in the imperial armies in Italy and Sicily in the 1030s and 1040s), the Byzantines had only rarely needed to confront it themselves. Most of the warfare they had been involved in since the 1060s had been against light-armed, highly mobile enemies such as Turks and Pechenegs. And whereas the Byzantine heavy cavalry of the later 10th century had been armed with lances and maces, they had advanced at a trot, not at the charge, with the aim of simply rolling over the enemy force facing them.

In spite of efforts under the emperors of the Komnenos dynasty, many indigenous units were re-equipped and trained in western style, so that the result

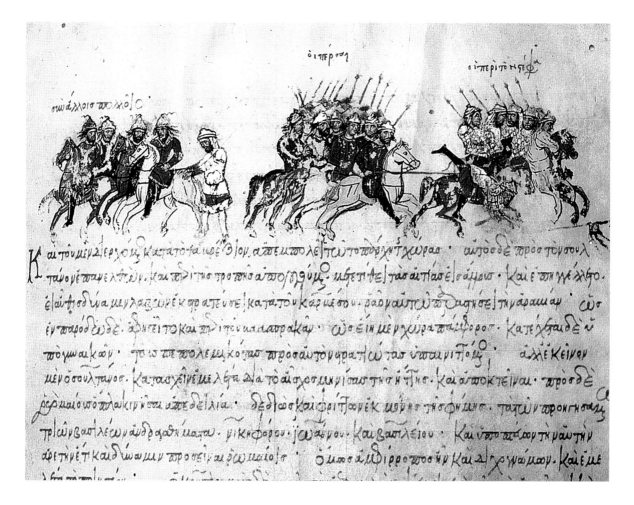

A battle between the cavalry of the Byzantines and the Seljuks. The History of John Scylitzes, folio 234v. (Werner Forman Archive/ Biblioteca Nacional, Madrid)

was an army no different from any other multi-ethnic, polyglot mercenary army in its tactics and formations. The difference lay in the superior order and tactical dispositions of the imperial troops, when these were properly exploited by an able commanding officer, and this is still evident on occasion in the later years of the 12th century. By the middle of the 13th century, and following the fall of Constantinople to the armies of the Fourth Crusade, while Byzantine technical terms, titles, and names for types of unit continued to be employed in the shrinking territories of the empire, tactics, armour and weaponry were no different from those of the surrounding cultures and states with whom the Byzantines were alternately at peace and war.

STRATEGY

Strategic dispositions evolved to meet the needs of the moment. In the 6th century and up to the period of the Arab invasions the units established in garrisons along and behind the frontier were called *limitanei*, frontier soldiers, usually comprised of the older legions and auxiliary regiments, while the field armies were largely formed of more recently established units, and located across the provinces, often well behind the frontier, in strategic bases from which they could meet any incursions into Roman territory. One result of the loss of the eastern and Danubian provinces during the 7th century was the disappearance of the former and the withdrawal into Asia Minor of the latter. In the later 10th century new and much smaller territories under *doukes*, 'dukes', grew up along both the eastern and northern frontiers, serving both as a zone of defence and as a springboard for further advances. At the same time, the old themes became increasingly demilitarized with the growth in the use of mercenaries, as we have also seen. The collapse of the later 11th century brought with it a need to reorganize, and although the changes wrought by the Komnenoi produced a series of new *themata* and new frontiers in Asia Minor, the basic principles of 11th-century strategy – an in-depth defence based in fortresses and similar strongpoints supported by a single imperial field force based in and around Constantinople – were maintained. The last two centuries of the empire, from the 1250s until 1453, saw no substantial change, although numbers were very much reduced as the empire's resources shrank.

LOGISTICS

There can be little doubt that one reason for the empire's survival from the 7th century on was its effective logistical administration. The road system, although both greatly reduced in scope and degraded in quality when compared with that of the Roman period, remained an important asset. In addition, the carefully managed fiscal system was closely tied into the needs of the army, and although the exact administrative and organizational structures evolved over the period in question, the arrangements for supplying the soldiers in either peacetime or war were effective. Resources were collected in either money or in kind, depending upon a number of variables: whether the areas in question supported enough market activity; whether the agricultural or other resources needed by the army were available and could be stored; what the particular needs of the army at that point in fact were; and how many soldiers and animals needed to be fed and housed over what length of time. The effects of an army on the land and its population were well understood, and there are in the written sources of the period both recommendations to commanders not to keep concentrations of troops for too long on Byzantine territory and descriptions of what happened when this advice was not followed.

When a campaign was planned, local fiscal officials liaised with the central authorities and the military records department at Constantinople, so that the right amount and type of supplies were provided for the numbers involved. The outlay was often very heavy, and accounts from the 10th century show just how

*The Martyrdom of
St Demetrios on a
15th-century Byzantine
icon. This icon contains
some interesting and realistic
features, including the varied
helmets, typically European
straight swords and Balkan
rectangular shields. (Photo
by David Nicolle, Benaki
Museum, Athens)*

heavy the burden could be, especially when the emperor and his household were on the expedition. Each of the regions through which the army passed had to put aside adequate supplies of grain, meat (usually on the hoof) and oil or wine for the required numbers of troops. Large expeditionary armies – which would generally be divided into several smaller columns, each taking a separate route and heading for a pre-arranged rendezvous on the frontier – numbered as many as 20,000 or more, and very occasionally as many as 30,000; but the average theme force might be no more than 3,000–4,000, often far fewer, confronting armies of the same size, or shadowing larger forces until they could be ambushed or taken on in a full-scale battle. Providing resources for such armies involved a considerable organizational effort. In addition to food, horses and pack-animals had to be provided, weapons and other items of military equipment replaced and, for expeditions intended to take enemy strongholds, wagons or carts found to carry siege machinery and artillery. While food and supplies were generally provided by the districts through which the army passed, weapons and other equipment, as well as cavalry mounts and pack-animals, might come from more distant provinces. In a 10th-century account, for example, detailing some of the preparations for an expedition by sea, some provinces were commissioned to produce a certain number of weapons: the region of Thessaloniki was ordered to deliver 200,000 arrows, 3,000 heavy infantry spears and 'as many shields as possible'; the region of Hellas was asked to produce 1,000 heavy infantry spears; while the governor of Eurippos in Greece,

Gold hyperpyron of Alexios I (1081–1118) Obverse showing enthroned figure of Christ. (Barber Insititute of Fine Arts, University of Birmingham)

and the commanders of the themes of Nicopolis and of the Peloponnese all undertook to provide 200,000 arrows and 3,000 heavy infantry spears. The same document specifies also that other governors or officers were commissioned to levy thousands of nails and similar items from their provinces for ship construction.

Military manuals stressed that excess personal baggage and servants should not be taken by the officers or wealthier men, since it caused problems in respect of food and transport; and while many commanders clearly enforced such regulations, there is evidence that many did not and that discipline in this area was slack – with all the consequences that brought with it. The imperial household, on the other hand, necessitated a vast amount of 'excess baggage', since the luxuries to which the emperors were accustomed were rarely left behind. The imperial baggage train in the later 9th and 10th centuries was supposed to have almost 600 pack-animals of one sort or another, to carry the household tents, carpets and other furniture – including a portable commode with gilded seat for the imperial person(!), folding tables, cushions, tableware, a private portable chapel, a portable 'Turkish' bath, with supplies, high-quality wines, meat and fowl, spices and herbs, as well as medicines and various other items for personal use. Large numbers of gifts in the form of both cash – gold and silver coin – and richly decorated luxury cloths and items of clothing were also taken, in part intended as rewards to the provincial officers, in part as gifts and bribes for foreign guests of distinction or even deserters from the other side. The attitude of the generals, who were generally members of the social élite and wealthy in their own right, varied. Some led a fairly ascetic life while on campaign, winning the respect of their men and other observers by sharing the soldiers' lifestyle; others insisted on taking as many home comforts along with them as they could, in part in order to stress their own status. Yet in general, the system of campaign organization and logistics was efficient and effective, and kept Byzantine armies in the field in even the most difficult circumstances. Sometimes, of course, in particular in the context of the guerrilla warfare of the frontier regions, this logistical apparatus was irrelevant: soldiers had to live off the land and move in unpredictable directions in order to keep track of and to harass enemy columns. But even here the provincial fiscal apparatus made it possible to claim back through the following year's tax assessment what could be demonstrated to have been consumed by the army, although this, like all such systems, tended to be cumbersome, inefficient, slow and unfair.

Where Byzantine armies failed it was generally due to poor leadership, or to a combination of poor morale and lack of discipline, themselves often a direct result of the quality and abilities of the commanding officers. They defended their territory, with varying success, for some 600 years, from the 6th and 7th centuries

Gold nomisma of Theophilos (829–842). Reverse showing busts of Michael II and Constantine, Theophilos' son. (Barber Institute of Fine Arts, University of Birmingham)

well into the 12th century, if we include the counter-offensives in Asia Minor under the emperors Alexios I, John II and Manuel I Komnenos in the period from the 1080s to the 1170s. For in spite of some often very heavy defeats, they nevertheless maintained the territorial integrity of the eastern Roman state and were even able, on several occasions, to go over to the offensive. The logistical arrangements maintained by the empire were a major, if not the major, contributory factor to this. Only when the political and economic environment in which the empire had to survive had changed sufficiently for it no longer to be able to maintain this logistical basis did the medieval east Roman state ultimately fail.

LIFE IN THE BYZANTINE ARMY

SOLDIERS

There is no doubt that the majority of ordinary soldiers in the army throughout the history of the empire were of fairly humble status. The better-off ordinary soldiers among the thematic armies in the 9th and 10th centuries appear to have held a relatively high position in their communities, however, partly because of their special fiscal and legal status: they were exempt from extra taxation and a range of state impositions in terms of labour service or providing housing and supplies for other soldiers, officers or imperial officials, to which the ordinary population was always subject; and they could bestow their property without having to adhere strictly to Roman inheritance law about the division of property among heirs. This gave soldiers of all types, even when they were not especially well paid, an enhanced social prestige, set them apart somewhat from the ordinary population, and gave them a sense of group identity and solidarity.

The sources for recruitment and length of service for the period after the middle to the end of the 6th century are not very informative. Before that time, it seems that the traditional Roman regulations probably applied, with a minimum recruitment age of 18 years and a minimum height requirement of about 5 ft 6 in. There is reason to believe that the minimum age for recruitment in the 9th and 10th centuries was still 18 and the maximum 40. Service beyond the age of 40 was not unusual, however, and several examples of soldiers who served beyond that age are known. Some sources suggest that many officers stayed on long after their useful career was over, as a result adversely affecting the military effectiveness of their unit.

There were important differences between the requirements applied to recruits to 'professional' units, such as the tagmata, and the provincial or thematic armies, with many of the regulations governing admission to the first group being retained from the late Roman legislation, whereas thematic soldiers were required merely to appear at the regular muster parade appropriately equipped – with mount, provisions for a certain number of days, shield and spear. Some restrictions on recruitment also existed, prohibitions on the enlistment of heretics were applied, at least in theory. Priests and monks were forbidden to join the army, while those convicted of adultery or similar crimes, those who had already been dishonourably

ολεα· ἀλλὰ ματῶν τὴν αἰτίαν τῆς τοῦ προκοπίου σφαγῆς· τῆς

ἐξορίαν καταπόκουαελον ἐρᾶτηρõικιιαρέιχε· παρέπεμφε

ΒΑΣΙΛΕΙΟΣ

κο πορᾶν τὸν· καιπρωρᾶαλλων πορε ξ νωη ρ 8ρου με ραραυτοῦ·

παρκαππωτὸν· ειαλόυπεστõυτο ναρδ ακλιαι δαῖõ õιπαιδ θεσαι

The enthroned emperor Basil accepts tribute from the general Leon, but because of Leon's behaviour towards Procopius, he is arrested by two soldiers. The History of John Scylitzes, folio 100a. (Werner Forman Archive/Biblioteca Nacional, Madrid)

discharged, and so forth, were technically disqualified from enlisting. But it is impossible to know to what extent such regulations were observed. It is most likely that in the situation that developed from the middle of the 7th century most of the formal regulations of the Roman period had become irrelevant. The application of such regulations was in any event not possible for foreign units, especially Muslims, Franks and others outside the sphere of Byzantine religious–political authority, nor to others, such as Armenians, who may have belonged to non-Orthodox communities. The further away from Constantinople, the more likely such regulations are to have been ignored. By the 10th century the greater diversity in origins, military value and contexts in which soldiers for different types of unit were recruited must have led to an equal diversity in their conditions of enlistment and service, not just between simple thematic soldiers and soldiers of the imperial tagmata but between foreign units and the mercenary soldiers recruited for specific campaigns.

All soldiers paid by the government, whether tagmata or themata, were listed in military registers, copies of which were maintained in their province and in the government department responsible at Constantinople. Foreign units employed as mercenaries under their own officers could be treated in the same way or paid through their leaders, who would receive a lump sum at regular intervals to be distributed to the men. Leave was granted on a rotational basis, and for periods of between 30 days and three months, depending on the situation of the unit in question – whether on active service, for example, or in winter quarters. The

Byzantine soldiers of the 12th–13th centuries. From top infantryman, cavalryman, and man-at-arms. (Angus McBride © Osprey Publishing Ltd)

number of men who could be absent at any given time was restricted, and officers who permitted more men to be away could be punished. But it is not clear whether these rules were observed or to which types of unit they were applied.

Soldiers received no state benefits when they retired, other than their protected fiscal status and special legal privileges, although there was a great deal of official rhetoric about how the emperor and the state should look after those who fought for the faith and for God's empire on earth. Until the end of the 6th or middle of the 7th centuries there was a system of state pensions or annuities, but the conditions of the 7th century probably made such arrangements financially impossible for the hard-pressed government. For the ordinary soldiers of the field armies in the provinces this was reflected in the state's acceptance and probable encouragement of their being supported directly from their own households, which by the later 8th century, if not long before, resulted in the majority of thematic soldiers holding landed property from which their duties could be supported. They had to supply provisions for a limited period, equipment and

A gold solidus minted in 945 with the figure of Emperor Constantine VII holding an orb surmounted by a cross. (Werner Forman Archive/Barber Institute of Fine Arts, University of Birmingham)

weaponry, and mounts when they were called up for the yearly campaigning season. When such provincial soldiers were too old to serve actively, they will simply have returned to their farms or traditional occupations. Soldiers could thus be divided into several categories according to the conditions under which they were recruited: self-supporting thematic militia, full-time theme soldiers supported by state salaries and other emoluments; professionals recruited for particular regiments or for particular campaigns. All shared the same legal rights, however, until the introduction of ever larger numbers of foreign mercenaries in the 11th and 12th centuries rendered this picture much more complex.

Many men who had completed their service in the army (as well as many who were trying to avoid conscription or who had deserted) entered a monastery. Most of the evidence concerns senior officers, but there is nevertheless some information on ordinary soldiers opting for this mode of retirement, in particular those who had no family cares. Official regulations forbidding serving soldiers to join a monastery were repeated from the late Roman legislation. Adopting the monastic life catered for the spiritual well-being of the individuals concerned and provided a degree of economic security. It offered at the same time a way through which the soldier could atone for the sins he had committed in terms of killing the enemies of the empire and of his faith while serving the emperor. The number entering monasteries among the officers of the provinces was substantial enough for an Arab historian to remark on the fact, and to note that those who pursued this life forfeited the continuation of their cash salary, to which they were otherwise entitled as bearers of an imperial title.

OFFICERS

There was no 'officer corps' in the Byzantine army, although it is clear that the majority of men who commanded units beyond the level of a squad or troop came from the wealthier elements in society, whether in the provinces or in Constantinople, and that service at court in one of the palace units functioned as a sort of training school. The sources tell us quite a lot about the middle and upper levels of officers, and until the 12th century it is clear that there was always a substantial meritocratic element in advancement. Social background and education played a role, but it was perfectly possible for an able and competent soldier or lower-ranking officer to rise to high position. In all aspects of Byzantine society social connections and kinship always played an important role too, and training and ability were generally mediated through personal ties; for example, an officer might advance his career through service initially in the retinue of an important officer, from where he might receive a junior appointment in a local regiment, rising through the various grades, or being transferred to a senior position elsewhere. Some careers developed within families serving in the same unit – there are several examples of officers' sons entering their father's unit as simple troopers or soldiers before being promoted to junior and then more senior officer grade; in other cases, we hear of privileged young provincial men sent to Constantinople where, with the help of an influential relative or patron, they were appointed to a junior post in the guards before further promotion. In one case, which was probably not untypical, a young man was appointed first to a small corps of elite guards in the palace, before receiving a junior command at the capital, then a middling provincial post, before being promoted to a senior position, all in the course of some 10 years or so.

By the middle of the 11th century the growth of a powerful provincial aristocracy had brought some changes to this structure. The provincial élite itself provided a major source of recruits to the middle and senior officers' posts in the empire, and during the later 9th and 10th centuries came to monopolize most key provincial military commands. The increasing use of mercenaries reduced at the same time the importance and status of the provincial, thematic soldiery, who blended back into the mass of the peasantry from which they were drawn, thereby losing their distinctive social position.

DISCIPLINE AND TRAINING

The Byzantine army, at least as represented in the narrative histories and in the military treatises, prided itself on its order and discipline. Life in the army involved a very different sort of daily routine from life in civilian contexts or from that in less disciplined and organized neighbouring armies. A 6th-century military handbook makes this abundantly clear: 'Nature produces but few brave men, whereas care and training make efficient soldiers,' notes the author. Levels of discipline varied and were a major cause of concern to commanders and to the authors of all the military treatises. There are plenty of cases of mutiny and unrest among the provincial armies and the examples of troops panicking when the commander was thought to have been killed or injured is evidence of the variable psychological condition of the troops. The extent to which proper discipline was actually enforced is not very clear in the limited sources. Usually it was the most able commanders who were most likely to apply military discipline effectively, partly a reflection of their personal character and ability to inspire confidence among the soldiers – a point also recognized in the military treatises. Financial generosity, either on the part of individual commanders or officers, or the government, was a crucial ingredient in encouraging soldiers to follow orders and accept the discipline necessary for effective fighting.

Discipline also varied according to the categories of troops. A strict code certainly prevailed in elite units such as the imperial tagmata and in units which had a particular loyalty to their commanding officer. One story recounts the tale of an officer who was upbraided by the emperor himself for his unkempt appearance while at his post in the palace. Discipline was probably least effective in the militia-like thematic forces, but under competent officers it seems to have been effectively maintained. There existed an official code of military discipline which is frequently included in the military handbooks, and effective leaders seem on the whole to have applied it. Nikephoros II is reported to have awarded punishment to a soldier for dropping his shield because he was too tired to continue carrying it. When his officer ignored the order, he too was punished severely, on the grounds that the first had endangered his comrades as well as himself, while the latter had compounded the crime and further endangered the well-being of the whole force. Constantine V in the 8th century, Nikephoros II, John I Tzimiskes, Basil II in the late 10th century and Romanos IV in the later 1060s were all regarded with approval as strict disciplinarians, as was Alexios I in the late 11th century. Yet discipline often broke down.

There are some hints in the sources about the exercises carried out by the soldiers, descriptions corroborated by accounts of similar exercises in the tactical manuals and handbooks. Nikephoros Phokas put on a series of military games and

The reverse of a gold histamenon nomisma of Isaac I Komnenos showing the emperor standing with a sheathed sword. (Barber Institute of Fine Arts, University of Birmingham)

mock battles in the hippodrome at Constantinople in the 960s – they were so realistic and frightening that a panic occurred which claimed many lives. But whatever the textbooks said about the value of such exercises, sensible commanders appear generally to have been aware of the limitations of the different sorts of troops under their command. The treatises on warfare often include quite simple, easily managed tactical manoeuvres for the great bulk of the thematic infantry, who were on the whole not well equipped and potentially unreliable. In contrast the well-trained and well-equipped heavy cavalry and elite units were expected to implement quite complex manoeuvres, frequently under enemy attack, on the battlefield. Skills and training, discipline and morale went hand in hand.

The sort of exercise in particular skills which cavalry troopers had to carry out is illustrated in a late 6th-century manual:

> [The trooper] should shoot rapidly, mounted on his horse and at a canter, to the front, to the rear, to right and to left; he should practise leaping onto his horse. When mounted and at a canter he should shoot one or two arrows rapidly and put the strung bow in its case … and then take the lance which he carries on his back. With the strung bow in its case he should hold the lance in his hand, then quickly replace it on his back and take the bow.

As well as these individual skills with bow, lance or sword, the troops were drilled in formation, so that, in larger or smaller bodies, they could be wheeled, moved from column into line and back again, form a square against heavy cavalry attack, form into a wedge to break through an enemy formation, and so forth. Success on the battlefield often depended on the effectiveness with which such manoeuvres might be carried out, although it was also admitted that things should be kept as simple as possible to avoid confusion or being caught unprepared mid-way through a manoeuvre – there are examples of battles in which one of the reasons for the collapse of the imperial forces appears to be due to such errors.

LIFE ON CAMPAIGN

Life as a soldier in the Byzantine army must have varied enormously from century to century as the empire's fortunes changed, and depending on the commanding officers, the type of unit, and so forth. We have very little evidence about individual soldiers, but there is a good deal of information that can be gleaned from the wide range of written sources about what the life of an ordinary soldier might have been like, for example during the campaign under the general Bardas Skleros in the Balkans in 971.

In the spring of 970 the empire faced an invasion from a large Rus' force deep into imperial territory in Thrace, where they took the local garrisons by surprise and were able to sack the fortress of Philippoupolis before advancing along the road to

Constantinople. Since the emperor John had most of his effective field units in the east, where they were campaigning near Antioch, he appointed Bardas Skleros, together with the patrikios Peter, both experienced commanders, to take a medium-sized force – numbering some 10,000 – and scout the enemy dispositions in the occupied territories. As a secondary objective they were to exercise the troops and prevent enemy raiders committing further depredations. At the same time, spies – disguised in Bulgarian and Rus' costume – were sent into enemy-held territory to learn as much as they could about the Rus' commander Svyatoslav's movements. Svyatoslav soon learned of the advancing imperial column, and in response despatched a force of both Rus' and Bulgar troops, with a supporting detachment of Petchenegs with whom he was temporarily allied, to drive the Romans off.

The march north followed the established pattern. Bardas needed to move quickly, and so forced the pace somewhat. Within imperial territory he could rely on the co-operation of local officials to supply his troops; once in enemy territory his soldiers and their animals had to live off the land. But regardless of where they were, the army always entrenched for the night. The scouts and surveyors sent ahead to locate an appropriate site had to ensure both an adequate water supply as well as good defensive properties, and preferably in relatively open country to avoid the possibility of surprise attack. On this campaign the latter was difficult since the army passed through hilly and wooded scrubland for much of its route. Byzantine camps followed a standard pattern. The commander's standard was set up in the centre and the subordinate officers – Bardas had divided his force into three divisions of about 3,500 men – were assigned to share the four quarters into which the camp was divided. The various units pitched their tents around the perimeter, as nearly as possible in battle order so that, in the event of a surprise attack or the need to sally out quickly, they would be ready for action. The camp itself consisted of a simple ditch dug by the soldiers themselves, with the earth thrown inside, stamped down and surmounted by the spears and shields of the troops. The spears might be set up as *triskelia*, made by roping three together with the point outermost, acting as a particularly effective barrier behind the trench. Most camps had either two or four transverse roads with the troops' tents placed in the intervals, and where the force was of mixed infantry and cavalry the latter were placed within the former for protection. Where circumstances and manpower permitted, the camp was to have been at least two and a half bowshots across so that the animals could be quartered safely in the middle sections. The largest camps, which could contain a major field army of over 20,000 men and animals with their baggage, were more than a mile along the side, with a v-shaped trench some six to eight feet in depth.

Each unit had to set up its own rotating watch within the camp; but the commanding officer also set up a watch for the camp as a whole. Each unit along

ABOVE
The ancient and medieval fortress at Acrocorinth, Greece, controlling entry to the Peloponnese. (akg-images/Rainer Hackenberg)

OPPOSITE
Conquest of Constantinople by the crusaders of the Fourth Crusade in April 1204. Illumination from the 14th-century Histoire de la conquête de Constantinople par les croises en 1204. *Bibliothèque Nationale, Paris. (akg-images)*

the perimeter provided soldiers for this patrol, called the *kerketon*, and through the use of a regularly changed password had complete authority over access to and egress from the camp. Other units had to be sent out to forage for supplies and fodder for the horses, and they were in turn accompanied by supporting troops for protection – it was important to pitch camp and secure the immediate area before sunset so that supplies could be got in as quickly as possible. Leaving camp after sunset was usually prohibited, except for the outer line of pickets, groups of four men sent out to cover the major approaches to the camp when it was clear that no enemy was yet in the immediate vicinity.

The men were organized in tent-groups of eight, called *kontoubernia*, sharing a hand-mill and basic cooking utensils as well as a small troop of pack-animals. Soldiers were issued with two main varieties of bread: simple baked loaves, and double-baked 'hard tack', referred to in late Roman times as *bucellatum* and by the Byzantines as *paximadion* or *paximation*. In campaign conditions, it was normally the soldiers themselves who milled and baked this. The hard tack was more easily preserved over a longer period, was easy to produce, and demanded fairly simple milling and baking skills. Hard tack could be baked in field ovens – *klibanoi* – or simply laid in the ashes

Sachiez que M. et C.
et quatre vinz anz aprés
l'incarnation notre sei-
gnor Ihesu crist. A l'apostoille
Innocent apostoille
de Rome et Phelipe
roi de France. et Ricchart roi d'Engleterre et un saint home en Fran
ce qui ot nom Folques de Nuilli.
Cil Nuillis si est entre Ligni sor
marne e Paris. et il ere prestre qui
tenoit la parroiche de la ville. Et
cil Folques dont ie uos di comença
a parler de deu par France et par
les autres terres entor. et notre sires
fist maint miracles por lui. Sachiez que la renomee de cel saint home
ala tant que le vint a l'apostoille
de Rome Innocent. et l'apostoile
l'enuoia en France et manda al
prodome que il prechast de croiz par
s'autorité. et aprés i enuoia un sien
cardonal maistre perron de
capues croisié. et manda par lui
le pardon tel come uos dirai. Tuit
cil qui se croissaroient et feroient le
seruise deu un an en l'ost seroient
quittes de toz les pechiez que il auo-
ient faiz dont il seroient confés.
Por ce que li pardons fu issi granz.
si s'en esmurent mult li cuers des genz.
et mult s'en croissierent por ce que
li pardons ere si granz.
A l'autre an aprés que cil preu-
dom folques parla en si de deu

ot un tornoi en la campaigne a un cha
stel qui ot nom Aicris. et par la
grace de deu si auint que tibauz
quens de campaigne et de brie prist
la croiz. et li quens loeys de blo-
is et de chartain et ce fu a l'entree del
auent. Or sachiez que al quens
Thybau ere iones hom. et n'auoit
pas plus de xxii anz. Ne li
quens loeys n'auoit pas plus
de xxvii anz. Cil dui ere cre-
neuou le roi de france et si co-
sin germain et neuou le roi
d'engleterre de l'autre part.
Auec ces ii contes se croisierent
ii mult haut home. l'un
Symons de montfort e Rao-
ul de mommarni. qui fu grant
la renomee par les terres qu'ot
cil ii haut home se croisierent.
Et l'autre ere Thibaut de
Champaigne se croisa garniers
l'euesques de troies. li quens
Garniers de berenel Josfroi de Jo
en ville qui ere seneschaus de
la terre. Robert ses freres. Gautiers de Gaignon. Gautiers de
mombeliart. Eustaces de che-
neleine. Guis de plaissie ses
freres. Jeans d'ardillieres. Ogi-
ers de saint cheron. oulains de cru-
illi. Josfroi de Vilehardoin. li
mareschaus de campaigne. Josfroi li
niers. Guillaumes de nuilli. Gautiers de saint unne. Lienars

of camp fires, an advantage when speed was essential, and this was the case during this expedition – although the soldiers much preferred the best such bread, baked in thin oval loaves cooked in a field-oven, and then dried in the sun. The ration *per diem* included two to three pounds of bread and either dried meat or cheese; wine was also issued, but it is not clear how often or in what circumstances. The amount of meat relative to the rest of the diet was often minimal or absent altogether, but would still provide a reasonable amount of nutrition, since ancient strains of wheat and barley had considerably higher protein content than modern strains, and it has been shown that the bread ration of ancient and medieval soldiers provided adequate nutrition for the duration of a campaign season even without much meat.

The camp routine was marked by the trumpet signals for the evening meal, lights out and reveille; trumpet signals were also employed to issue commands to the various units and divisions to strike camp, assemble in marching order and begin the march. Leaving camp was always a dangerous time, for as the troops defiled through the main entrances they were for a while exposed to archers or even a rapid hit-and-run charge by enemy horsemen. A particular order for exiting camps was laid down and followed, and once the army was out of the entrenched area it would be drawn up for a while in a defensive formation until the troops fell into the marching order for the day.

The speed at which armies moved varied according to terrain, weather and the number and types of troops. Unaccompanied mounted troops could cover distances of up to 40 or 50 miles per day, provided the horses were regularly rested and well nourished and watered. Small units generally moved more rapidly than large divisions, even up to 30 miles per day for infantry in some contexts. Average marching speeds were much slower: three miles per hour for infantry on even terrain, two and a half on broken/hilly ground. Mixed forces moved at the speed of the slowest element; but speed also depended on the conditions of the roads or tracks followed, the breadth of the column, and its length. The longer the column, the longer it took for the rearmost files to start moving off, which would thus arrive at the next camp later than the foremost groups, the delay between first and last units being proportional to the length and breadth of the column. Thus a division of 5,000 infantry, which is what Bardas probably had at his disposal, marching at the standard infantry rate of about three miles per hour over good ground, ordered five abreast and with each row occupying a (minimal) two metres would stretch over a two-kilometre distance. There would be a gap of at the very least about 20 minutes, if not more, between the front and rear elements. The whole army would have extended back some 14 miles. The rearmost units would be well over one hour behind the van.

A screen of scouts was deployed well ahead of the column, followed by a van division, including cavalry, ahead of the main contingent of cavalry and infantry.

The baggage train, to which a group of units was assigned on a rotational basis for protection, was placed in the centre, and other units patrolled at some distance, where the terrain allowed, on either flank. On open terrain in enemy country the army would march over a broader front in a formation that could be rapidly deployed into battle order; and for passing through narrow passes or across rivers another formation was employed.

As the march progressed some of the scouts returned to inform the general that the enemy was not far away, near the fortress town of Arkadioupolis (mod. Luleburgaz). The three divisions were given separate tasks: two were concealed in the rough scrub and wooded terrain through which the track led in the direction of the enemy, while the general took command of the third section of the army himself. Leaving the two divisions in ambush with clear instructions, he himself led a fierce and unsuspected charge against the foremost enemy units, made up of Pecheneg mounted archers. In spite of the greater numbers in the enemy force, he managed to lure the enemy out of their encampment and withdraw in good order, encouraging more and more of the enemy to pursue but, on the assumption that the Byzantine troops were indeed losing, without any clear plan of attack or order. It must have seemed as though the outnumbered Byzantine force, which managed with difficulty to avoid being completely surrounded, was doomed. Yet discipline, training and leadership told, and Skleros finally ordered the prearranged signal to be given for the whole force to fall back. Meanwhile the two corps that lay in ambush prepared themselves: the order was given to remain absolutely silent, to place all supernumerary baggage animals with their attendants well to the rear, to check their weapons, and to deploy into a battle order appropriate to the terrain. One of the priests who accompanied the force offered up a quick prayer – a standard practice before battle. As the van division approached, drew level with and then withdrew beyond them, a single trumpet-call ordered them to break cover and charge into the flank of the unsuspecting enemy. Caught in the open in close combat, the Pechenegs, a war-like Turkic people from the Eurasian steppe, had no chance to deploy at a distance suitable for the use of their archery and, after being brought to a halt – at which point the van division about-faced and counter-attacked in its turn – they turned and fled. The Rus' and Bulgar troops, meanwhile, who had been hurrying to catch them up, on the assumption that the Romans had been routed, suddenly found themselves caught up in the panic. As the rout became general and the Roman forces pushed home their advantage, heavy casualties were inflicted on the fleeing enemy troops. A contemporary source remarks that the Romans lost some 550 men and many wounded, as well as a large number of horses, a direct result of the fearsome archery of the Pechenegs. The combined enemy force, however, lost several thousand. The short encounter won an important breathing space for the emperor John, furnishing him also with vital information about the

Gold hyperpyron of Alexios I. Obverse showing enthroned figure of Christ. (Barber Institute of Fine Arts, University of Birmingham)

composition, fighting abilities and morale of the enemy. The defeat of the enemy force gave the emperor time to organize a major offensive, an offensive which was, in the event, far more successful than was originally planned.

After any encounter with the enemy the commanding officers held a muster to establish casualties. Specially detailed soldiers were deputed to check the fallen, and to carry or help the wounded back to the temporary Roman camp, where the divisional medical attendants and surgeons tried to deal with those wounds that were not likely to be fatal. Far more men died of wounds than in battle itself, of course. In a contemporary treatise instructions are given that the wounded were to be taken back towards imperial territory with a section of the rearguard, transported on the pack-animals no longer required for the army's supplies. Occasional references in the chronicles of the period bear this out. There survives a medical treatise, certain sections of which deal with the problems of extracting arrowheads, with fractured or broken bones, and related injuries. Chronicles dating from the 6th to 12th centuries give accounts of the treatment of various wounds: the removal of an arrowhead from the face (the victim survived), of a javelin from the skull (survived the extraction, but died as a result of the infection which followed), and the treatment of deep slashes in the back and thigh (the victim died from blood loss).

THE WORLD AROUND WAR

The medieval eastern Roman world was a society in which the virtues of peace were extolled and war was condemned. Fighting was to be avoided at all costs. Yet the Byzantine empire nevertheless inherited the military administrative structures and, in many ways, the militaristic ideology of the non-Christian Roman empire at its height. The tensions which these traditions generated were resolved by a political-religious ideology or world view which melded Christian ideals on the one hand, with the justification of war as a necessary evil on the other, waged primarily in defence of the Roman world and Orthodoxy – literally, correct belief. From the 4th and 5th centuries on in the eastern Mediterranean and Balkan regions this blending of ideas generated a unique culture, that could adhere unreservedly to a pacifistic ideal, yet on the same grounds could legitimate and justify the maintenance of an efficient and effective military apparatus.

This attitude is neatly summed up in the introduction to a legal codification promulgated by the emperors Leo III and Constantine V in the year 741:

> Since God has put in our hands the imperial authority … we believe that there is nothing higher or greater that we can do than to govern in judgement and justice … and that thus we may be crowned by His almighty hand with victory over our enemies (which is a thing more precious and honourable than the diadem which we wear) and thus there may be peace…

Byzantine emperors could justify their wars on the basis that they were fighting to preserve peace, to extend the territory of the Christian world, and to defend God's Chosen People – for in Christian Roman terms, the mantle of the Chosen People had been transferred to the Christians with the coming of Christ. There was always a tension between the pacifism of early Christianity, however, and the imperial Roman, but Christian, need to fight to defend the empire's territorial integrity, or to recover 'lost' Christian lands and peoples. Christianity never evolved an ideological obligation to wage war against 'infidels' presented in the terms of Christian theology, even if, at times, and on an ad hoc basis, individuals have spoken and acted as though such a justification could be made. The 13th canon of St Basil specifically states that those who took life in warfare should abstain from communion for a period.

Tenth-century ivory plaque with a representation of Jesus in the act of benediction. On the sides are depictions of the the evangelists. Byzantine work of art preserved at the Louvre Museum, Paris. (©2006 Alinari / Topfoto)

As Christianity spread across the empire during the 2nd and 3rd centuries, pragmatism often won the day, and it seems that considerable numbers of Christians served in the imperial armies at this time. This could not banish particular conflicts of interest, however – military service required acceptance of the emperor cult, that is, the emperor as a god – and a whole range of pagan traditions and rituals. The result is that the history of the first three centuries of Christianity, and the 3rd century in particular, is full of tales of persecution and martyrdom, as individual recruits refused to conform to the ceremonial and ritual observances associated with life in the army. As a compromise solution, the 3rd-century Christian thinker Origen argued that Christians formed a special type of army that did not fight wars for the emperor physically, but instead prayed for the success of the state, which made possible their continued existence and the expansion of their community. This compromise was developed as a response to the criticisms made by pagan commentators about Christian communities and their pacifism. In the end, it was the argument about the continued existence of the Roman state being the necessary condition for the survival and expansion of Christianity which won the day, and led to the more pragmatic compromise noted already.

The favour shown to Christianity by the emperor Constantine I, and his deathbed baptism, however, led during the course of the 4th century to a substantive reformulation of imperial political ideology, and this changed the situation dramatically. The Christianization of the emperor cult solved one of the most difficult issues at a blow – an earthly emperor selected by God to lead the Christians, now consonant with the Roman people – was clearly acceptable, whereas an emperor who was supposed to be a divinity was not. Two perspectives evolved from this situation. The first was the officially sanctioned view which encouraged support for the state, as personified by the orthodox emperor, and all its undertakings. Leading churchmen, while expressing their hope that violent conflict could be avoided and that bloodshed would not be necessary, went on to state clearly that it was praiseworthy for a Christian to take up arms against the enemies of the state. The Christianization of society developed rapidly thereafter, and as the government became dominated by Christians, so by the end of the 4th century it became impossible to obtain a government post without being a Christian.

The association between warfare and Christianity, the struggle for survival of the 'Chosen People', led by the emperor chosen by God, at the head of his armies became quite explicit. All warfare was thus about defending Christianity and the Christian empire. At the same time a desire for peace, and a regret that war should be necessary, were constant motifs in imperial and Church ideology. There were constant reminders of the heavenly support which Byzantine armies received. Successful warfare without God's help was impossible. A late 6th-century text notes that:

> we urge upon the general that his most important concern be the love of God and justice; building on these, he should strive to win the favour of God, without which it is impossible to carry out any plan, however well devised it may seem, or to overcome any enemy, however weak he may be thought.

The idea is repeated throughout the Byzantine period. Roman defeats were seen as the result of God's anger with the Romans, the chosen people, who were being

A 12th-century icon with the figure of Demetrios in enamel. (Werner Forman Archive/Museum of Islamic Art, Berlin)

The Byzantine Empire *c.*1204–1250

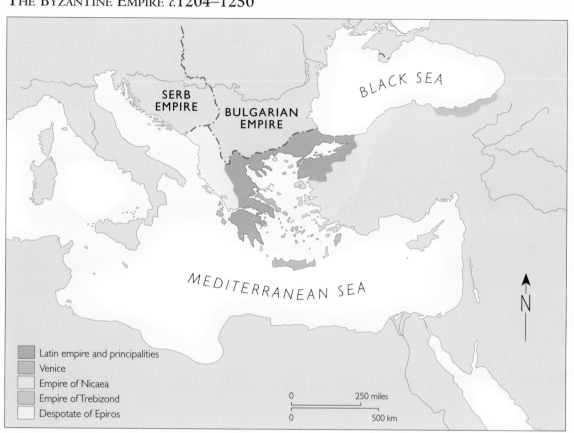

SERB
EMPIRE

BULGARIAN
EMPIRE

BLACK SEA

MEDITERRANEAN SEA

N

Latin empire and principalities
Venice
Empire of Nicaea
Empire of Trebizond
Despotate of Epiros

0   250 miles

0   500 km

punished for their sins. Only when the Romans returned to the path of righteousness and corrected their sins would success once again attend Roman arms, and this idea underlies much of the thinking in the actions of individuals and groups in Byzantine political history and political theory.

There was thus no notion of Holy War as something special, to be waged under specific circumstances against particular enemies. The Byzantine self-image was one of a beleaguered Christian state fighting the forces of darkness, with foes against whom it had constantly to be on its guard and to evolve a whole panoply of defensive techniques, among which warfare was only one element, and by no means necessarily the most useful. In this sense, one might argue that all war was 'holy war', since all enemy action threatened the lands and beliefs of the Romans.

The notion that soldiers who fell in battle might be rewarded in heaven was considered upon occasion, and was reinforced after the development of Islamic Jihad, a development of which the Byzantines were quite aware. Thus in the 10th century, for example, the soldier-emperor Nikephoros II – known by the somewhat chilling epithet as 'the white death of the Saracens', suggested that this might be an appropriate way to encourage soldiers to fight. But the idea was rejected by the Church and was never really revived. It may have been an element of folk belief, of course, but it was certainly never given any official recognition. A prayer to be said before the soldiers marched into combat is recorded in two 10th-century texts, and it gives a good idea of this combination of Christian with warlike motifs:

> Lord Jesus Christ, our God, have mercy on us. Come to the aid of us Christians and make us worthy to fight to the death for our faith and our brothers, strengthen our souls and our hearts and our whole body, the mighty Lord of battles, through the intercession of the immaculate Mother of God, Thy Mother, and of all the saints. Amen.

There is a mass of evidence, therefore, dating from the 4th century up to the very last years of the empire, for the public and official acceptance by both Church and court, as well as by the ordinary population, of the need to wage war; for the fact of divine support for such warfare; and for the need to maintain and rely on heavenly aid in waging war. Although the notion of 'holy war' in the sense understood by the Crusaders, or by non-Muslims as typical of Islam, flickered briefly into life in the Byzantine world, especially in the context of the aggressive fighting of the 10th century, it never developed beyond this. The ways in which warfare on behalf of the Christian Roman state were understood did go through a certain evolution, for it is apparent that the Byzantines were always conscious of the need to legitimize their wars, a need which generally became more pressing in a time of political and military expansionism such as the 10th century. While warfare could be justified, therefore, loss of life on the Roman side was in particular to be avoided or minimized, if at all possible. The emperor Constantine V characterized as 'noble' his campaign into Bulgaria in 772–73 because no Roman soldiers died; while by the time he compiled his military handbook or *Tactica* c.900, the emperor Leo VI clearly expresses the idea that war has to be justified in accordance with Orthodoxy and the continued existence of the Roman state. As long as Roman interests, however defined, were at stake, then warfare was acceptable and just. War with other Orthodox Christians was, of course, to be avoided. But even this could be justified if the one true empire, that of the Romans, was at risk or subject to attack by the misguided rulers of such lands.

WARFARE AND EAST ROMAN SOCIETY

Warfare was for much of the Byzantine world, throughout much of its history, the normal state of affairs. Its effects were manifested in a number of ways. To begin with, the ordinary population of the empire was directly affected by hostile activity in those areas most exposed to enemy attack, they suffered the destruction of their crops and

dwellings, the theft or slaughter of their livestock, and if they were themselves caught, possible death or enslavement. There survive some short but evocative inscriptions from the frontier regions of Asia Minor, dating to the middle Byzantine period, which commemorate individuals who died of their wounds following a battle or raid; other accounts tell of relatives carried off into captivity or lost in the confusion of an enemy attack and never seen again. And the literate élite was just as aware of these aspects: warfare imposed itself upon many facets of Byzantine literary culture, in saints' lives, in speeches in praise of emperors, in funeral orations, in sermons and homilies to church congregations, in private letters addressed to individuals. Themes such as death, loss of property and so forth occur frequently, and in some cases the terror inspired by a sudden enemy raid is graphically portrayed. Letters often bewail the effects of warfare, with references to the tears of orphaned children and widowed mothers, the destruction of crops, homes, monastic communities, the enslavement or death of populations, driving off of livestock and so forth.

A miniature from a manuscript of the 11th-century Cynegetica, *Pseudo-Oppian, cod.gr.479.fol.59.r. Three men catch fish in a net, presumably at night, as a light is fixed to the boat's stern. (Werner Forman Archive/Biblioteca Nazionale Marciana, Venice)*

OPPOSITE
*Soldier from Byzantine
Macedonia (left), c.1295
wearing armour seen in
Byzantium and neighbouring
Serbia during the period
c.1280–1330, and perhaps
until c.1350. This Epirote
Byzantine soldier of the
14th century (centre) carries
the long straight-sided
triangular shield which
had displaced the
almond-shaped shield by
the late 13th century. Right,
Byzantine or Bulgarian
infantryman, c.1350.
Contemporary pictures show
that the equipment of the
average soldier was virtually
identical on both sides of the
Bulgaro-Byzantine frontier by
the mid-14th century. This
particular warrior is typical.
Shields varied in shape, the
Bulgarians favouring the
conventional Western
European heater-shield over
the longer, straight-sided
triangular Byzantine variety,
and also still used bucklers.
(Angus McBride © Osprey
Publishing Ltd)*

The presence of Byzantine troops was no less onerous, however. The very existence of an army brought with it the need to supply and provision it, to supply materials and livestock for it when it was on campaign, to provide lodgings and billets for officers and soldiers, and so on. There were extensive and burdensome logistical demands wherever an army was present, not just a question of demands made by the army on local populations, but also the fact that government intervention into the local economy often affected the economic equilibrium of the affected districts. This could either take the form of fixing artificially low prices for the sale of produce to the army, thus harming the producers, or of sudden heavy demand for certain produce, thus driving up prices for those in the private sector. The civilian population might also be compelled to bake bread and biscuits for the troops as well as providing other supplies and, in addition, they were subjected to the plundering and pillaging of the less well-disciplined elements of the army. Quite apart from this was the potential for conflict between soldiers and civilians, for the outcome was seldom favourable to the latter.

Additional levies in grain were particularly onerous, and there are frequent complaints in the written documentation concerning this and related burdens, usually a result of either special requirements for particular campaigns or the normal operational demands made by the troops in a particular region. In addition to these demands, provincial populations had to provide resources and manpower for the maintenance of the public post, the dromos, with its system of posting stations and stables, stud farms and breeding ranches, mule-trains and associated requirements. The postal system served the needs of both the military and the fiscal administration of the state. It helped with the movement of military supplies and was responsible for the rapid transit of couriers and imperial officials of all kinds, as well as important foreigners – diplomatic officials or prisoners of war, for example. The households that were obligated to carry out certain duties for the post were, like households that had to support a soldier, released from the extraordinary state impositions, and this was an important aspect of the smooth running of the provincial postal system.

The nature of the burden which the provincial population bore in support of the army can be seen particularly clearly in a series of documents of the later 10th and especially the 11th century. It consisted of imperial grants of exemption from the billeting of soldiers, the provision of supplies for various categories of troops in transit, the provision of horses, mules and wagons for the army, and the delivery of charcoal and timber for military purposes. Some accounts in chronicles detail the sort of requirements needed to mount major military expeditions – large numbers of draught-animals, wagons and foodstuffs, for example, and increases in demands for supplies of all kinds; all were provided by requisitions from the local peasantry who suffered considerably from this form of indirect taxation.

Economic and demographic disruption affected not just the people who lived in the provinces or towns that suffered during periods of fighting. It also directly threatened the government's control over its resources and the ability of the Church to maintain its spiritual authority and to supervise the communities most affected. Some worries about supposed 'pagan' practices and folk beliefs appear in texts and letters of the time, for example. Archaeological and written information about populations fleeing from the path of invaders or the movement of settlements to more secure sites testifies to the effects of warfare in certain areas. And it took a long time for the worst affected areas to recover. Again, the evidence suggests as long as three centuries before economic and demographic decline was halted. And the effects of warfare were also visible on a day-to-day basis, in the structure of defended settlements, the shrinking and abandonment of towns, the ubiquitous forts and fortresses guarding key strategic points, crossroads, passes, valleys, bridges. And according to several reports the more gruesome effects of warfare could be seen on the battlefields themselves: in one text the author describes how the bones of the soldiers slain at a conflict a few years beforehand could still be seen littering the ground over which the battle was fought. Yet, while warfare disrupted social and cultural life, it also influenced the patterns of daily existence. Different cultural traditions evolved in regions regularly affected by fighting and enemy action, especially in the east. The seasonal nature of the fighting had quite a lot to do with this, for in many areas distinctive cultures and societies developed on both sides of the frontier, engendering values and ways of life very different from those of the interior or the metropolitan districts around Constantinople, for example, also encouraging intercultural contacts, influences and traditions very different from the mainstream. We should bear in mind that soldiers and their families were no more exempt from these effects than the rest of the population. But while the parents of young men called up for military service wept and lamented as they said goodbye to their sons, the more privileged were able to deploy powerful contacts to have them released from serving in the army: on grounds of economic hardship, for example!

The negative aspect was to some extent balanced by an alternative set of views, however. Popular approval and enthusiasm for war could be encouraged, and the emperors exploited court ceremonial at Constantinople specifically to this end. Triumphal processions, accompanied by displays of booty and prisoners, hymns of thanksgiving, the acclamations reminding the emperors (and the crowd who were in earshot) of their Christian duty to defend Orthodoxy and the empire, all were directed to achieve a particular consensus about warfare and the emperor's duty to defend orthodoxy. Poets were commissioned to write and declaim verse accounts of the emperor's courage, strategic skill and military achievements: the poet George of Pisidia thus composed a series of laudatory poems in the 620s and 630s about the victories of the emperor Heraclius over Avars and Persians, while in the 10th century Theodosios the Deacon similarly praised the victories of the emperor Nikephoros II Phokas. Other members of the cultural and political élite composed letters in praise of the emperor's deeds in war, so that the glorification of military deeds and of individual leaders or emperors was part of the staple production of composers in verse and prose. As an unfortunate but necessary means of achieving a divinely approved end, warfare could thus be given a very positive gloss. Such views were not necessarily shared by the many thousands of peasants and townspeople who suffered over the centuries.

The degree to which warfare was fundamental to the fabric of late Roman and Byzantine society and historical development is evident in our sources. The physical appearance of the Byzantine countryside, social values, cultural attitudes, government fiscal and administrative organization, themes in literature and art; all these different aspects of cultural and material life were directly influenced by the beleaguered situation of the medieval east Roman state and its need to fight wars.

CIVILIAN LIFE

The effects of warfare and fighting on individuals and on local communities at different times and the evidence for the non-military perception and perspective on war have already been alluded to in earlier chapters. One of the problems of Byzantine history is the fact that the written evidence, upon which historians have to rely for knowledge of people's opinions and attitudes, was nearly always produced by members of relatively privileged social strata. We thus have very little real idea of what ordinary people – peasants, merchants, craftsmen, simple soldiers – actually thought about their world. Of course, we can try to establish through the writings of the educated something of the views and beliefs of the non-literate, or

Byzantine mosaic, 6th century, showing an allegory of Autumn, found at Madaba in Jordan. Much of the population of the Byzantine Empire was tied to agriculture and the land, and state demands on these peasants became increasingly oppressive through the centuries. (akg-images/ Jean-Louis Nou)

at least non-writing part of society, and we can also work out through the actions taken by certain groups at certain times something of what they thought and why. For example, while writing for a limited and very élite readership, the Princess Anna Komnena, writing early in the 12th century, presents a graphic description of the effects of warfare on the provinces in the years before her father, the emperor Alexios I, had (in her view) rescued the empire from its troubles:

> Cities were wiped out, lands ravaged, all the territories of Rome were stained with blood. Some died miserably, pierced by arrow or lance; others were driven from their homes or carried off as prisoners of war... Dread seized on all as they hurried to seek refuge from impending disaster in caves, forests, mountains and hills. There they loudly bewailed the fate of their friends ... mourned the loss of sons or grieved for their daughters... In those days no walk of life was spared its tears and lamentation.

It is because they tended to act in large groups, and in specific circumstances about which we often possess quite a lot of information, that soldiers are a very good group to study in this respect. Unfortunately, less can be said through direct evidence about civilians.

It is clear that the presence of soldiers was rarely, if ever, welcome, except perhaps when a community or the local population at large was suffering directly from enemy attacks. Whether the army was engaged in fighting the enemy or not, whole communities or individuals might still suffer at the hands of unruly or poorly disciplined soldiers. In the 10th century, members of a small monastic community on the island of Gymnopelagesion in the Aegean were forced to abandon their homes because of the frequent 'requisitioning' of their animals and crops by passing vessels of the imperial fleet. There are plenty of other examples: Armenian soldiers, for instance, notorious (at least in the view of the Greek sources) for their lack of discipline and poor behaviour, were especially feared by the ordinary populace of the countryside; and an 11th-century source recounts the tale of a local girl who had been robbed by a unit of Armenian troops passing through. Byzantine writers themselves often remarked on the fact that Roman troops could be poorly disciplined and even ravage imperial territory for their supplies when these were not forthcoming or thought to be inadequate. One commentator sums up the general attitude to soldiers when he makes reference to 'the troublesome presence of soldiers'.

Villages which lay on major routes, particularly those frequently used by the army, regularly had to provide accommodation and board for the officers and imperial officials – fiscal, military and others – who would frequently pass through while carrying out their duties. Although the disadvantages of having to put up such people was the cause of frequent grumbling, it also meant that the village was

The production and sale of silk formed an important part of the economy of Constantinople. This 10th–11th century example with a design of stylized lions is thought to have been used as a wall hanging. (Werner Forman Archive/ Erzbischoslichen Diozesan Museum, Cologne)

never short of news, since inevitably the attendants of the officials in question would be willing to pass on gossip to those with whom they came into contact in the course of their duties.

In the late 11th century the Archbishop Theophylact of Ohrid in the Byzantine provinces of Bulgaria complained in the strongest terms about the oppressive weight of the state demands on Church tenants. He was especially concerned with the labour demanded for the repair, maintenance or construction of fortifications, but he was equally vehement about special conscriptions for the army, which took men away from an already weakened local population. The oppressive demands of the imperial fiscal officials was often such that Theophylact remarks on the flight of considerable numbers of villagers to the forests, in order to escape such oppression.

While the situation seems to have worsened in the later 11th century and afterwards, these requisitions and demands and the hardship they caused remained a major burden on the rural population of the Byzantine empire until its last years.

Many Byzantine peasants were tenants of local landlords who extracted relatively high rents, technically to cover the taxation on the estate's lands, but frequently including a fairly high private rent for the landowner. As the wealthier officials and their families bought land and office and increased their hold on the key posts in government and the provinces, so the general situation of the rural population began to worsen as landlords increased rents and the government demanded more in taxes to maintain its own machinery and the army. There were many other trades and occupations, of course – merchants and traders, village craftsmen such as the smith, the potter and the leatherworkers, the townspeople of the larger cities who had trades ranging from gold- and silversmiths to butcher, baker, clothiers, fullers and dyers, cobblers, silk importers and exporters, dairy traders, and every other provider of foodstuffs, finished goods and services we might expect to find in a large town. Until the economic boom of the later 10th and 11th centuries, however, such urban activity was limited on the whole to a few major cities such as Constantinople, Thessaloniki, Trebizond on the south-east coast of the Black Sea, or Attaleia on the southern coast of the Asia Minor peninsula. Yet all these developments were affected in fundamental ways by the fact that war was a normal state of affairs for inhabitants of much of the Byzantine world, and for much of the time. The presence of soldiers as fighters, as peacekeepers, as oppressors and as liberators was a part of this, and the demands made by the army and the government for its soldiers were, as we have seen, the central pillar of the state's financial system. Everything was based on the need to recruit, supply, equip and organize soldiers, and both the economy of the state – the issue of gold coin, for example – and the local economies which comprised the empire were directly affected by this fundamental fact.

DEATH OF AN EMPIRE

The Byzantine empire survived for some 500 years from about 600 in a form which grew increasingly away from its late Roman roots. Yet although there were many substantial changes in its geographical extent, institutional arrangements and social structure, it remained until the early 13th century the recognizable descendant of the eastern Roman empire of Justinian. However in the 11th and 12th centuries, the international political and economic context in which the Empire had to survive began to change in ways that set up substantial challenges to it and, more importantly, to the ways in which it worked and was able to respond.

Deep cultural differences and an increasing divergence between the Greek eastern Mediterranean and south Balkan world, on the one hand, and the Latin-dominated lands of central and western Europe had become increasingly marked across the 8th, 9th and 10th centuries. The situation worsened as western economic strength and political and military aggression began to be a serious problem for the medieval east Roman state in the later 11th century, with the Normans on the one hand and the German emperors on the other presenting serious threats to Byzantine political authority, control and prestige in the Balkans, and with the growing challenge to Byzantine maritime power from Italian commercial centres such as Venice and Genoa. The crusading movement, western prejudices about Greek perfidy and effeteness, and the expansion of the Seljuk emirates in Asia Minor, transformed alienation and suspicion into open conflict.

The real threat now came no longer from the Islamic world to the east, but from the Christian west, and the first conclusive indication of the changed balance of power came in the form of the Fourth Crusade. Intending to attack Egypt, the crusading forces had found themselves heavily indebted to the Venetians, who had hired them the ships and provided some of the finance needed for the expedition. The Venetians had been looking for an opportunity to intervene in the confused situation at Constantinople in order to consolidate their trading privileges and their hold over the commerce of the eastern Mediterranean. The presence at Venice of Alexios IV Angelos, a pretender to the imperial throne, rendered the task of the Venetians in requesting a diversion to Constantinople fairly easy. In 1203, the crusader army arrived before the walls of the Byzantine capital and within a short time had succeeded in installing Alexios IV as co-emperor with his blind father, Isaac II, whom his uncle Alexios III had deposed, and who had been

THE BYZANTINE EMPIRE IN ITS LAST YEARS

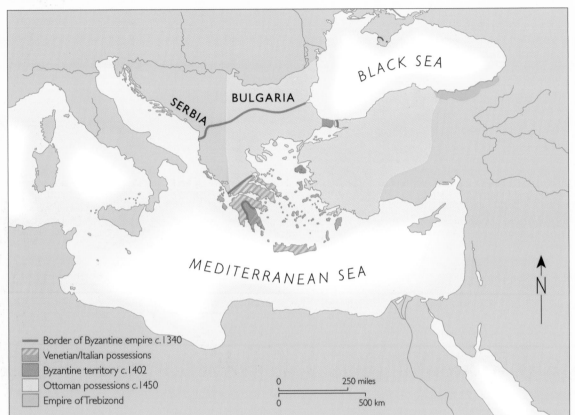

SERBIA

BULGARIA

BLACK SEA

MEDITERRANEAN SEA

N

— Border of Byzantine empire c.1340
▨ Venetian/Italian possessions
▨ Byzantine territory c.1402
☐ Ottoman possessions c.1450
▨ Empire of Trebizond

0   250 miles

0   500 km

OPPOSITE
*The outer container of a
reliquary of the True Cross,
c.955, one of the richest and
most elaborate ensembles of
Byzantine enamel to have
survived the sack of
Constantinople in 1204.
It was taken by a German
leader of the western forces
and has been in Germany
ever since. (Werner Forman
Archive/ Cathedral Treasury,
Limburg, Germany)*

brought out of prison after the latter fled the city. Once installed, Alexios IV found
it impossible to pay the promised rewards and, as the situation worsened, he found
himself increasingly isolated. Early in 1204 he was deposed and murdered by
Alexios Doukas (Alexios V); but this only exacerbated the problem. Although the
new emperor strengthened the defences and was able to resist an initial crusader
attack, the city fell on 12 April. The booty taken was immense – an eyewitness
asserts that so much booty from a single city had not been seen since the creation
of the world. The city, full of precious objects, statues, liturgical and ceremonial
vestments and objects, which had never before fallen to violent assault,
was mercilessly sacked and pillaged for three days. Much destruction occurred,
with innumerable artefacts destroyed and precious metal objects melted down
or stolen – some of the most spectacular objects can still be seen in Venice today.
The capture of Constantinople in 1204 and the establishment of a Latin empire
finalized the split between east and west, for the Latin patriarchate was not

recognized by the Orthodox populations of the Byzantine or formerly Byzantine regions. The patriarch Michael Autoreianos, elected in Nicaea in 1208, was recognized as the true patriarch of the Constantinopolitan Church.

After the capture and execution of the fleeing Alexios V, a Latin emperor was elected in the person of Baldwin of Flanders, the empire's lands were divided among the victors, and Venice was awarded the coveted provinces and maritime districts. Greece was divided among several rulers and the principality of Achaia (in the Peloponnese) and the duchy of the Archipelago, the kingdom of Thessaloniki and the duchies of Athens and Thebes were established.

In spite of this catastrophe, the empire survived and several counter-claimants to the imperial throne asserted their position. A branch of the Angelos family established an independent principality, the Despotate of Epiros, in the western Balkans, which lasted until the end of the 14th century. The family of the Komnenoi governed a more or less autonomous region in central and eastern Pontus, where the 'empire' of Trebizond now appeared; and at Nicaea, where the noble Constantine Laskaris continued to exercise effective control over much of Byzantine western Asia Minor, the empire of Nicaea evolved, its first emperor being Constantine's brother Theodore, the son-in-law of Alexios III, and thus possessed of a certain legitimacy. Apart from these territories, the Bulgarian Tsar Kalojan was in the process of establishing an independent Bulgaria, and was even able to capture the Latin emperor in 1205 after decisively crushing his army. By the 1230s the Bulgars were threatening to reduce the Byzantines of Epiros to vassal status.

The Latin empire based at Constantinople had a bleak future. The rulers of Epiros tried with help from the German emperor Frederick II, and later with King Manfred of Sicily, to establish a balance in the Balkans, with the intention of recovering Constantinople. But the emperors of Nicaea were in a better position strategically and politically and succeeded in making an alliance with Genoa. They thereby achieved a balance of power with Venice at sea. During the 1240s and 1250s they extended their territories in the southern Balkans, recovering a substantial area from its Frankish rulers. In Asia Minor a stabilization of the frontier with the Seljuks was achieved for a while, and in 1261, taking advantage of the absence of most of the Latin garrison of Constantinople on an expedition, a small Nicaean force was able to gain entry to the city and reclaim it for the empire. Constantinople was the capital of the east Roman empire once more. By the end of the 13th century, parts of central Greece were once again in Byzantine hands, while they also controlled much of central and south-eastern Peloponnese.

Nevertheless, the last two centuries of Byzantine rule in Asia Minor and the southern Balkans saw the loss of Asia Minor, and the reduction of the empire to a dependency of the growing Ottoman Sultanate. The empire simply did not have the

Gold hyperpyron of Michael VIII. Obverse showing the Virgin Mary within the walls of the city. (Barber Institute of Fine Arts, University of Birmingham)

resources to fight on several fronts, and even to fight on one for more than a short period proved an impossible burden. But the empire's strategic position made warfare unavoidable, while the imperial political ideology meant that emperors continued to look for ways of recovering former territory and lost glory. For a while in the second half of the 13th century, and under the able emperor Michael VIII (1259–82), the empire marked up several successes. It was able to expand into the Peloponnese and to force the submission of the Frankish principalities in the region. Alliances with Genoa and the kingdom of Aragon and, briefly, with the Papacy, enabled the empire once more to influence the international scene and to resist the powers which worked for its destruction and partition. But the international environment soon became much less favourable. For with the transfer of imperial attention back to Constantinople the Asian provinces were neglected at the very moment that the Mongols arrived in eastern Asia Minor, where they weakened Seljuq dominion over the nomadic Türkmen tribes, allowing them unrestricted access to the ill-defended Byzantine districts. By the 1270s most of the south-western and central coastal regions were lost, independent Turkish principalities or emirates, including the fledgling power of the Ottomans, posed a

Gold hyperpyron of Manuel I. Reverse showing the emperor standing. (Barber Insitute of Fine Arts, University of Birmingham)

growing threat to the remaining districts, and by the mid-1330s, the remaining Aegean regions had been lost. The Mercenary Catalan Grand Company, hired by the emperor Andronikos II in 1303 to help fight the Turks and other enemies, turned against the empire when its demands for pay were not met and, after defeating the Burgundian Duke of Athens in 1311, seized control of the region, which it held until 1388. Other mercenary companies behaved similarly. The empire no longer had the resources to meet any but the smallest hostile attack, and could soon hardly even afford to hire the mercenaries upon which it relied to defend itself.

In 1390 the last fortress in Asia Minor fell to the Ottomans. Part of the empire's failure can be ascribed to the vicious civil wars that were fought between factions of the ruling dynasty: war began in 1321, lasted until 1325, flared up again in 1327, and broke out again in 1341. The Serbian ruler Stefan Urosh IV Dushan (1331–55) soon became involved on one side, while the other hired Turkish mercenaries to help in the fight. The struggle, which exhausted the small treasury, alienated the rural and urban populations who had to pay for it and failed to heal any of the rifts in the élite, ended with the victory of the emperor John VI Kantakouzenos in 1346. John had been supported by a faction of the clergy which had adopted a strongly anti-western view, a view that had important consequences for the last century of Byzantine culture and politics. But politically and economically the empire was in a desperate situation. The Serbs had absorbed Albania, eastern Macedonia and Thessaly, and all that was left of the empire was Thrace around Constantinople, a small district around Thessaloniki (surrounded by Serbian territory), and its lands in the Peloponnese and the northern Aegean isles. Each region functioned as a more or less autonomous province, so that Byzantium was an empire in name and by tradition alone. The civil wars had wrecked the economy of these districts, which could barely afford the minimal taxes the emperors demanded. Galata, the Genoese trading centre on the other side of the Golden Horn from Constantinople, had an annual revenue seven times as great as that of the imperial city itself!

During the civil wars, and as a result of their fighting for Kantakouzenos, the Ottomans began permanently to establish themselves in Europe. By the beginning of the 15th century, and with the exception of some limited areas in the

Peloponnese and a few Aegean islands, there remained no imperial possessions in Greece. The advance of the Ottomans in Europe led to the ultimate extinction of Byzantium. Having defeated and subjugated both Serbs and Bulgars by the end of the 14th century, the Ottoman advance caused considerable anxiety in the west. A crusade was organized under the leadership of the Hungarian king, Sigismund, but in 1396 at the battle of Nicopolis his army was decisively defeated. The Byzantines attempted to play the different elements off against one another, supporting first the western powers and then the Ottomans. Some Byzantines espoused a possible solution by arguing for a union of the eastern and western Churches, which would bring with it the subordination of Constantinople to Rome. But the monasteries and the rural population were bitterly hostile to such a compromise. It was even argued by some that subjection to the Turks was preferable to union with the hated Latins. Neither party was able to assert itself effectively within the empire, with the result that the western powers remained on the whole apathetic to the plight of 'the Greeks'.

In 1401 the Ottoman Sultan Bayezid began preparations for the siege of Constantinople, but the empire was saved at the last minute by the appearance of Mongol forces under Timur (Timur Lenk, known in English as Tamburlane or Tamerlane), who invaded Asia Minor and crushed the Ottoman forces at the battle of Ankyra in 1402. The Byzantines used the opportunity to strengthen their control in the Peloponnese, but the respite was of short duration. Timur died soon after his victory over Bayezid, his empire broke up in internecine conflict, and Ottoman power revived. The Sultans consolidated their control in Anatolia, and set about expanding their control of the Balkans. The Byzantine emperor John VIII travelled widely in Europe in a vain attempt to gather support against the Islamic threat. He even accepted the union with the western Church at the council of Florence in 1439; and a last effort on the part of the emperor led to the crusade which ended in disaster at the battle of Varna in Bulgaria in 1444. In 1453 Sultan Mehmet II set about the siege of Constantinople.

Constantinople, under its Turkicized name Istanbul (from the Greek *eis tin polin* – in the city) became the new Ottoman capital. The Aegean islands that remained to the empire were soon absorbed under Ottoman rule. The Byzantine principality in the southern Peloponnese, the Despotate of Morea, fell in 1460, and Trebizond, seat of the Grand Komnenoi, fell to a Turkish army in 1461. The east Roman empire – Byzantium – was no more.

WAR, PEACE, AND SURVIVAL

The Byzantine state survived as an important force in the Balkan and east Mediterranean region until the later 12th century because it maintained an effective fiscal apparatus that could support an efficient and well-organized army. It was as much the changes and shifts in the international situation as it was the internal evolution of Byzantine social and economic relations that led to its decline in the 13th century and its collapse and disappearance in the 14th and 15th centuries. One of the most important reasons for its longevity and its success in defending a territory surrounded on all sides by hostile forces was the system of logistical support that it maintained almost to the end. It was this system which permitted the state to allocate resources from the land to its armies as they needed them, to plan in advance the requirements for offensive operations, to hinder hostile appropriation of the same resources, and thus to make the conditions for enemy forces on Byzantine soil as difficult as possible. The taxation system ensured the raising of supplies in kind at the right time and in the right place, as well as of cash in order to purchase other requirements as well as mercenary soldiers, livestock, and so forth. Naturally, in reality this system was by no means as effective at all times as a simple description might suggest, and it often worked less to the advantage of the army than to that of the social élite, who could exploit it for their own ends. The whole apparatus worked often to the disadvantage of the producing population, who could be very oppressed by the incessant demands of this bureaucratic state.

Other factors also played a role. Tactical order and discipline were regarded by the Byzantines themselves as key elements in their success over the long term, and they were only too aware of what could happen when these were not respected or maintained. It is also the case that the Byzantine military were by no means unique in this respect. The Islamic armies were also well organized and operated under a strict discipline, while the crusaders in the late 11th century soon learned the value of particular formations and tight tactical discipline in dealing with the fast-moving and hard-hitting Seljuk horse archers. Yet it is clear that Byzantium had an edge over most of its enemies in this respect until the 11th century, even if tactical discipline did not always deliver the results expected because individual officers or commanders lacked the leadership and authority to impose and maintain it. On the other hand, Byzantium was not Rome, and it is important to bear this in

OPPOSITE
The church of St Eirene in Istanbul. (C. Hellier, The Ancient Art and Architecture Collection)

mind – the medieval east Roman empire was indeed a medieval empire, and it exhibited similar developmental traits in terms of social organization, political structures and economic evolution as many of its neighbours.

Another important aspect was leadership, the other side of the disciplinary coin, as it were. When Byzantine armies were well led, it usually meant that they were well-disciplined, fought in coherent units and obeyed the basic tactical rules of engagement appropriate to their equipment and weaponry. It also meant that they were, more often than not, victorious, because Byzantine leaders were supposed to observe the fundamental principle of east Roman warfare, namely that of ensuring that they fought only when they were fairly sure they could win, and at the same time that of minimising the loss of life on their side. This was not mere philanthropy, although that was certainly an important ideological element. It was common sense in such a beleaguered state, in which manpower was at a premium and demographic change could lead to serious problems for the armies. But there were plenty of foolish commanders, men whose vanity, arrogance or ignorance led them to throw the lives of their soldiers away in futile attacks or ill-considered actions. And it seems often to have been the case that these were the leaders who paid least attention to the fundamental principles of managing soldiers: discipline,

The reverse of a gold scyphate of Romanos IV, issued between 1067 and 1071. The future emperor Michael VII stands between his brothers Constantine and Andronikos. (Werner Forman Archive/ Barber Institute of Fine Arts, Birmingham)

tactical cohesion and esprit de corps. For with good leadership usually came good morale and self-confidence – crucial ingredients for successful fighting, especially in offensive warfare.

Even with well-equipped, disciplined and well-trained troops, the result of a battle in the medieval period, as well as at other times, was, in the end, unpredictable. The ultimate arbiter was a combination of the soldiers' morale and fighting skills, the quality of the leadership, and good luck. But as the emperor Leo VI points out in his *Tactica* in the early 10th century, the difference between the good general and the bad general was that the good general understood this, acted in a manner appropriate to the circumstances, and made sure that his dispositions could cope with sudden surprises or changes in the conditions of battle. Another writer, this time the son of a famous Byzantine general, noted at the end of the 11th century that he had never known a diligent and alert man who had not been able to make his own good fortune on the battlefield. And while it would be incorrect to suggest that Byzantine defeats were due only to the incompetence or arrogance of commanding officers, this did nevertheless play an important role.

The Byzantine world has attracted western popular and scholarly attention, not only because it stood at the crossroads of east and west, bridging very diverse cultures, but because it evoked a romantic lost medieval Christian world which was both eastern in its forms yet western in its cultural significance. For some, it had been a bastion of Christianity against Islam; for others, especially in the 16th and 17th centuries, it was a source of politically relevant information about the Ottomans who threatened Europe at that time. And it was to Byzantine authors and texts that later generations directed their attention in the context of increasing national self-awareness as interest grew in the pre-Renaissance and early medieval antecedents of the formerly Byzantine lands. And while both medieval Islam and the Byzantine world served to transmit the heritage of classical and Roman civilization to the Renaissance and beyond, it was in particular through collections of Byzantine manuscripts and books that many texts were preserved, influencing in this way the evolution and content of modern classical scholarship.

Byzantium was, in a sense, always at war, for as we have seen, it always had an enemy or a potential enemy on one front or another. This situation necessarily inflected the whole history of the empire and determined in part at least its social structure and the way in which the state as well as the political system could evolve. Byzantium made war against its enemies over a period of some 700 years, from the 7th to the 14th and 15th centuries. In this sense, we might also assert that war made Byzantium what it was.

Part II	# The Walls of Constantinople

INTRODUCTION

THE FOUNDING OF CONSTANTINOPLE

Constantinople takes its name from the Roman emperor Constantine the Great. In the year AD 324 he moved the capital of the Roman Empire eastwards to the site, then called Byzantium, where Europe gazed over into Asia.

Few cities have a more dramatic topography than Constantinople. The new capital was built on a promontory that projects out into the waters of the southern end of the Bosphorus, the narrow strait that connects the Sea of Marmara to the Black Sea. To the south of the promontory the Sea of Marmara spreads out around it like a lake. Beyond this sea to the west lie the straits known as the Dardenelles that give access to the Aegean and the Mediterranean. To the immediate north of the old city is a narrow bay called the Golden Horn. It is one of the finest natural harbours in the world and runs inland for almost seven miles. This was one of Constantinople's most priceless assets.

From ancient times the Bosphorus has been conventionally regarded as separating Europe from Asia. The dramatic and picturesque location of Constantinople on its western shores has therefore ensured that the city should acquire a tremendous symbolic value, giving the site the inevitable romantic associations that have arisen from its position as the 'bridge between east and west' or 'the crossroads of the universe'. It has been such a powerful concept that the image has tended to obscure any serious discussion of the strategic and military considerations that led to Byzantium being chosen as the new capital in the first place. As a result the good points of the strategic and topographical conditions have been exaggerated and the negative points diminished to paint a picture of Constantinople as the ultimate example of perfection attained in the natural strategic defence of a city.

PERA

CONSTAN=
TINOPOLIS.

Sautari

Turquia

Porta delmeso

Calchidona

PREVIOUS PAGE
This pictorial map comes from an 1485 edition of Liber Insularium by Buondelmonti, showing Constantinople and Pera. (Topfoto/The British Museum)

It is therefore somewhat surprising to note that the site of Constantinople was not always so favourably regarded. Byzantium had already existed for 1,000 years before Emperor Constantine came onto the scene, and for most of that time the apparent strategic advantages that we take for granted nowadays were either unrecognized or regarded as irrelevant. For example, the historian Polybius, who lived in the 2nd century BC, wrote that the site of Byzantium may have been favoured for security and prosperity by the sea, 'but as regards the land it is most disadvantageous in both aspects'. In this statement Polybius anticipated why Constantinople's mighty walls should be built in the first place. Byzantium only looked really formidable when viewed from the seaward side. From the landward side, the site looked very vulnerable indeed.

Whether vulnerable or not, the settlement of Byzantium on the promontory made the location into a position of considerable economic importance. It served naturally and inevitably as a gateway for trade in and out of the Black Sea, but for much of Constantinople's history this factor was far less important than the trade routes coming up from the south. The most important of these was the vital sea traffic that brought food. The Egyptian corn that fed the population until the 7th century not only had to travel a distance of 1,000 miles but had to be taken up the Dardanelles at a time when the prevailing winds were northerly.

Polybius' worries about the city's weak defensive points were specifically concerned with the western approach to Constantinople over the flatlands of Thrace that now constitute north-west Turkey. The only mountain ranges in that region run from east to west, and thus afford no natural protection against an invading army. There were also weaknesses to the north because there was no other natural harbour nearby on the Bosphorus, and there was also a long-running problem over water supply to the city.

The walls of Constantinople were raised as the solution to the problem of security from the west. Impregnable by nature to north, east and south, the city had to be made equally impregnable to the west by the hand of man. The results stand today as the greatest surviving monument of military architecture to arise out of the ancient world and the Middle Ages. Repaired and extended over centuries, the walls of Constantinople withstood sieges delivered by different armies with different weapons and techniques for over a millennium. They stand today partly in romantic ruin, partly as restorations, but everywhere as a splendid testimonial to the men who built and defended them.

THE FIRST FORTIFICATIONS OF CONSTANTINOPLE

When Constantine the Great, an experienced soldier, made his momentous decision to turn Byzantium into his capital, his first thoughts naturally turned towards its defence. So, in 328 the emperor himself traced the limits of the future capital on foot and with his spear in his hand. Some defensive walls had existed from ancient times, but Constantine immediately arranged for new walls to be built. These included an important land wall from the Golden Horn to the Sea of Marmara. The limits that his new walls now enclosed trebled the area formerly occupied by the old Greek city.

The rebuilding of the city as the new imperial capital inevitably encouraged a substantial growth in population. One happy result of this was that when the invading Goths appeared before Constantine's wall in 378, following their victory at the battle of Adrianople, they were dissuaded from attacking the city because of the evidence of such a large multitude to oppose them. But the growing population could not forever be housed conveniently within the confines of Constantine's original city plan. Such was the demand for building plots for housing alone that areas of land were reclaimed from the sea. On a larger scale Emperor Valens, for example, erected the fine aqueduct that bears his name in the 4th century. This was an enormous project, the scale of which can be gauged from the fact that when it was repaired during the 9th century 6,000 labourers had to be brought in for the purpose.

By the time of the reign of Emperor Theodosius II (408–450) the city was threatening to burst the confines that Constantine had erected. Something had to be done, but by the first half of the 5th century the population explosion in Constantinople was not the most important consideration occupying imperial minds. Rome, the former capital of the Empire, had been captured by the Goths. The Huns had also crossed the Danube, and although they had been driven back there was a real fear that they would return to pose a direct threat to Constantinople.

It was therefore most fortunate for the Byzantine Empire that when the hour came, along too came the man. His name was Anthemius, and he headed the Byzantine government during the minority of Emperor Theodosius II. From the time of his appointment as Praetorian Prefect of the East in 405, Anthemius applied himself with vigour to whatever task the empire demanded of him. The first task was the expulsion of the Huns from the Balkans. The second resulted in the walls of Constantinople.

The so-called Theodosian walls (nothing so grand could bear the name of anyone less than the ruling emperor) were the results of Anthemius' skilled and dedicated work. His walls set in stone the limits that Constantinople was to possess and to defend until modern times. Today, tourists to Istanbul can find Anthemius' limits marked on the map as the 'Old City': an apparently tiny element in the modern sprawl that now stretches far up the Bosphorus past the two recently built suspension bridges. But that sprawl is modern Istanbul. The Theodosian walls defined what for the next 1,500 years was to be understood as Constantinople.

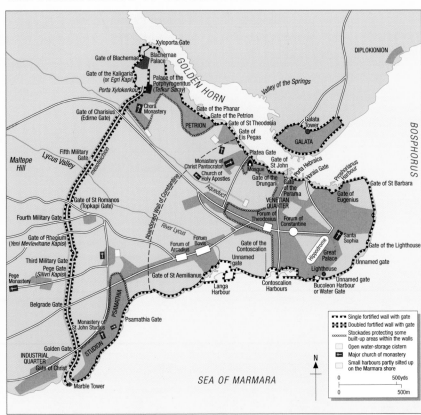

THE FORTIFICATIONS OF CONSTANTINOPLE

THE THEODOSIAN WALLS

The Theodosian walls were built about 1½ miles west of Constantine's original fortifications. The area occupied by the city was therefore greatly increased, and, most suitably for the city that had inherited the mantle of Rome, the completed Theodosian walls of Constantinople enclosed seven hills.

From the moment that Anthemius' designs began to take shape the erection, maintenance and repair of the new fortifications of the city became an undertaking in which all citizens were required to assist in one form or another. On that point the laws were very strict, and neither rank nor privilege exempted anyone from their obligation to carry out the work. One-third of the annual land tax of the city went towards the cost of the walls, and any additional expenditure was provided by requisitions laid upon the inhabitants. There does not seem to have been much grumbling about the matter. Indeed, there was a genuine enthusiasm for a project that promised increased security, and the government harnessed such enthusiasm

A tower in the Theodosian walls, c.447. A cutaway section of one of the towers of the Theodosian walls, showing how the two levels of the towers were entirely separate. The lower room was entered from the city, the upper from the battlemented walkway. (Peter Dennis © Osprey Publishing Ltd)

in various ways. One subtle ploy was the way the government appealed to the citizens' generosity through the circus factions, chariot-racing teams, such as the Blues or the Greens, that they supported. The supporters were great rivals when cheering on their side from the terraces of the Hippodrome, but worked together on the walls when the city was threatened. Records show that in 447, when repairs

Towers and walls of the inner wall between the Golden Gate and the Belgrade Gate. The first tower is octagonal. Although damaged here, we can also clearly see the outer wall, the other small wall outside the outer walk, and the moat, here flooded. (Stephen Turnbull)

were being undertaken, the Blues and Greens supplied 16,000 men between them for the building effort.

The walls designed by Anthemius were completed in the year 423, the fifth year of the reign of Theodosius II, who was then about 12 years old. They survive today as the inner wall of the fortification line that extends from the Sea of Marmara to the ruins of the Byzantine Palace of the Porphyrogenitus (Tekfur Saray). The increase in the area they enclosed also necessitated an extension of the sea walls along the northern and southern shores of the city, although these works were not carried out until some time later.

The first challenge faced by the original line of the Theodosian walls was provided by nature. In 447, only 34 years after their construction, the greater part of the new walls, including 57 towers, was flattened by a series of mighty earthquakes. The timing could not have been worse as Attila the Hun was advancing on Constantinople. Fortunately, in a splendid confirmation of the energy and commitment to their defence that the citizens of Constantinople had shown before, the government and people rose to the challenge and restored the fallen walls in less than three months. These new walls helped to save Constantinople from Attila, although some sources tell of an epidemic among his followers.

Strangely enough, we do not know for certain the name of the man who took the lead in this great endeavour. He may have been called Constantine or Cyrus, and he was the then Praetorian Prefect of the East. Our anonymous hero went much further than mere restoration, and took the opportunity to make the city into a much stronger fortress than even Anthemius had dared to contemplate. An extra wall was built outside Anthemius' wall, with a broad and deep moat in front of it. When the work was complete the city lay behind three lines of defence and 192 towers flanked the walls. It was these walls that were to prove impregnable for the next 1,000 years and survive to this day.

THE LATER WALLS

Although the Theodosian walls described above constitute the greater part of what is now visible on the ground, even the most cursory visitor cannot help but notice that towards the northern extremity of the walls there is a change in design. Just before they head downhill towards the Golden Horn, the Theodosian walls come to an abrupt end and are replaced by a wall of more complex and different construction. This is something of a puzzle. Surely the Theodosian walls originally extended all the way to the Golden Horn, so why were they replaced?

The explanation begins in 627 during the reign of Emperor Heraclius, when the quarter called Blachernae was actually a suburb outside the line of the Theodosian walls. It contained a church called the Church of the Theotokos, or Mother of God, and it was believed that the holiness of the site and the relic it contained would protect it from danger. But in 627 Constantinople was attacked by the Avars, who devastated the area around. Even though the church suffered no harm it prompted the realization that a wall should enclose it for extra security. Blachernae therefore received the protection of a wall, and further additions were made in 813 under Emperor Leo V (the Armenian) in the face of threats from the Bulgarians.

The Blachernae area grew in importance over the next few centuries. It even acquired one of Constantinople's most important buildings. This was the imperial palace of Blachernae, which became the favourite residence of the imperial court during the reign of Alexios I Komnenos (1081–1118). It was a peaceful spot away from the hustle and bustle of the city, but its remoteness made it a prime target for any attack, so there was a constant need to review the defences in this quarter and, if necessary, enhance them. Additions were therefore made, and the walls that now surround the Blachernae Palace area are the walls built during the reign of

Cross-section and plan of the Thedosian walls. This plate shows a complete cross-section and plan of a typical stretch of the Theodosian walls. The section shows the different layers of defence. On the plan are the different shapes of tower. (Peter Dennis © Osprey Publishing Ltd)

Emperor Manuel I Komnenos (1143–80). According to the historian Niketas Choniates, the camp pitched by the armies of the Fourth Crusade in 1203 lay 'on a hill overlooking the wall built by Emperor Manuel'. These were the final pieces of the jigsaw that now make up the walls of Constantinople.

DESIGN AND DEVELOPMENT

THE MATERIAL STRUCTURE OF THE WALLS

A cross-section of the Theodosian walls of Anthemius reveals three layers of defence. From the city side outwards, there is first the inner wall. A narrow walkway divides this from the outer wall, which is both lower and weaker. A wider outer walkway ends with another low wall that is the inner side of the moat. On the other side of the moat the ground is flat.

The standard building materials of Constantinople were squared stone, brick and lime mortar. To these could be added marble, sometimes in the form of reused pieces taken from older sites. The region around the Sea of Marmara offered a rich variety of natural stones, for which there were numerous quarries. The stone sections in the walls were built from tertiary limestone brought from the quarries located about three miles to the west of the Golden Gate.

Bricks must have been produced locally, although no remains of Byzantine kilns have been found. Mortar was made by mixing lime with various aggregates, often brick dust and fragments. Byzantine mortar was particularly strong once it had hardened. The other building material seen in some places on the wall would have been roof tiles used for decoration, for example to make an arch-shape to frame an inscription.

The foundations of Byzantine churches were constructed of brick or stone, and if possible cut to the bedrock, so the city walls were probably underpinned in a similar way. Byzantine walls were generally constructed of alternating bands of brick and stone. Squared stone faced both the inner and outer surfaces of the wall, and mortared rubble filled the space in between the facings. The Theodosian walls were no exception to this general pattern. The bricks normally formed a levelling course, extending through the thickness of the walls and binding the two faces together, so that when a brick course appears on the outside of a wall, we should expect to see the same course on the inner.

In the inner wall six brick courses, each containing five layers of bricks, were laid at intervals through the thickness of the walls to bind the structure more firmly. The bricks used are from 1ft to 1ft 2in. square and 2in. thick. They are sometimes stamped with the name of their manufacturer or donor, and occasionally bear the name of the contemporary emperor and some indication of where they were made.

RIGHT
Looking from inside the city we see a military gate, a walkway, an outer staircase and the arches of the inner wall in a section near the Edirne Gate. (Stephen Turnbull)

OPPOSITE
The peribolos, the area between the inner and outer walls, looking north from the Belgrade Gate. Some of the fiercest fighting during the 1453 siege occurred in this area between the two defences. (Stephen Turnbull)

The inner wall

The strongest part of the wall along its entire length was the inner wall. This magnificent structure, nearly all of which is still visible either as ruins or modern reconstruction, stood on a higher level than the outer wall and was loftier, thicker and flanked by stronger towers. The inner wall rises some 30ft 6in. above the present exterior ground level and about 40ft above the level within the city, with a thickness varying from 15ft 6in. near the base to 13ft 6in. at the top. There was a battlemented row along the outer edge 4ft 8in. high. This was the main defensive platform, and was reached by flights of stone steps set at right angles to the wall above ramps of masonry.

The inner wall originally sported no fewer than 96 towers. They were spaced between 175 and 181ft apart and were from 57 to 60ft high with a projection of 18 to 34ft. Their shape is interesting, because while most are of square cross-section some are hexagonal, while others are heptagonal or octagonal. Although lying along the wall, the towers were part of the same construction, but were built as separate structures. This ensured that different rates of settlement would not cause them to break apart.

Wooden or vaulted floors usually divided each tower into two chambers. The lower chamber was entered from the city by a large archway. This entrance provided most of the light and air for the room, because defensive considerations did not permit large windows. This chamber had little to do with the defence of the city but served as a storeroom or guardhouse. In some cases a narrow postern

gate in the angle of the wall allowed access to the walkway between the two sets of walls. Further security considerations also meant that, as a general rule, the lower room had no means of communication with the room above. This was instead entered only from the battlement level by an arched doorway. The upper room was well lit by comparatively large windows that allowed the defenders a good field of view and also permitted them to fire freely upon attackers. A flight of stairs allowed access to the third and uppermost defensive level of the tower. This was the battlemented roof. In times of siege catapults, and later cannon, could be mounted.

The outer wall

The terrace between the inner and outer walls was called the *peribolos*, and accommodated the soldiers who defended the outer wall. It was between 50 and 64ft wide. Beyond lay the outer wall, which was a modest structure compared to the inner wall. It was nonetheless a vital line of defence, and during the fierce sieges of 1422 and 1453 the most desperate fighting occurred here.

The outer wall is from 2ft to 6ft 6in. thick, rising some 10ft above the present level of the peribolos and about 27ft 6in. above the present level of the terrace between the outer wall and the moat. Its lower portion is a solid wall that retains the embankment of the peribolos. The upper portion is built for the most part in arches, faced on the outer side with hewn blocks of stone, and is frequently supported by a series of such arches in concrete. The arches strengthened the wall and allowed the construction of a battlement and parapet walk on the upper surface. The arches also formed chambers 8ft 6in. deep where soldiers could be safely sheltered and accommodated.

The towers in the outer wall are much smaller than those in the inner wall. They are some 30 to 35ft high, projecting about 16ft beyond the curtain wall, and are spaced out so as to alternate with the towers of the inner wall. They appear to have been designed in alternate shapes of squares and crescents, although later repairs have spoiled the pattern. Each tower had a chamber on the level of the peribolos that was provided with small windows. The lower portion of most of the towers was generally a solid substructure, but in the case of the square towers it was often a small chamber reached from the outer terrace by a small postern gate and leading to a subterranean passage running towards the city.

The outer terrace and moat

The terrace between the outer wall and the moat is about 61ft wide. It was known as the *parateichion*, and its main function was to extend the distance between the besiegers and the besieged.

The moat is over 61ft wide and over 20ft deep. On its inner and outer sides (the scarp and counterscarp) there is masonry 5ft thick, and buttresses support it. The small defensive wall on the scarp is about 6ft 6in. high. Across the moat are found long low walls that appear to divide the moat into several compartments. These contain hidden aqueducts for the supply of water to the city.

THE GATES OF THE CITY

The Theodosian walls were pierced by ten main gates and several small postern gates. Postern gates were few in number for security reasons and almost all were located in the inner wall. The main gates can be divided into two types: the military gates that led to different parts of the fortifications and the public gates that were the entrances to the city by means of bridges across the moat. The two series followed each other in alternate order, the military entrances being known by numbers and the public gates by proper names. Both the public and the military

The battlemented walkway of the inner wall looking south from the Belgrade Gate into the city. (Stephen Turnbull)

gates shared a common overall design. All were double gateways because they had to pierce two walls. The inner gateway, being the principal one, was built into the inner wall of the Theodosian line. Two large towers that projected far beyond the curtain wall guarded all the gateways. The towers were of very similar design to the towers found along the length of the walls as described above. The Belgrade Gate provides an excellent example of this, showing how the projecting walls would allow defenders to achieve good flanking fire and to protect the outer gateway by archery. The other intention behind the design was that the distance across the peribolos between the two sets of gates should be made deliberately as narrow as possible. By contrast, the gates in the outer walls were quite modest affairs, consisting of a simple gated arch not much higher than the outer wall level.

THE SEA WALLS

As the line of the land walls expanded outwards under Constantine I and Theodosius II so the sea walls grew to meet them. They are of similar construction to the land walls, but nowhere were they as formidable, and nowadays they exist only as short stretches of fragments, though some have been restored.

The sea walls of Constantinople were always less spectacular in appearance than the land walls, and were to some extent less important in the city's defence. As long as the emperor retained control of the sea, a city accessible only by water through the narrow defiles of the Dardanelles and the Bosphorus had little to fear from a naval attack. This immunity was compromised when the Ottomans and the Italian republics became maritime powers. But even then the position of the city rendered a seaborne attack a difficult proposition. The northern shore of the city could be put beyond the reach of an enemy by stretching a chain across the narrow entrance to the Golden Horn, while the currents in the Sea of Marmara could always carry an attacking fleet out to sea or fling it against rocks. According to Villehardouin, it was the fear of these currents that dissuaded Dandolo's crusaders from attacking along the coastline of the Sea of Marmara.

The chain on the Golden Horn passed between two towers and was supported in the water by wooden floats. It is first mentioned in connection with the siege of 717–18 when Emperor Leo lowered the chain in the hope of enticing the enemy fleet into the harbour. It was also used by Nikephoros Phokas against an expected Russian attack during the 960s, but in 1203 the crusading army simply removed it once they had captured the northern anchor point to which it was secured. It managed to frustrate Mehmet the Conqueror in 1453, who as a result was driven to the ingenious and successful method of dragging his ships overland. In the long history of the Byzantine Empire there was only one instance of a successful naval assault on Constantinople. This was the capture of the city in 1204 by the Venetian crusaders after they had destroyed the chain's anchor tower.

The need for sea defences also provided some concern in 1351 when a powerful Genoese fleet sailed to attack Constantinople in support of certain claims put forth by the Genoese colony at Galata. On its way through the Sea of Marmara the Genoese fleet captured the fortified town of Heraclea. This event caused great consternation in the capital, and in view of the enemy's approach the reigning emperor promptly put the sea walls in order, repairing them where they were ruined, raising their height and ordering all houses in front of them to be removed. He also increased the height of the towers.

THE GOLDEN GATE c.850

This plate shows the Golden Gate as it would have appeared during the reign of Emperor Michael III (842–867). The Golden Gate is actually a Roman triumphal arch erected in about 390. When Theodosius II decided to extend the city walls two decades later, he incorporated the Golden Gate within his new land walls. We see the gate here in its dual role of fortification and major entrance to the city. The sculptures that adorn it are ones that are known to have existed at the time of Michael III and consisted of two Winged Victories, female figures representing the fortune of the city, and four bronze elephants. (Peter Dennis © Osprey Publishing Ltd)

RIGHT
The chain that was slung across the Golden Horn during sieges is preserved in the Military Museum in Istanbul. Each link is about 2ft long. It was only broken once in a siege, that occasion being the capture of Constantinople during the Fourth Crusade. (Stephen Turnbull)

OPPOSITE
The southern tip of the walls at the Sea of Marmara, looking from the Golden Gate towards the sea. (Stephen Turnbull)

REPAIRING AND MAINTAINING THE WALLS

The walls of Constantinople had to be kept in a good state of repair, so designated officers, known variously as Governors of the Walls or Counts of the Walls, had the job of taking charge of repairs and maintenance.

Most of the damage the walls sustained came from the effects of weather or earthquakes, not war. The walls were so strong that little battle damage was sustained until very late in their history when gunpowder was employed. Earthquakes, by contrast, led to the initial rebuilding at the time of Attila the Hun and to damage in 542, 554 and 558. The latter disaster occurred during the reign of Justinian, who was so despondent that he refused to wear his crown for the next 30 days. The subsequent rebuilding, however, was thorough enough to allow the great general Belisarius to repel the Huns from the walls when the raiders appeared again in 559. Repairs were also undertaken when danger threatened, as happened early in the 8th century when a further attack by the Arabs was expected. The most extensive work in the wall's history after 447 was made in 1345 when the entire length of the walls was repaired and strengthened in the face of an attack by a rival emperor.

The most important example of the walls being restored after war damage occurred following the 57 years of Latin occupation of the city that resulted from the disaster of the Fourth Crusade in 1204. When Emperor Michael VIII Palaiologos made his triumphant entry to the city in 1261 he was shocked and dismayed by the ruinous condition of the city and its walls. During the initial siege of 1203 catapult stones had rained down on the Blachernae Palace and a battering ram had broken through a section of the walls. There had then been years of looting and neglect. A recent

Artillery damage in the mesoteichion. The destruction wrought by Mehmet the Conqueror's artillery and the subsequent ravages of time allow us to see the interior of a tower on the inner wall. (Stephen Turnbull)

estimate concludes that during the Latin occupation one-sixth of the area of Constantinople was ravaged by fire and between one-sixth and one-third of its buildings destroyed.

The repair of the walls was one of the new emperor's top priorities, because an attempt by the Latin forces to regain control was daily expected. The land walls were in such a bad condition that even when the gates were closed it was easy to get in and out of the city, but at that time there was more concern about the sea walls. The Genoese were now established across the Golden Horn in Galata, and their ships passed defiantly up and down below the sea walls. There was no time to build from stone, so as a temporary measure Michael VIII immediately ordered that the height of the sea walls be increased by about 7ft by the addition of wooden screens, which were covered in leather hide to make them fireproof. Later in his reign Michael VIII is believed to have had a second line of sea walls built so that they matched the fortifications of the land walls. However, the new line cannot have been very substantial because no trace of them has survived and some authorities doubt if they were ever built at all.

Like the Theodosian walls, the later sections around the Blachernae Palace were repaired time and again, and several inscriptions testify to this. For example, in 1317 Empress Eirene, the consort of Andronikos II, died and left a large sum of money that the emperor devoted to the restoration of the walls. A later inscription mentions repairs undertaken by John VII Palaiologos in 1441, just over a decade before the fall of Constantinople to the Ottomans. The outer wall received the major attention on this occasion.

TOUR OF THE SITE

FROM THE MARBLE TOWER TO THE GOLDEN GATE

The best way of understanding the layout of the walls of Constantinople and the succession of construction phases is to take a hypothetical tour from one end to the other. We will begin at the southern extremity where the Theodosian walls reach the Sea of Marmara. Heading north we will pass the Golden Gate and the Yedikule fortress, taking in the major stretches of the best preserved wall. We will then descend into the Lycus Valley, rising up again to the Palace of the Porphyrogenitus. The line of walls that follows are the later ones that take us down to the Golden Horn.

As noted above, the walls of Constantinople enclose an area running from the Sea of Marmara in the south to the natural harbour of the Golden Horn to the north. They are anchored at their southern extremity by the so-called Marble Tower. This handsome structure stands on a little promontory by the sea. Its lower half is faced with marble, and is unlike any other structure along the entire length. It is likely that the Marble Tower did not primarily form part of the

The Marble Tower stands on a little promontory by the sea. Its lower half is faced with marble, and is unlike any other structure aong the entire length of the walls. It is likely that the Marble Tower was an imperial sea pavilion. (Stephen Turnbull)

123

The Gate of Christ, so called because of the monogram 'XP' above it. The Gate of Christ was also known as the first Military Gate. (Stephen Turnbull)

defensive structure, but was instead an imperial sea pavilion, a sort of fortified villa for the imperial party. The tower also served for some time as a prison, and one can still see the chute down which the bodies of the executed were thrown into the sea.

The first tower of the Theodosian walls lies just to the north of the Marble Tower. It is in a fine state of preservation, as is the first of the ancient gateways to the city. This is the Gate of Christ, so-called because of the monogram 'XP' above it. The Gate of Christ was also known as the First Military Gate. Just to the north the railway cuts through the circuit of the walls between the seventh and eighth towers of the inner wall. The eighth tower of the inner wall forms the south-western corner of Yedikule, the Ottoman 'castle of the seven towers' described below, while the ninth and tenth towers are the two marble towers flanking the famous Golden Gate. These towers are also part of Yedikule, as is the eleventh and last tower in this first stretch of the Theodosian Walls. Immediately beyond this last tower is Yedikule Kapisi, the modern name of a small portal that was the public entrance into this part of the city in Byzantine times. In the interior above the arch of this gate there is the figure of an imperial Byzantine eagle represented in white marble.

THE GOLDEN GATE

Probably the most interesting part of the Yedikule complex is the Golden Gate. Although it was completely integrated into the defensive system many centuries ago it is actually a Roman triumphal arch erected in about 390 by Theodosius I. At that time the city walls had not been built and the triumphal arch, as was customary, stood by itself on the road called the Via Egnatia. The arch was of the

The Golden Gate was originally a Roman triumphal arch. It was walled up for defence during the last two centuries of the Byzantine Empire. (Stephen Turnbull)

The twin towers outside the Golden Gate showing the means whereby this originally triumphal arch became integrated into the defensive system. (Stephen Turnbull)

usual Roman form, with a triple arcade consisting of a large central archway flanked by two smaller ones. The outlines of the arches can still be seen clearly although the openings were bricked up in later Byzantine times. The name Porta Aurea (Golden Gate) probably comes from gold decorations on the arches. Travellers described them as 'glittering with gold'.

The facade was decorated with sculptures, the most famous of which was a group of four elephants placed there to commemorate the triumphal entry of Theodosius the Great after his victory over Maxentius. When Theodosius II decided to extend the city walls two decades later he incorporated the Golden Gate within his new land walls. It was presumably in connection with this new wall that he built the small marble gate outside the triumphal arch. The arch itself would have had no gates, except for ornamental iron or bronze grilles, and would have been indefensible. The outer gateway thus became part of the general system of defence and, together with the curtain walls that join it to the city walls near the polygonal towers, forms a small courtyard in front of the Golden Gate.

On many occasions after the time of Theodosius the Great the Golden Gate became the scene of triumphal entries by Byzantine emperors: Heraclius in 629 after he saved the empire by defeating the Persians; Constantine V, Basil I, and Basil II after their victories over the Bulgars; John I Tzimiskes after his defeat of the Russians; and Theophilos and his son Michael III after their victories over the Arabs. Perhaps the most emotional of all these triumphal entries was that of 15 August 1261, when Michael VIII Palaiologos rode in triumph and gratitude through the Golden Gate on a white charger after Constantinople was recaptured from the Latins who had taken it during the Fourth Crusade of 1204. This was the last time an emperor of Byzantium rode in triumph through the Golden Gate. In its last two centuries the history of the empire was one of continuing defeat, and by that time the Golden Gate had been walled up for defence, never again to open.

FROM THE GOLDEN GATE TO SILIVRI KAPISI

From the Golden Gate to the next gate, Belgrad Kapisi (the Belgrade Gate), it is possible to walk either on top of the great wall or on the terrace below, for the fortifications along this stretch are in quite good condition. All of the 11 towers that guard the wall along this line are still standing, as are all but one of those in the outer wall. An inscription on the eighth tower of the inner wall records repairs by Leo III and Constantine V in the years 720 to 741, and one on the tenth tower of the outer wall states that John VIII Palaiologos restored it in 1434.

The Belgrade Gate was known in Byzantine times as the Second Military Gate. It was also called Porta tou Deuterou, because it led to the military quarter of Deuteros, where the Gothic soldiers had their barracks during the early Byzantine period. This was the largest of all the military gates and may also have been used by the general public, as indeed it has been ever since. The gate came by its Turkish name because Suleiman the Magnificent settled in its vicinity many of the artisans he brought back with him from Belgrade after his capture of that city in 1521.

A view looking up to the outer and inner walls from the area just north of the Golden Gate. The towers of the Yedikule fortress can be seen just behind the line of the inner wall. (Stephen Turnbull)

The stretch of walls from Belgrad Kapisi to the next town gate, Silivri Kapisi, is also in good condition, with all 13 towers still standing in the inner wall and only one missing in the outer. The third and fourth towers of the inner walls both bear inscriptions of Leo III and Constantine V; while the fifth, tenth, and twelfth towers have inscriptions of John VIII, the first dated 1440 and the second and third 1434.

Silivri Kapisi was known in Byzantium as the Pege Gate, or the Gate of the Spring, because it was near the celebrated shrine of Zoodochus Pege. Like all of the larger gates, it is a double gate with entrances through both the inner and outer walls. On the southern tower beside the gate there is an inscription dated 1438 and recording a repair by Manuel Bryennius, a nobleman in the reign of John VIII, and on the north tower there is an inscription of Basil II (976–1025) and his brother Constantine VIII (1025–28). The most memorable day in the history of this gate was 25 July 1261. On that day a small body of Byzantine troops led by Alexios Strategopoulos overpowered the Latin guards at the gate and forced their way inside, thus opening the way to the recapture of Constantinople and the restoration of the Byzantine Empire to its ancient capital.

FROM SILIVRI KAPISI TO YENI MEVLEVIHANE KAPISI

All of the original 15 towers are still standing in the stretch of wall between the two gates of Silivri Kapisi and Yeni Mevlevihane Kapisi, but neither they nor the walls themselves are as well preserved as those closer to the Sea of Marmara. Between the fifth and seventh towers there is a curious indentation in the wall. This is known as the Sigma because its shape resembles the uncial form of that Greek letter. Just beyond the Sigma is the Third Military Gate, now walled up. Over this little gate there once stood a statue of Theodosius II, builder of these great walls. The statue did not disappear until the 14th century. The second tower of the inner wall bears an inscription of Leo III and Constantine V, and on the tenth tower is one with the names of Leo IV (775–80), Constantine VI (780–97), and Empress Eirene (797–802).

Yeni Mevlevihane Kapisi takes its modern Turkish name from the headquarters of a group of Mevlevi dervishes that once stood outside the gate. In Byzantium it was called the Gate of Rhegium, and sometimes also the Gate of the Reds after the circus faction that built it. The gateway is remarkable for the number of inscriptions preserved upon it. One inscription mentions the Red faction and is undoubtedly of 447, when the final phase of the Theodosian walls was completed by Constantine, Prefect of the East. This great feat is commemorated in two inscriptions on the south corbel of the outer gate, one in Greek and the other in Latin. The Greek inscription merely gives the facts of construction. The Latin one is more boastful, reading, 'By the command of Theodosius, Constantine erected these strong walls in less than two months. Scarcely could Pallas herself have built so strong a citadel in

so short a span.' There is also an inscription on the lintel of the outer gate recording a restoration by Justin II (565–78), his wife Sophia, and Narses, the eunuch who succeeded Belisarius as commander of the Byzantine army.

FROM YENI MEVLEVIHANE KAPISI TO PORTA XYLOKERKOU

The stretch between these two gates forms the centre of the long arc of walls. The seventh tower of the inner wall bears the names of Leo III and Constantine V, along with this inscription: 'Oh Christ, God, preserve thy city undisturbed and free from war. Conquer the wrath of our enemies.' Between the ninth and tenth towers the Fourth Military Gate, now closed up, pierces the inner wall. On the first tower of the wall north of this gate there is an inscription mentioning a certain Georgius. This is believed to have been removed from a nearby church and placed in the walls during the restoration by John VIII in 1438–39, evidence that many buildings near the walls were torn down to strengthen them against the impending siege by the Turks.

The stretch of fortifications between the two gates of Romanos and Charisius (Top Kapi and Edirne respectively) was known in Byzantium as the *mesoteichion*. This part of the walls was the most vulnerable in the whole defence system,

The Belgrade Gate was known in Byzantine times as the Second Military Gate. It was where the Gothic soldiers had their barracks during the early Byzantine period. This was the largest of all the military gates and the public may also have used it, as indeed they have ever since. (Stephen Turnbull)

Silivri Kapisi was known in Byzantium as the Pege Gate, or the Gate of the Spring, because it was near the celebrated shrine of Zoodochus Pege. Like all the larger gate, it is a double gate with entrances through both the inner and outer walls. (Stephen Turnbull)

because here the fortifications descend very noticeably into the valley of the Lycus, the stream that entered the city midway between the two gates. During the last siege in 1453 the defenders on the mesoteichion were at a serious disadvantage because they lay below the level of the Turkish guns on either side of the valley. For that reason the walls in the Lycus Valley are the most badly damaged in the whole length of the fortifications, and most of the defence towers are mere piles of rubble or great shapeless hulks of masonry. The course of the ancient river Lycus is today marked by the broad new road, called Vatan Caddesi, which breaches the walls midway between Top Kapi and Edirne Kapisi. Just inside the walls between this breach and the Fifth Military Gate is the area called Sulukule. Since late Byzantine times this has been the Gypsy quarter of the city, and, despite frequent attempts by the authorities to evict them, the Gypsies still live there in ramshackle wooden houses built right up against the Theodosian walls. The section of walls in this area was originally known as the Murus Bacchatureus. According to tradition this is where Constantine XI had his command post during the last siege. He was last seen there just before the walls were breached, fighting valiantly.

The Fifth Military Gate is known in Turkish as Hucum Kapisi (the Gate of the Assault) to preserve the memory of that last battle. On the outer lintel of the gate there is an inscription recording a repair by one Pusaeus, dated to the 5th century. On the eighth tower there is an inscription of John VIII dated 1433 and another by one Manuel Iagari in the reign of Constantine XI (1449–53). The latter inscription is the latest record of a repair to the walls, and it was probably placed there at the time of the preparations for the final siege in 1453.

The Yeni Mehlev Gate. Yeni Mevlevihane Kapisi takes its modern Turkish name from the headquarters of a group of Mevlevi dervishes that once stood outside the gate. (Stephen Turnbull)

The Edirne Gate (the Gate of Charisius) stands at the peak of the sixth hill and is thus at the highest point in the old city, 40ft above sea level. This gate has preserved in Turkish form one of its ancient names, as from here the main road went to Adrianople (the modern Edirne). It was also known in Byzantium as the Gate of Charisius, or sometimes as the Porta Polyandriou, the Gate of the Cemetery. This latter name came from the large necropolis outside the walls in this area. The graveyard still exists and displays large Turkish, Greek and Armenian burial grounds, the latter two probably dating from Byzantine times.

It was through the Edirne Gate that Mehmet II made his triumphal entry after his capture of Constantinople early in the afternoon of 29 May 1453, and a plaque on the southern side of the gate commemorates that historic event. Just inside the Edirne Gate to the south stands the splendid Mihrimah Sultan Camii, one of the great imperial mosques of Constantinople.

The Theodosian walls continue on for about 700 yards beyond Edirne Kapisi, at which point they give way to the stretch of walls constructed in later times. The inner wall in this stretch is well preserved and has nine towers that are more or less intact. At the very end of the existing Theodosian walls, just next to its last tower, are the remains of a small postern that played a fateful role in the final hours of the last siege. This is the Porta Xylokerkou, the Gate of the Wooden Circus, named after a hippodrome that once stood outside the walls in this area. At the climax of the last battle on 29 May 1453 this gate was left open and unguarded for a few moments, and it was through here that the Janissaries first made their way into the city. It was also from the tower beside the Porta Xylokerkou, the very last bastion on the long line of the Theodosian walls, that the Turkish ensign first waved over Constantinople.

Towers of the inner wall and damaged sections of the outer wall shown near the Topkapi Gate where a modern road cuts through the wall. (Stephen Turnbull)

THE PALACE OF THE PORPHYROGENITUS

Just beyond this gate there stands one of the most remarkable buildings remaining from the days of Byzantium. It is known in Turkish as Tekfur Saray, the Palace of the Sovereign, but it is better known in English as the Palace of the Porphyrogenitus. The palace was probably built in the latter part of the 13th century or early in the 14th century and served as one of the imperial residences during the last two centuries of Byzantium. It is a large three-storied building wedged in between the inner and outer fortifications of the last stretch of the Theodosian walls. On the ground floor an arcade, with four wide arches, opens on to the courtyard, which is overlooked on the first floor by five large windows. The top floor, which projects above the walls, has windows on all sides, seven overlooking the courtyard, a curious bow-like apse on the opposite side, and a window with the remains of a balcony to the east. The roof and all of the floors have disappeared. The whole palace, but especially the facade on the court, is elaborately decorated with geometrical designs in red brick and white marble.

FROM THE PALACE OF THE PORPHYROGENITUS TO THE GOLDEN HORN

Just beyond Tekfur Saray the Theodosian walls come to an abrupt end and walls of later construction continue the fortifications. As noted earlier, there has been much discussion about the original course of the Theodosian walls from Tekfur Saray down to the Golden Horn. It would appear that they turned almost due north at Tekfur Saray and from there followed a more or less straight line down to the Golden Horn, whereas the later walls are bent in an arc farther out to the west. Stretches of what are undoubtedly the original Theodosian walls can be seen at Tekfur Saray and also along a nearby street where the ruined walls are quite impressive and picturesque. Like so many other ruins in Istanbul, squatters inhabit them.

The stretch of wall from Tekfur Saray to the Golden Horn is quite different from the Theodosian fortifications. It is a single bulwark without a moat, but to make up for this deficiency it is thicker and more massive than the main Theodosian wall, and its towers are stronger, higher and placed closer together. The Emperor Manuel Komnenos (1143–80) built the first part of this section of the walls. This wall begins just beyond Tekfur Saray, where it starts westward almost at right angles to the last fragment of the Theodosian wall and then turns right at the third tower.

The Palace of the Porphyrogenitus. Just in front of the ruins may be seen the remains of the Porta Xylokerkou, the Gate of the Wooden Circus, named after a hippodrome that once stood outside the walls in this area. (Stephen Turnbull)

133

The Edirne Gate (the Gate of Charisius) stands at the peak of the sixth hill and is thus at the highest point in the old city, 40ft above sea level. This gate was originally called the Porta Adrianopoleos, as from here the main road went to Adrianople (the modern Edirne). (Stephen Turnbull)

The wall of Manuel Komnenos is an admirably constructed fortification consisting of high arches closed on the outer face. It contains nine towers and one public gate, now called Egri Kapi. Most authorities identify Egri Kapi with the ancient Gate of the Kaligaria. It was here that his friend George Phrantzes, the chronicler who would later write a history of the fall of Byzantium, last saw Emperor Constantine XI alive. On the night of 28 May 1453 the emperor, accompanied by Phrantzes, stopped briefly at the palace after returning from his last visit to Hagia Sophia. According to Phrantzes, Constantine assembled the members of his household and said goodbye to each of them in turn, asking their forgiveness for any unkindness he might ever have shown them. 'Who could describe the tears and groans in the palace?' Phrantzes wrote, 'Even a man of wood or stone could not help weeping.' The emperor then left the palace and rode with Phrantzes down to the Gate of the Kaligaria. They dismounted there and Phrantzes waited while Constantine ascended one of the towers nearby, whence he could hear the Turkish artillery preparing for the final assault. Soon after he returned and mounted his horse once again. Phrantzes then said goodbye to Constantine for the last time and watched as the emperor rode off to his command post on the Murus Bacchatureus, never to be seen again.

The Turkish name Egri Kapi, the Crooked Gate, is so called because the narrow lane that leaves the city here must detour around a tomb that stands almost directly in front of the portal. This is the supposed tomb of Hazret Hafiz, a companion of the Prophet, who, according to tradition, was killed on this spot

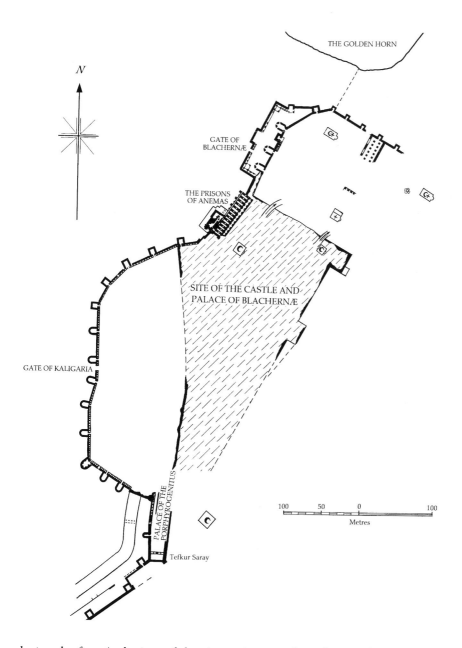

THE GOLDEN HORN

GATE OF
BLACHERNÆ

THE PRISONS
OF ANEMAS

N

SITE OF THE CASTLE AND
PALACE OF BLACHERNÆ

GATE OF KALIGARIA

PALACE OF THE
PORPHYROGENITUS

100   50   0   100
Metres

Tefkur Saray

Plan of the Blachernae Quarter, showing how the later walls spread outwards to enclose this vital strategic area. (© Osprey Publishing Ltd, artwork by John Richards)

during the first Arab siege of the city in 674–78. Several sainted Arab heroes of that campaign are buried in the vicinity, all having been dispatched to Paradise by the defenders on the walls of Constantinople.

From Egri Kapi one may continue along the path just inside the walls to see the remainder of the wall of Manuel Komnenos, which ends at the third tower past the gate. The rest of this section of wall, from the third tower to where it joins the retaining wall of the Blachernae terrace, appears to be of later construction. The

One of the first towers in the newer wall. Emperor Manuel I Komnenos (1143–80) built the first part of this section of the walls. This wall begins just beyond the Tekfur Saray, where it starts westward almost at right angles to the last fragment of the Theodosian wall and then turns right at the third tower. The wall of Manuel Komnenos is an admirably constructed fortification consisting of high arches closed on the outer face. It contains nine towers and one public gate. (Stephen Turnbull)

workmanship here is much inferior to that in the wall of Manuel Komnenos. This can clearly be seen where the two join without bonding, just beyond the third tower from Egri Kapi.

Four towers, all square and also much inferior to those in the previous section, guard this section. The wall of Manuel Komnenos bears no dated inscriptions. The later northern one has three: one dated 1188 by Isaac II Angelos; another 1311 by Andronikos II Palaiologos; and the third 1441 by John VIII Palaiologos. There is also in this northern section a postern, now walled up, which is thought to be the ancient Gyrolimne Gate or the 'Gate of the Silver Lake'. This was an entrance to the Palace of Blachernae, whose outer retaining wall and two towers continue the line of fortifications in this area.

The fortification from the northern corner of the Blachernae terrace to the Golden Horn consists of two parallel walls joined at their two ends to form a kind of citadel. The emperor Heraclius built the inner wall in 627 in an attempt to strengthen the defences in this area when the city was being threatened by the

Blachernae today, showing the ruins of the so-called Prison of Anemas in the outer circuit of the walls. (Stephen Turnbull)

Avars and the Persians. The three hexagonal defence towers in this short stretch of wall are perhaps the finest in the whole system. In 813, when Krum the Bulgar threatened the city, Leo V decided to strengthen the defences in this vulnerable area by building an outer wall with four small towers, a fortification thinner than the older one behind it and much inferior in construction. These walls were pierced by a single entryway, the Gate of the Blachernae. That part of the gate that passed through the wall of Leo has now collapsed, but it is still open through the Heraclian wall, passing between the first and second towers.

The Wall of Leo stands 77ft to the west of the Wall of Heraclius, running parallel to it for some 260ft, after which it turns to join the walls along the Golden Horn. Its parapet walk was supported upon arches, which served at the same time to buttress the wall itself, a comparatively slight structure about 8ft thick. In order to increase the wall's capacity for defence it was flanked by four small towers, while numerous loopholes pierced its lower portion. Two of the towers were on the side facing the Golden Horn, and the other two guarded the extremities of the side looking towards the country on the west. The latter towers projected inwards from the rear of the wall, and between them was a gateway corresponding to the Heraclian Gate of Blachernae.

In 1081 the friends of Alexios Komnenos sallied from the city through the Gate of Blachernae to raise the standard of revolt against Nikephoros III Botaneiates. It was at the imperial stables outside the gate that they obtained horses to reach as fast as possible the Monastery of SS. Cosmas and Damianus, preventing any pursuit by hamstringing the animals they did not require. In 1097 Godfrey de Bouillon and his crusaders encamped on the hills and plains outside this stretch of wall.

The area of the citadel between the walls of Leo and Heraclius is quite fascinating to visit and study. It has been much improved in recent years and has been attractively landscaped as a public park. At the northern end of the citadel the walls of Leo and Heraclius come together and link up with the sea walls along the Golden Horn.

THE LIVING SITE

STRATEGIC CONSIDERATIONS

The maintenance and manning of the walls of Constantinople was but one small part of the overall Byzantine strategy for the defence of the empire utilizing the limited resources as necessary. The careful defence of Constantinople was backed up by a vigorous diplomatic effort that was not merely aimed at avoiding the shedding of Christian blood. On the contrary, the whole future of the state, and the security of its apparently huge and mighty walls depended upon having friends to aid you and enemies whose intentions one could understand. Preparation was of the greatest importance, as the *Chronicle* of Theophanes reminds us for the Arab attack in 714:

> then the Emperor commanded each man to be able to pay his own way for three years' time, and ordered those unable to do so to abandon the city. He made sails and began to build warships, Greek-fire-carrying biremes, and huge triremes. He restored the land and sea walls, and installed arrow-shooting engines, stone-throwing engines and catapults on the gates. He stored up a great amount of produce in the imperial granaries and secured it as best he could, and strengthened the city to the best of his ability.

It is also worthy of note that there were several occasions when strategic considerations led to a siege of Constantinople's walls being abandoned as a result of a victory gained many miles away. The best example concerns the year 1090, when the Patzinaks, a warlike nomadic people from the plains of southern Russia, reached the walls of the capital after a series of hotly contested struggles with imperial troops. As if this was not enough, Constantinople was also assailed by sea from the fleet of Tzachas the emir of Smyrna. He had once been a prisoner of the imperial court, and that experience had shown him that any decisive blow against Constantinople had to include a movement from the sea.

In his dire need Emperor Alexios I Komnenos allied himself with another nomadic group called the Cumans, and with their help defeated the Patzinaks at the battle of Mount Levunion. The Patzinaks were completely wiped out. As Anna Komnena, Alexios' daughter and biographer, wrote, 'An entire people, numbering

myriads, was exterminated on a single day.' Tzachas' seaborne blockade was neutralized and had to be abandoned. The walls of Constantinople were safe again.

THE WALLS AND THE ARMY

The walls and gates of Constantinople may have been formidable, but they always depended upon a supply of men to defend them. Although modern research has shed light on the overall organization of the Byzantine army, much less is known about the soldiers whose job it was to guard the capital from Constantinople's walls. When danger threatened soldiers were found wherever possible, and there is no evidence that divisions of garrison troops had any special names or titles, or that garrison soldiers were distinguishable from any of the mercenaries who lived in the city. The garrison would therefore appear to have consisted of any standing troops who were ready at a moment's notice to defend the walls against attack. They were distinguishable only from the palace guards.

The best example of a garrison in action in Constantinople is a group of Catalan mercenaries who were given the job of defending the Golden Gate fort on behalf of John Kantakouzenos in 1352. We are told that their commander Juan de Peralta had known John Kantakouzenos since their days in Serbia some years earlier, so these mercenaries can probably be identified as the group of 'Latin' or 'German' mercenaries who had deserted Stephen Dushan in Serbia. The function of the Golden Gate garrison was twofold: to defend the city if the rival emperor John V Palaiologos attacked it and to maintain John Kantakouzenos' hold over the city. This was no idle threat. The people were warned that if they surrendered to John V Palaiologos they would face both John Kantakouzenos' Turkish allies and the garrison of the city.

There are also records of occasions when troops were sent from Constantinople to garrison other towns then under threat. For example, when Andronikos III besieged Apros in 1322, 220 cavalry, 200 archers and 30 crossbowmen, sent from Constantinople, reinforced the town's garrison. This was a great help to a local force that consisted of 100 cavalry, archers and slingers, and a force drawn from those living nearby who 'came together because of the war'.

The garrisoning of Constantinople, however, involved considerations that went far beyond the fighting quality of the men stationed on its walls. Defence of the capital was as much a political need as a military one, and required a delicate balancing act. Large numbers of troops in and around the capital always represented a potential threat to the emperor's safety. Hence the small numbers employed as bodyguards, and the preference for foreign troops such as the Varangian guardsmen. In any case, the maintenance of a large permanent garrison would have been an enormously expensive proposition. The cost of maintaining the Byzantine army was the empire's largest item of expenditure, and when there was a major threat to Constantinople regional forces could be sent to the city quite speedily.

OPPOSITE
The Conquest of Constantinople by Tintoretto (1518–1594). The conquest of Constantinople by the crusaders of the Fourth Crusade on 12 April 1204. Venice, Palace of the Doge. (akg-images/Cameraphoto)

The aqueduct of Valens. The growing population led in 373 to the building of the first aqueduct to take water into the heart of the city. This was the aqueduct of Valens, named after the emperor who commissioned it. The aqueduct still stands as a striking monument in the middle of busy Istanbul. (Stephen Turnbull)

The Varangian Guard

Of all the mercenaries employed to serve in Constantinople none are better known than the famous Varangian Guard, who were recruited from the Scandinavian north. Forging their way from their own inhospitable lands the Northmen, first of all from Sweden, reached the Volga and later by the so-called 'Varangian Way' came down from Russia by way of the Dnieper and the Black Sea to Constantinople. They came first as pirates, then as traders and finally as the most trusted guards of the Byzantine emperors. During the first half of the 11th century Harold Hardrada served in the Varangian Guard. Later that same century in the aftermath of the Norman Conquest, many Anglo-Saxons from England joined their ranks, the earliest written record of their presence being 1088.

The Varangians are frequently referred to in the Byzantine chronicles as 'axe-bearing warriors'. Their axes were wielded wherever their emperor needed them, and this included service on the walls of Constantinople. The best records of the Varangians manning the walls date from the Fourth Crusade. The chronicler Niketas Choniates tells us that when the crusaders tried to enforce a landing at the imperial pier on the Golden Horn near Blachernae they were driven back by the great bravery of the allies of the Greeks who included the Pisans and the 'axe-bearing barbarians'. Villehardouin tells us that English and Danes manned the wall, and that 'the fighting was very violent, and there was a hand to hand fight with axes and swords, the assailants mounted on the wall and prisoners were taken on both sides'. He also tells us that when the Latins sent envoys to the Emperor Isaac, Englishmen and Danes were posted at the gate of the city and all along the road to the Blachernae Palace, fully armed with their formidable axes.

The service by the Varangian Guard does not seem to have lasted much beyond the restoration of Byzantine power under Michael VIII. There is however a reference of 1329 to 'the Varangians with their axes' who were accustomed to guarding the keys of any city in which the emperor was staying. There is no mention of them in action during the sieges by the Ottomans in the 14th and 15th centuries, and the only trace of them left in Istanbul today is an interesting and unique memorial to the Varangian Guard high up in the southern gallery of the church of Hagia Sophia, where on a balustrade a Varangian guardsman carved his name, 'Halvdan', in Viking runes.

WATER AND FOOD SUPPLY

No matter how strong a city's walls might be, its population has to be supplied with food and water, and Constantinople was no exception. The original site of Byzantium was poorly supplied with natural water sources. The stream called the Lycus that has long since disappeared once flowed into the city, and there were a few small springs. At a further distance two streams once known as the 'Sweet Waters of Europe' flowed into the Golden Horn.

The first aqueduct to bring water to Byzantium was built by the Emperor Hadrian. Records note that it soon proved inadequate, and the growing population of the new capital founded by Constantine led in 373 to the building of the first aqueduct to take water into the heart of the city. This was the aqueduct of Valens, named after the emperor who commissioned it. The aqueduct still stands in the middle of busy Istanbul, straddling a multi-lane highway. What we see today was only part of a huge network that took about 30 years to complete and was described by Gregory of Nazianzus as 'a subterranean and aerial river'.

But to bring water in is one thing. It also needed to be stored, so very large underground and surface cisterns and reservoirs were added within the city walls. In 626, during the siege of Constantinople by the Avars, the besiegers cut the aqueduct of Valens, but the act had no serious consequences. This was probably because the damage was slight, and also because of the storage facilities. For example, Justinian built the Yerebatan Saray, the huge pillared underground cistern that is one of the great sights of Istanbul, during the 530s. Curiously, knowledge of this colossal urban reservoir was lost in the century following the conquest by the Ottomans. It was only rediscovered in 1545 when Petrus Gyllius, a traveller to the city engaged upon the study of Byzantine antiquities, heard that the inhabitants of this area obtained their water supplies by lowering buckets through the floors of their houses, while some even caught fish there!

The Varangian Guard, probably the best-known Byzantine regiment, was composed of men from the far north of Europe, and served the Byzantine emperor. Sometime after 860, a treaty stipulated that the Emperor should receive a levy from the Rus', Scandinavians settled in Russia. This treaty may not have been honoured, but later treaties probably were, and Rus' bands fought for Byzantium, though not as regular units in permanent Byzantine employ. In 988, Emperor Basil received a large group of men from Prince Vladimir of Kiev, and these men were immediately established as the emperor's bodyguard. The Varangian Guard were renowned for their ferocity, and served the emperors of Byzantium for centuries. Pictured is a Rus' mercenary, c.950 (1). Many of the Scandinavians who settled in Russia were soon influenced by the dress of their Slav and Asiatic neighbours. This man wears a mixture of Slav and Asiatic clothes, and his tattoos are indicative of an Asiatic trait adopted by some Rus'. A Varangian guardsman of c.1000 (2), carries the distinctive two-handed axe. His other gear is a mixture of Scandinavian and Byzantine items. A Varangian guardsman of c.1030 (3), wears dress uniform, silk clothes, a scarlet cloak, and carries a shield and axe. (Angus McBride © Osprey Publishing Ltd)

As for food supply, by 1200 the empire had lost its richest provinces for good, notably Egypt, once the source of grain that had fed the population up to the time of Heraclius. This could have posed serious problems, particularly when an attack loomed, but Constantinople was actually able to feed itself from its lands in Thrace and the fields round the Aegean. Ships and carts ferried the grain to Constantinople, where it was stored and distributed through a commercial network.

SIEGE WEAPONS AND THE DEFENCE OF THE WALLS

The defenders of Constantinople had several types of siege weaponry at their disposal. Various forms of catapults designed to throw stones or arrows were used both to defend Constantinople and attack it until the early 15th century, but it is not clear how much continuity there was between the Roman war machines of the 4th and 5th centuries and the later Byzantine weapons. The classic Roman model was the two-armed horizontally mounted torsion-powered catapult. This was a device that required considerable technical knowledge and expertise both to produce and to maintain. The crucial factor of having equivalent torsion levels in both springs required great mathematical and engineering knowledge, and this does not appear to have been available in abundance from the 5th and 6th centuries onwards. Instead the Byzantine historian Procopius described the use of the onager, the familiar Roman torsion catapult that used one vertical arm threaded through some form of torsion spring in a horizontal plane. Such machines could throw stones and incendiary missiles. They had the disadvantage of having to be constructed very solidly to give the stability they needed to operate, but these skills were generally available. The *Tactica* of Leo tells of field artillery units that accompanied the infantry. They were wagon-mounted and with a single pole, which rules out the two-armed torsion catapults. At the siege of Adrianople by the Goths in 378 the defenders hurled a huge stone ball from an onager against a densely packed group of Goths. No damage was done, but the incident caused considerable alarm and impressed the besiegers.

The Byzantines also used machines that projected bolts or arrows. Procopius again describes these, and the language he uses to illustrate their operation implies that they were not torsion devices but received their stored energy from tension. As words for bow appear in the long names he uses for the weapons some form of siege crossbow is more than likely. Procopius also gives a good indication of the force that could be mounted behind the flight of one of these bolts. During Vitiges' siege of Rome in 536 a bolt hit a Goth as he sat halfway up a tree, shooting arrows from a hand bow. The bolt nailed him to the tree and he hung there, pinned to the trunk!

While the one-armed onager seems to have survived under the Byzantine Empire, the Avars introduced other stone-throwing weapons in the late 6th century. These were based neither on torsion nor tension, but made use of the energy given to a lever by a team of men pulling ropes in unison. These were the traction trebuchets, the forerunners of the later and larger counterweight trebuchets that made their appearance in Western Europe in the late 13th century. The traction trebuchet originated in China and had travelled west. Counterweight trebuchets would certainly have played a part in the defences of Constantinople once their use had been established after the Crusades.

THE SEA WALLS OF CONSTANTINOPLE *c.*1000

The sea walls were never as strong as the land walls, but served their purpose when well defended. A Byzantine *dronon* is testing a Greek fire projector just outside the harbour of Bucoleon on the Sea of Marmara, and the performance is being watched from

the battlements by the Varangian Guard. In the centre background is Hagia Sophia, to the left the Church of SS Sergius and Bacchus, and to the right the Church of St Eirene. (Peter Dennis © Osprey Publishing Ltd)

GUNPOWDER WEAPONS AT CONSTANTINOPLE

By the last two decades of the 14th century the Byzantines had begun to accumulate gunpowder weapons, spurred on by the growing threat on their doorstep posed by the Ottomans. The earliest were medium-sized cannon about 3ft in length and with a calibre of up to 10in. Only a few large bombards were to be found in Byzantine arsenals. By the middle of the 15th century handguns also began to appear.

In 1390 there took place a coup d'état that resulted in the emperor John V Palaiologos being besieged in the Golden Gate fortress by his grandson John VII Palaiologos. This incident is interesting because it may have involved the earliest use of gunpowder weapons at Constantinople, but the actual passage in the chronicles is ambiguous, as it refers to the attackers 'beating' against the walls. Guns are first definitely mentioned when Bayezid the Thunderbolt's Turks came to besiege the city in 1396. The Ottomans had no firearms of their own but made use of conventional siege machinery such as trebuchets. The defenders, however, did possess cannon, although the source tells of them being used by the 'Franks' (probably the Genoese) of Galata, and that the noise and smoke they produced, together with crossbow bolts and stones from slings, caused the Turks to withdraw. These cannon may therefore have been Genoese weapons that were not under the control of the Byzantine forces.

By the time of the siege of 1422, a fight that was to be the dress rehearsal for 1453, the Turks had their own artillery, and in a major eyewitness source about this siege John Kananos describes how the Turks used 'falcons' (short fat cannons) along with other siege weapons such as 'tortoises', the covered wagons

This interesting and evocative stretch of damaged wall lies in a section immediately to the north of the Golden Gate. Artillery was a vital factor in the fall of Constantinople in 1453, not merely because of the number of guns possessed by Mehmet the Conqueror, but the sensible use he made of them. (Stephen Turnbull)

used to protect miners. The defenders had cannon too, so the Turks built barricades 'in order to receive the arrows of the bows and of the crossbows of the Romans, and the stones of the bombards'. The Byzantines had roughly the same level of technology as the Ottomans, although the eventual lifting of the 1422 siege was credited not to the success of the Byzantine artillery, but to the miraculous intervention of the Virgin herself, who appeared on the walls and inspired the defenders.

Such apparitions had saved Constantinople in the past, but it would be an exaggeration to blame such touching faith for the extraordinary fact that during the next 30 years the Byzantines do not seem to have made any progress in developing their artillery. Nor did they attempt to remodel any part of their huge medieval walls to withstand a possible bombardment on a contemporary scale. The reasons for such failures are probably very mundane ones of Constantinople's severe economic problems, which led to a simple shortage of cash to buy the guns or to hire the experts who could both cast and use them. Indeed, many of the cannon that were eventually used to defend Constantinople during the siege of 1453 appear to have been made available to them as gifts, a practice promoted later by Pope Pius II as a way of helping the Byzantines. It was a gesture that most crowned heads of Europe could easily afford, and it was also a safer alternative to going on crusade to provide military help to Constantinople.

Economic problems just before the fateful siege of 1453 were partly to blame for the well-known story (recounted originally by the chronicler Doukas) that tells how a Hungarian artillery expert named Urban approached the Byzantine emperor with an offer to cast guns for the defence of the city. This was the opportunity for which the defenders of Constantinople had been waiting, but because the price he demanded was too high he was sent away. Urban immediately turned to Sultan Mehmet II, who hired him for four times the fee he had asked. Urban's creations were the two giant bombards. He had boasted that these cannon could reduce 'even the walls of Babylon'. They took three months to make and were test fired at Adrianople (Edirne), where:

> public announcements were made ... to advise everyone of the loud and thunderous noise which it would make so that no one would be struck dumb by hearing the noise unexpectedly or any pregnant women miscarry.

The enormous cannon were each transported to Constantinople by 70 oxen and 10,000 men. Following the advice of his artillerymen, Mehmet II positioned his siege guns against the weakest and most vulnerable parts of the wall. The targets included the imperial palace of Blachernae at the north-western corner of the city and the Gate of St Romanos in the middle wall. The bombardment, which was to last 55 days, soon began to cause massive destruction, and the chronicler Kritovoulos has left a fascinating description of what happened when one of the enormous stone balls hit its target:

> And the stone, borne with enormous force and velocity, hit the wall, which it immediately shook and knocked down, and was itself broken into many fragments and scattered, hurling the pieces everywhere and killing those who happened to be nearby.

From the Byzantine side the defenders hit back with their own artillery weapons. The available guns were distributed along the walls and used as required, either against Turkish siege machinery or as anti-personnel weapons together with crossbows. As Doukas recounts:

> [These guns] fired, with the help of powder, five or ten bullets at a time, each about the size of a Pontic walnut, and having a great power of penetration. If one of these hit an armed man, it would go right through his shield and his body, and go on to hit anyone else who happened to be in his way, and even a third until the force of the powder diminished. So one shot might kill two or three men.

Possibly the finest restored section of the Theodosian walls lies here to the north of the Belgrade Gate. The complete system of inner wall, towers, peribolos, outer wall, outer walkway, small parapet and moat are shown here. (Stephen Turnbull)

149

THE SIEGE OF 1204

The later walls around the Blachernae quarter of Constantinople as the crusaders would have seen them during the siege of 1204. The fortification from the northern corner of the Blachernae terrace to the Golden Horn consists of two parallel walls joined at their two ends to form a kind of citadel. The Emperor Heraclius built the inner wall in 627. In 813, when Krum the Bulgar threatened the city, Leo V decided to strengthen the defences in this vulnerable area by building an outer wall with four small towers. These walls were pierced by a single entryway, the Gate of the Blachernae. To the right, we see the so-called Prison of Anemas. (Peter Dennis © Osprey Publishing Ltd)

There was some initial success as the Byzantines settled down to the effects of the Turkish bombardment. Soon they could repel whatever siege engine they could see, reports Leonard of Chios, but the Turks responded by hiding their war machines from view. The Byzantine artillery faced several other problems, one of the most serious being that the flat roofs of the towers in the medieval walls were not sufficiently strong to act as gun emplacements. As Leonard of Chios put it, 'the largest cannon had to remain silent for fear of damage to our own walls by vibration'. Chalkondylas even wrote that the act of firing cannon did more harm to the towers than the Turkish bombardment. Even the largest of the Byzantine

cannon was smaller than the Turkish equivalents, and when it burst a great fury rose against the artilleryman. He was suspected of having been bribed by the Sultan and would have been executed, but was finally released for lack of evidence.

A very damaged octagonal tower from the inner section of the Theodosian walls, located just to the south of the Golden Gate. (Stephen Turnbull)

GREEK FIRE

Greek fire was the secret weapon of the Byzantine Empire. Its introduction can be dated quite exactly, because Theophanes, who finished his *Chronographia* in 815, described how the Arabs continually attacked Constantinople from 674 to 678, but finally gave up. One factor in this was the chemical process introduced a few years earlier by an architect-engineer called Kallinikos that produced Greek fire. Incendiaries using naturally occurring mineral oils had been known about for some time. Naphtha, for example, was obtained by the filtration of crude oil. The particular feature of Greek fire that made it so revolutionary, and so much a state secret, was that it used petroleum that had been distilled, although many of the accounts of so-called naphtha-throwing may also involve what was actually distilled petrol.

Most accounts of Greek fire in the defence of Constantinople are to do with naval warfare. The burning petrol would float on the surface of the sea and destroy the hulls of enemy ships. It would, however, dissipate rather quickly and carry only a short distance. For this reason it was thickened with resinous substances. The means of delivery in Constantinople was by siphons, which were effectively ancient flamethrowers. These siphons were mounted on Byzantine ships, and were often given the shapes of animal heads at the ends of the tubes. Emperor Leo's *Tactica*, written in the 8th or 9th century, tells us how the men who worked the bronze flame-throwing pumps were protected by iron shields, and that the blazing jets, which may have been of a considerable size, made the noise of rumbling thunder. Smaller handheld versions also apparently existed. One account says that the pumps were worked by compressed air, which could mean that the petrol was forced out using some sort of piston-bellows. Another implies that flexible pipes formed part of the overall apparatus, because the siphon could be directed to left or right at the will of the operator, or even at a high elevation to fall on to the enemy ships from above.

The repulse of the Arab sieges of Constantinople involved Byzantine ships sailing out of Constantinople and attacking them with Greek fire. A later large-scale use took place during the Russian attack on Constantinople in 941:

> The Greeks began to fling their fire all around; and the Rus', seeing the flames, threw themselves in haste from their ships, preferring to be drowned in the water rather than burned alive in the fire.

The Greek fire projectors were mounted on a swivel so that they could be aimed in any direction. A good example of seaborne use is 1103 when Emperor Alexios Komnenos used Greek fire against the Pisans near Rhodes.

Greek fire could also be used against troops on land or to set fire to siege weapons. There are not many references to this, but it is interesting to note the employment of Greek fire during the final siege of Constantinople in 1453. It was used on one occasion then as a defensive weapon for a ship arriving with grain. Turkish attempts to intercept it were beaten off using Greek fire. It was also very useful against siege towers. We are told that a German, reportedly named Johannes Grant, directed the fire. He sprayed Greek fire on to an enormous siege machine, presumably a belfry lined inside and outside with three layers of ox hide. The machine had already helped bring down the tower of St Romanos during the night, but the defenders repaired it very quickly, astounding the Sultan by their endeavours.

Greek fire was also used when the Ottoman soldiers stormed the walls. Fire was poured down on to the unfortunate souls climbing up, and we are given a nightmare picture of the soldiers falling into the moat screaming with pain. The maces and whips of guards beat more of these forlorn hope troops forward, while the Janissaries in the background cut down any who fled. But by 1453 gunpowder was the decisive weapon, and attempts to use Greek fire from ships against the Turkish troops were cut short by cannon fire. It was the end of an era in more ways than one.

Further detail concerning Greek fire has come from the fact that its use eventually spread as far as China and entered the repertoire of Chinese siegecraft around 900. A detailed description of the Chinese version is given in the *Wu Jing Zong Yao* of 1044. Chinese illustrations are also more detailed and realistic than Byzantine ones, and show that the Chinese Greek fire container was made of brass and fitted with a horizontal pump, which terminated in the gunpowder ignition chamber, and a small-diameter nozzle. When the handle was pushed in and out vigorously petrol was squirted out. It is unlikely that Byzantine ones were much different, and the Chinese author recommends placing these machines on the ramparts or the outworks of cities. An excellent account of the Chinese use of Greek fire concerns a battle on the Yangtze near Nanjing in 975 between the Song and the Tang, where things did not quite go according to plan because 'he quickly projected petrol from flame throwers to destroy the enemy. The Song forces could not have withstood this, but all of a sudden a north wind sprang up and swept the smoke and flames over the sky towards his own ships and men.' It was a scenario that may well also have happened in the Byzantine Empire.

THE SUPERNATURAL DEFENDERS OF CONSTANTINOPLE

A western traveller to Constantinople early in the 15th century surmised that God had spared the city more for the holy relics it contained than for anything else. It was a perceptive observation, because the city's inhabitants believed that they enjoyed the protection of a secret weapon even more potent than Greek fire. This was the firm belief that God and his saints provided supernatural help, and one particular way in which their spiritual help was guaranteed lay in the possession of relics. The body of St Stephen the first martyr, the head of John the Baptist and the leather tunic of the pillar-dwelling St Symeon Stylites all had their sanctuaries within Constantinople along with numerous other relics of saints. In 944 as a result of his victories John Curcuas carried to Constantinople the famous portrait of Christ believed to have been painted by St Luke, which had been granted to Abgar, King of Edessa. It was recorded that by this act 'Constantinople would thereby acquire greater strength and would be kept for all time unharmed and unravaged'.

But of all the supernatural defenders of Constantinople none was held in more esteem or relied on more fully than the Blessed Virgin Mary, the Theotokos

The Virgin Mary was honoured as Constantinople's greatest protector, stronger than any wall or weapon. Here she is depicted in a mosaic in the gallery of Hagia Sophia, now the Aya Sofia mosque. Dressed in purple, the colour of the robe in which she was seen on the walls in visions, she is holding the Christ Child. She is flanked by portraits of Emperor John II Komnenos and his wife the Empress Eirene. (Stephen Turnbull)

(Mother of God). Constantinople was her city and the churches dedicated to her outnumbered all others. The most important of all these churches was the one at Blachernae that originally lay outside the Theodosian walls but was later enclosed for safety. During the 5th century Constantinople acquired its most precious relic in the form of the robe of the Virgin. The city also possessed her shroud, her girdle and the swaddling clothes in which Jesus had been wrapped. In the succession of perils to which the walls of Constantinople were subjected their ultimate salvation was invariably ascribed to the protection of the Mother of God. Any reverses such as burning of outer suburbs by attackers were explained a God's punishment for sins. Prayers were then offered to the Virgin, and these appeared to save the city time and time again.

The most touching images of the Virgin as the protectress of Constantinople concern her miraculous appearance on the city's mighty walls. Icons bearing her image were paraded round the walls in time of siege, and in times of direst need she was seen standing on the walls and inspiring the defenders. Such an incident allowed the chronicler to place an excuse for failure into the mouth of the besieging Avars in the *Chronicon Pascale* account of the siege of 626: 'And this is what the godless Chagan said at the moment of the battle: "I see a woman in a stately dress rushing about on the wall all alone."' In accounts of other sieges there was usually a focal point of one of the relics of the Virgin, such as in 860 when the Virgin's robe was dipped into the sea.

THE PERIBOLOS, 1422

The inner terrace between the inner and outer walls was called the peribolos, and accommodated the soldiers who defended the outer wall. It was between 50 and 64ft wide. Beyond lay the outer wall, which was a modest structure compared with the inner wall. This plate shows a memorable moment during the Ottoman siege of 1422, when a vision of the Virgin Mary on the wall heartened the defenders. (Peter Dennis © Osprey Publishing Ltd)

Gratitude to the Virgin Mary is described by John Kananos in his account of the 1422 siege. On that occasion she had appeared on the walls during an attack, and greatly inspired the defenders:

The Romans, though exhausted from fatigue, leapt and were glad. They clapped their hands and rendered special thanks to God. They shouted hymns to the Most Holy Virgin, glorifying her from the depths of their hearts, saying, 'This is in truth a rich, celebrated, memorable, extraordinary and remarkable miracle worthy of admiration.'

This is another restored section near Silivri Kapisi, known in Byzantium as the Pege Gate, or the Gate of the Spring. The contrast between the modern additions and the ancient masonry are of course very marked. (Stephen Turnbull)

The miracle was even confirmed by the enemy:

> The army of the Turks confirmed by an oath sworn to Mersaites, spoken of by all at the hour of battle, that on arriving at the walls of the city with an irresistible force to scale them and pursue the Romans and conquer the city, they saw a woman dressed in purple robes walking on the ramparts of the outer fortifications, and having seen her shudders and fright immediately entered everybody's soul. So because of the woman fear overtook them and the city was liberated.

As will be recounted below, Kananos noted that that the women of Constantinople were very active in the defence, approaching near enough to the 'front line' to get hit by arrows, so the apparition may just have been an interpretation put upon an action of some brave wife or sister. However, it is by no means improbable that the Turks should seize upon an apparition of the Virgin as an honourable excuse for their failure to take the city.

THE ROLE OF THE CITIZENS

When danger threatened it was not only the mercenaries in the city or the palace guard that rushed to its defence. All accounts indicate that the ordinary inhabitants rallied round, and there is no better illustration than the story of how the walls of Constantinople were defended during the siege of 1422 by citizens as well as soldiers, as related by John Kananos:

> The volley of arrows fired at the ramparts darkened the sky and forced all the defenders to duck for cover, thus giving the Turks the impression that their ploy had actually succeeded in clearing the walls at one go. Siege towers were wheeled forwards, and scaling ladders flung against the towers. Who in fact did not tremble at that hour? Who did not shiver at the sight? Which ear could stand the sound, which eye the spectacle?

But then a miracle happened, and a change of heart came over the defenders.

> They led each other out from their hiding places, for, those who formerly were fainthearted or fleeing, were unexpectedly transformed into brave and noble warriors who despised both blows and ugly wounds, and by the hope of the Most Holy Virgin they armed themselves with swords and stones and fell upon the godless plunderers. Even as smoke disperses a swarm of bees, one encouraged another, every person and age group with the weapons they had, some even with just their hands, others with swords and staves. They fastened ropes to the platters off which they had been eating their food, or the ends of barrels, and used them as shields. Some even went to fight without these but fought bravely and with valour armed only with stones as if they were wearing a complete suit of armour.

Here, for John Kananos, the religious motivation takes over completely. They encourage each other to fight 'especially for the true faith of the Christian'. They talk of throwing themselves into battle 'as the martyrs ran into the stadia of the tyrants'. They fought furiously 'as if drunk', and after a tremendous struggle drove the Turkish army back off the walls, decapitating a few unfortunates whom they caught on ladders and presenting the heads to the emperor. All the townspeople joined in, including priests and monks, and many women:

> They came as far as the outer fortifications, and some carried stones up to the walls for the fighting Romans and encouraged them… Others took eggs and cloth to treat the injuries, while others would give a drink of water and wine to those who were burning with thirst from the fatigue of combat … some were struck by missiles and suffered wounds.

THE WALLS OF CONSTANTINOPLE UNDER SIEGE

All the designs, all the precautions and prayers, all the strategies of defence of the great walls of Constantinople were put to the test on several memorable occasions during the city's long history when enemies placed the city under siege. This chapter examines how the walls played their part in the defence of the city on several occasions, although reference has already been made to the 1397 siege by Bayezid the Thunderbolt, and the role of the walls during the 1422 siege, so eloquently described by John Kananos, has been adequately covered above. The 1453 siege will be covered in depth in Part III.

Usually attacks were directed against the land walls, but the sea walls also came under threat. In addition to the incidents listed below there are also other examples of Constantinople changing hands during wars between rival emperors, but none of these actions involved prolonged sieges. The pattern then tended to be that of opportunism or treachery, as for example when Alexios I Komnenos entered the city with the connivance of German mercenaries stationed in the capital. Three days of plunder and riot followed.

THE SIEGE BY THE AVARS AND PERSIANS, 626

The mighty appearance of the walls alone acted as a sufficient deterrent to drive back Attila the Hun in the 4th century. The siege of the city by the Avars and Persians in 626 therefore became the first test ever placed upon the walls of Constantinople. It was also one of the most severe encounters. The Persians had overrun all the Roman provinces in the Near East and were now allied with the Avars, who were steadily dominating the Balkans. Constantinople was well prepared to withstand the siege although the Avars were preparing a huge operation. The Avars possessed the most up-to-date siege engines in the form of traction trebuchets. These originated from China, and their first use in the European theatre is recorded in Thessalonica in 586. They also had mobile armoured shelters (the medieval 'sows') and siege towers, the latter covered in hides for fire protection. The shelters were deployed around the walls when the Avars arrived on 29 July. On 31 July an attack was launched along the entire length of the Theodosian walls, but the main effort was concentrated against the central section, particularly the low-lying *mesoteichion*. More siege engines were brought

OPPOSITE
The siege of Constantinople in 1204 as depicted in the 14th-century Bible of Velislas. Prague, New University Library.
(Roger-Viollet/Topfoto)

up. Some had been constructed from prefabricated parts brought by the invaders, augmented by timber stripped from buildings near the ramparts. The *Chronicon Paschale* gives us a vivid account of the operation:

> And again on the following day he stationed a multitude of siege engines close to each other against that part which had been attacked by him, so that those in the city were compelled to station very many siege engines inside the wall. When the infantry battle was joined each day, through the efficacy of God, as a result of their superiority our men kept off the enemy at a distance. But he bound together his stone-throwers and covered them outside with hides; and in the section from the Polyandrion gate as far as the gate of St Romanos he prepared to station 12 lofty siege towers, which were advanced almost as far as the outworks, and he covered them with hides.

The Avars were soon joined by the Persians, but instead of providing the knock-out blow a blockade of the Bosphorus by the Byzantine fleet rendered them helpless spectators until the siege finished. The decisive moment occurred not on the walls but in the waters of the Golden Horn when a planned landing was intercepted. The victory was nonetheless ascribed to the protection of the Virgin Mary, one of whose principal churches lay at Blachernae, where the main fighting took place. On the night of 7–8 August the Avars burned their siege engines and the fires lit up the night sky. The walls of Constantinople had survived their first test.

THE SIEGE BY THE ARABS, 674–678

In the year 674 Constantinople faced a new threat from armies marching for the first time in the name of Islam. Reference has already been made to the crucial role played during this epic siege by Greek fire, but there were also assaults on the Theodosian walls. Unable to breach them, the Arabs pillaged up and down both sides of the Bosphorus and blockaded the city. But as winter approached they withdrew to an island 80 miles away. From this base they raided Constantinople for the next six years, but the city remained uncaptured. Among those killed in the attacks was Abu Ayyub (Eyüp), the standard bearer to the Prophet and the last surviving of his companions. His tomb is one of the holiest Muslim sites in Istanbul.

THE SIEGE BY THE ARABS, 717–718

More Muslim armies returned in 717, and the account of it mentions attacks on the walls:

> Maslama had drawn up the Muslims in a line (I had never seen a longer) with the many squadrons. Leo, the autocrat of Rum, [the emperor] sat on the tower of the

gate of Constantinople with its towers. He drew up the foot soldiers in a long line between the wall and the sea opposite the Muslim line. We showed arms in a thousand ships, light ships, big ships in which were stores of Egyptian clothing, etc., and galleys with the fighting men. Laith said 'I never saw a day more amazing for our advance by land and sea, the display of our arms, the display by the autocrat of Rum on the wall of Constantinople and their array of this armament. They set up mangonels and onagers. The Muslims advanced by land and sea, the Rum showed the same [tactics] and fled disgracefully.' Urnar and some of those from the ships were afraid to advance against the harbour mouth, fearing for their lives. When the Rum saw this, galleys and light ships came out from the harbour mouth against us and one of them went to the nearest Muslim ship, threw on it grapnels with chains and towed it with its crew into Constantinople. We lost heart.

The Blachernae section of walls, showing the wall of Leo and Gate of Blachernae. This was the main view of Constantinople that was seen by the crusaders in 1204, who encamped on a hill opposite. (Stephen Turnbull)

THE SIEGE BY KRUM THE BULGAR, 813

In the year 811 Emperor Nikephoros I was killed in battle against the Bulgars under their ruthless leader Krum. Krum added insult to injury by making a drinking cup out of the emperor's skull. Two years later Krum appeared outside

ABOVE
*The point where the
Theodosian walls give way
to the Komnenian walls
near the Palace of the
Porphyrogenitus. The change
in style is quite striking.
Several centuries separate
the two constructions.
(Stephen Turnbull)*

OPPOSITE
*The view looking along the
very damaged section of wall
north of the Golden Gate
towards the Belgrade Gate.
(Stephen Turnbull)*

the Golden Gate, where he intimidated the garrison by performing human sacrifices in their sight. There was no serious attack on the walls at this time, because Emperor Leo V suggested negotiation. The two leaders were to meet beyond the walls at the northern end in front of the walls of Heraclius. Both parties were to come unarmed, but Leo had placed three bowmen in ambush. Something warned Krum that all was not well and he escaped. His wounds were superficial, but he returned to Bulgaria swearing vengeance. He was unable to carry out his threats as he died soon afterwards.

THE SIEGE BY THE RUS', 860

According to the patriarch Photius, an eyewitness to the events, the Rus' attack of 860 was swift and absolutely unexpected 'as a swarm of wasps'. The Rus' had picked their moment well, because the emperor and his army were fighting the Arabs in Asia Minor, and the fleet was absent fighting the Arabs and Normans in the Aegean and Mediterranean. This exceptional double advantage by both land and sea suggests that the Rus' may have been informed of the situation, especially the absence of the fleet. The land defence of the capital was also weakened, because the imperial army that was fighting against the Arabs consisted not only of the troops stationed in Asia Minor but also of those regiments that were usually stationed in the neighbourhood of the capital and could therefore most easily rally to its defence. The coasts of the Black Sea, the Bosphorus and the Sea of Marmara, including its islands, were almost defenceless and helplessly exposed to Rus'

attacks. In the event deliverance from the Rus' threat was once more attributed to the intercession of the Virgin Mary. Having hurried back to the capital, the emperor took the relic of the robe of the Virgin Mary from the church at Blachernae. It was paraded round the walls and then symbolically dipped into the sea. Immediately after this was done a strong wind arose and the ships of the 'godless Russians' were wrecked.

ATTACKS AND SIEGES DURING THE FIRST CRUSADE, 1097

The frustrated soldiers of the First Crusade who had to pass by the great, and to them mysterious, city on their way to the Holy Land made an assault on the walls of Constantinople. While negotiations with the crafty Alexios I Komnenos were proceeding, the envoys of the crusaders were on one occasion detained so long by the emperor as to arouse suspicions of treachery on his part. A band of crusaders rushed from the camp, and in their attempt to enter the city and rescue their comrades set fire to the Gate of Blachernae. The incident is recounted in the *Alexiad* of Anna Komnena:

> A false rumour reached the others that the Counts had been thrown into prison by the Emperor. Immediately numerous regiments moved on Byzantium, and to begin with they demolished the palace near the so-called Silver Lake. They also made an attack on the walls of Byzantium, not with siege-engines indeed, as they had none, but trusting to their numbers they actually had the impudence to try to set fire to the gate below the palace which is close to the chapel built long ago by one of the Emperors to the memory of Nicolas, the greatest saint in the hierarchy.

ATTACKS AND SIEGES DURING THE FOURTH CRUSADE, 1204

Tragedy struck the walls of Constantinople when more crusaders returned a century later. The notorious Fourth Crusade of 1204 was the only occasion prior to the fall of the city to the Ottomans in 1453 that the walls were breached. The Fourth Crusade had originally been designed to conquer Egypt, but after the failure of the Third Crusade there was little interest in Europe for another crusade against Islam. The Fourth Crusade, summoned by Pope Innocent III in 1198, was the last of the major crusades to be directed by the papacy. The later crusades were directed by individual monarchs, and even the Fourth quickly fell out of papal control.

By 1201 the crusader army had gathered at Venice. The Venetians had agreed a fixed fee for transporting the army by sea, but far fewer crusaders had turned up than was expected. Venice would not let the crusaders leave without being paid the full amount agreed to originally. So the Doge Dandolo made a deal and had the crusaders attack Zara, a former Venetian possession in Dalmatia. By chance, a request then came for the crusaders to aid Alexios Angelos, the son of the recently deposed Byzantine emperor Isaac II, to claim his throne. So the army turned towards Constantinople.

The crusaders were still reluctant to attack fellow Christians, but the clergy convinced them that the Orthodox Byzantines were the next best thing to the Muslims. Unfortunately for them, Alexios Angelos had overstated his importance and it was quickly discovered when the crusaders arrived at the walls of Constantinople that the citizens preferred a usurper to an emperor supported by the hated 'Latins'. The crusaders and Venetians decided to place Alexios on the throne by force, and an unsuccessful amphibious assault was launched on the city in 1203. Twenty warships, the pathetic remains of the Byzantine navy, were sunk and the weight of the crusaders' navy broke the massive chain across the Golden Horn. Siege positions were taken up on the hill overlooking the Blachernae quarter. Assault was made with catapults and scaling ladders from ships in the Golden Horn:

Most authorities identify Egri Kapi with the ancient Gate of the Kaligaria. The Turkish name Egri Kapi, the Crooked Gate, arises from the fact that the narrow lane that leaves the city here must detour round a tomb that stands almost directly in front of the portal. (Stephen Turnbull)

The interior of the Yedikule fortress, showing how it was integrated into the existing Theodosian walls in 1457 by Mehmet the Conqueror. (Stephen Turnbull)

the Doge of Venice had not omitted to do his part, but had drawn up all his ships in battle formation in a line extending some three crossbow shots in length. Next the Venetians began to draw near to that part of the shore lying under the walls and towers. Then you could see their mangonels hurling stones from the decks of warships and transports, bolts from their crossbows flying across the water, archers loosing shower after shower of arrows, and the Greeks on their side fiercely defending the city from the top of its battlements, as the scaling ladders on the ships came so near that in many places swords and lances clashed one against the other. The din was so tremendous that it seemed as if both land and sea were crumbling in pieces. The galleys, however, did not dare come to shore.

The crusaders attacked the city the following year, again initially by sea on 8 April:

Thereupon, the enemy's largest ships, carrying the scaling ladders that had been readied and as many of the siege engines as had been prepared, moved out from the shore, and, like the tilting beam of a scale's balance, they sailed over to the walls to take up positions at sufficient intervals from one another. They occupied the region extending in a line from the Monastery of Evergetes to the palace in Blachernae, which had been set on fire, the buildings within razed to the ground, thus stripping it of every pleasant spectacle.

The crusaders were eventually able to knock holes in the walls small enough for a few knights at a time to crawl through; the Venetians were also successful at scaling the walls from the sea, though there was extremely bloody fighting with the Varangians.

THE SIEGE OF 1453

The bombardment of the Theodosian walls of Constantinople by Mehmet the Conqueror. The Byzantine emperor had concentrated his troops between the inner and outer walls.

It was the low-lying mesoteichion section of the walls across the Lycus Valley that was finally breached by the Turks.
(Peter Dennis © Osprey Publishing Ltd)

One of the most extraordinary features of the 1453 siege concerned Mehmet the Conqueror's successful effort to overcome the chain across the Golden Horn. He dragged his ships overland and launched them into the waters of the Golden Horn beyond the chain. (Stephen Turnbull)

Two men on one of the scaling ladders nearest the Petria Gate, which was raised with great difficulty opposite the emperor, trusting themselves to fortune, were the first from among their comrades to leap down onto the tower facing them. When they drove off in alarm the Roman auxiliaries on watch, they waved their hands from above as a sign of joy and courage to embolden their countrymen. While they were jumping onto the tower, a knight by the name of Peter entered through the gate situated there. He was deemed most capable of driving in rout all the battalions, for he was nearly nine fathoms tall [54ft] and wore on his head a helmet fashioned in the shape of a towered city.

The crusaders captured the Blachernae area and used it as a base to attack the rest of the city, but while attempting to defend themselves with a wall of fire, they ended up burning down even more of the city than they had the first time. Eventually, the crusaders were victorious, and inflicted a horrible and savage sacking on Constantinople for three days, during which many ancient works of art were stolen or destroyed.

When they reached the Golden Gate of the Land walls, they pulled down the new built wall there, ran forth, and dispersed, deservedly taking the road to perdition and utter destruction. The enemy, now that there was no one to raise a hand against them, ran everywhere and drew the sword against every age and sex. Each did not join with the next man to form a coherent battle array, but all poured out and scattered, since everyone was terrified of them.

THE WALLS BEYOND 1453

Many ruined sections of the walls today are as they were left after the Ottoman guns had done their damage. The major addition made to the walls of Constantinople by the Ottomans was the creation of the Yedikule fortress at its southern end. The Yedikule fortress is a curious structure, part Byzantine and part Ottoman. The seven towers that give it its name consist of four in the Theodosian walls itself, plus three additional towers built inside the walls by Mehmet the Conqueror in 1457. Yedikule in fact represents the only attempt by the Ottoman conquerors of Constantinople to enhance the fortifications of the city. The three inner towers are connected and joined to the Theodosian walls by four heavy curtain walls to form a five-sided enclosure.

Many buildings suffered during the final siege. The close proximity to the walls caused the Palace of the Porphyrogenitus to be badly damaged in the last siege, but after the conquest it was repaired and used for a variety of purposes. During the 16th and 17th centuries it served as an imperial menagerie, particularly for larger and tamer animals such as elephants and giraffes. The latter particularly amazed European travellers to the city. Before the end of the century the animals were moved elsewhere and the palace served for a while as a brothel. But it was soon redeemed from this misuse, for in 1719 the famous Tekfur Saray pottery was set up here. This pottery produced a new kind of Turkish tiles, the so-called Tekfur Saray type, inferior to those of Iznik and beginning to show European influence. The project, however, was short-lived, and by the second half of the 18th century the palace was in full decline and eventually lost its roof and floors. During the first half of the 19th century Tekfur Saray served as a poorhouse for Jews and in the present century it housed a bottle works before being abandoned altogether. Today it is a mere shell.

THE INFLUENCE OF CONSTANTINOPLE ON MEDIEVAL MILITARY ARCHITECTURE

Many were the rulers of western Europe who passed beneath the walls of Constantinople as they made their way towards a crusade in the Holy Land. The sight was no doubt most impressive, and made its mark upon the military architecture that these monarchs commissioned on their return. King Edward I of England is the most quoted example, and it is no coincidence that the walls and towers of 13th-century Caernarfon Castle bear a strong superficial resemblance to the monumental 5th-century wall of the Byzantine emperor Theodosius II. Edward I commanded an army on the Seventh Crusade and would without doubt have been impressed by the high curtain interspersed with polygonal, round and square towers and its banded masonry. Caernarfon Castle was intended by Edward to be symbolic of his conquest and new government of Wales, and he constructed his new hourglass-plan castle, with high curtain walls, polygonal flanking towers and great twin-towered gatehouses. Edward's symbol had to be novel, vast and majestic and derived in some way from imperial Rome, hence its Roman/Byzantine appearance. Even the masonry was made to look like the walls of Constantinople by using limestone from the Penmon quarries in Anglesey, whose tiers of courses were interleaved every so often with darker brown sandstone courses from quarries in Menai. But in reality the whole project must have been a great disappointment to him. Begun in 1283, it was never finished.

REPAIRS AND RESTORATION

The walls of Constantinople were kept in constant repair throughout the Middle Ages. During the 20th century restoration took the place of repairs in

Caernarfon Castle, built by Edward I of England in humble imitation of Constantinople. (Stephen Turnbull)

This staircase in the inner wall is being rebuilt and shows very clearly the use of brick and stone. It is also a welcome indication that the most recent rebuilding work is being carried out in an appropriate and sensitive manner. (Stephen Turnbull)

a programme that was much criticized at the time. The restorations were financed in part by UNESCO, but the exigencies of the municipal authority caused the project to be rushed. The work was divided among 11 contractors, with a 'scientific consultant' assigned to each, when one could be located. In most areas the walls were over-restored and refaced rather than being repaired. Perhaps they now give a clearer idea of how the elaborate defensive system once worked, but all sorts of historical evidence may have been destroyed in the process. There does not appear to be any coordination between teams, or a plan for the publication of the results. With the change of government in 1994 the work was abruptly halted.

The programme's inadequacies, however, only became really apparent on 17 August 1999, when an earthquake of a magnitude of 7.4 on the Richter scale caused some damage to the walls. Several towers were damaged, five of them seriously. There was less effect on the southern part of the walls, although one octagonal tower lost its southern half. Several rectangular towers were damaged near the Belgrade Gate, and part of the wall fell by the Topkapi Gate. Two towers that had been restored in the 1970s and a segment of wall near the Edirne Gate also suffered. One interesting observation that was made after the earthquake was that, in many areas, the cosmetic additions of recent restorations simply fell away from the historic fabric, almost as if the walls were showing contempt for the shoddy work that had been done on them! Professor Zeynep Ahunbay, chair of Historic Preservation at Istanbul Technical University, is quoted as saying:

> The restoration campaign of the 1980s has been criticized due to its resort to the reconstruction of ruined towers and gates instead of stabilizing and consolidating the dangerous structures. The behaviour of 20th-century repairs during the recent earthquake ... constitutes a good lesson for future restorations.

Part III Constantinople 1453

THE ORIGINS OF THE CAMPAIGN

The fall of Constantinople to the Ottoman Turks in 1453 is sometimes regarded as the end of the Roman Empire, or as the absorption of a redundant relic by a new and expansionist superstate. In reality, the siege and conquest of Constantinople was neither; nor was it such a one-sided affair as it might seem. The real importance of 1453 lies not in the disappearance of something ancient, but in the birth of something new: the Ottoman Empire in its fully developed form, an empire which would endure until 1922.

To the Ottomans the Balkans were Rum-eli, Rumelia, 'the land of the Romans'. They looked upon it as the Spanish Conquistadores regarded America: as a land where the conquerors had a free hand, where the local people were ripe for conversion, and where conqueror society was dominated by the masculine virtues of courage and fortitude. By the mid-15th century, however, the Ottoman élite was divided between those who clung to the old heroic ideal of autonomous *ghazi*, (religiously inspired) frontier warfare, and those in favour of a new military and administrative centralization. Whereas the feudal élite generally opposed centralization, the *kapi kulu*, or 'slaves of the gate', favoured a concentration of power around the sultan. Although the *kapi kulu* were theoretically slaves, many were free-born, and proudly claimed the title of *Kul*. This might best be described as 'sultan's man', and Sultan Mehmet II, the conqueror of Constantinople, had advisers from both traditions.

The conquest of the Byzantine capital had been a dream of Islamic armies ever since their first assaults in the 8th century. Alongside such Islamic motivation, the Turks focused their own dream of the *Kizil-Elma*, or 'Red Apple' to which destiny led the Turks, upon Constantinople. Sultan Mehmet II and his immediate predecessors had adopted the title of Sultan-i Rum, 'ruler of the Romans' and thus claimed to be the heirs of Byzantium and Rome. In fact Ottoman Turks were often called Rumiyun by Muslims further east.

PREVIOUS PAGE
The Turkish army camp before Constantinople in 1453. This illustration from the book Avis directif pour faire la passage d'Outre-mers dates from 1455, from the workshop of Jean Mielot. Bibliothèque Nationale, Paris. (akg-images)

The last Byzantines also called themselves 'Romans', but their emperors held very little territory. The remaining lands, however, could serve as naval bases for the Ottomans' powerful maritime rivals in Italy, while the only major European power facing the Ottomans on land was Hungary. In 1444 the Ottoman Empire had almost been cut in two by a combined naval and land crusade. Even the Byzantine Despot of Morea in southern Greece, the future Emperor Constantine XI, had struck northwards into Ottoman and vassal lands. For Mehmet II, who became sultan aged 12 in July 1444 when his father, Murad II, abdicated, the events of that year were a personal humiliation. The Grand Vizier, Çandarli Halil, persuaded Murad to return, defeated the Hungarians at Varna and forced the Byzantines back. Two years later Murad formally reassumed the title of sultan while young Mehmet was sent to govern a small Anatolian province. Mehmet II

The old city of Istanbul as seen across the Golden Horn from shipyards on the northern side where the floating boom would have been attached. The area on the other side now occupied by the Yenicami (New Mosque) would have been the Venetian quarter of Constantinople. (David Nicolle)

may have smarted from his temporary deposition, but he also noted that his father's army crossed the Bosphorus under the protection of guns which held back the Christian galleys. It was a lesson well learned, for on this same spot Mehmet subsequently built the great fortress of Rumeli Hisar.

To the Ottomans, the Byzantine emperor was merely the *Tekfur*, an Armenian term for king, while his great city of Constantinople was a pale shadow of its former self. In fact, the emperor was a vassal of the Ottoman sultan, as were his subordinates, the despots of Morea. The sultan's capital was Edirne, in Thrace, some 100 miles (160km) west of Constantinople. Far to the east, the Byzantine Empire of Trebizond (Trabzon) was a separate state ruled by a rival dynasty, while to the north the little Byzantine principality of Mangoup in the Crimea was little more than an offshoot of the Genoese colonies on the Crimean coast. Venice and Genoa dominated the seas and controlled most of the islands as well as several coastal enclaves around the Aegean and Black seas. The Black Sea was the crossroads of major trade routes linking Europe and Central Asia, Russia and the Middle East. At the centre was the Crimean peninsula, whose coasts were largely controlled by the Genoese. Venice and Genoa had also fought over the strategic north Aegean island of Tenedos (now Bozcaada) at the entrance to the Dardanelles.

The crusader principality of Athens was ruled by a family of mixed Italian-Catalan origin who had links with the Aragonese rulers of southern Italy. But all that remained of the once powerful Byzantine Despotate of Epiros were three coastal castles and the Ionian islands ruled by an Italian, Leonardo III Tocco.

The Muradiye Mosque in Edirne was built for Sultan Mehmet II's father in 1435. The Rumelian (European) provincial forces mustered alongside the sultan's own palace regiments at Edirne. (David Nicolle)

THE OTTOMAN EMPIRE AND ITS NEIGHBOURS, 1451–52

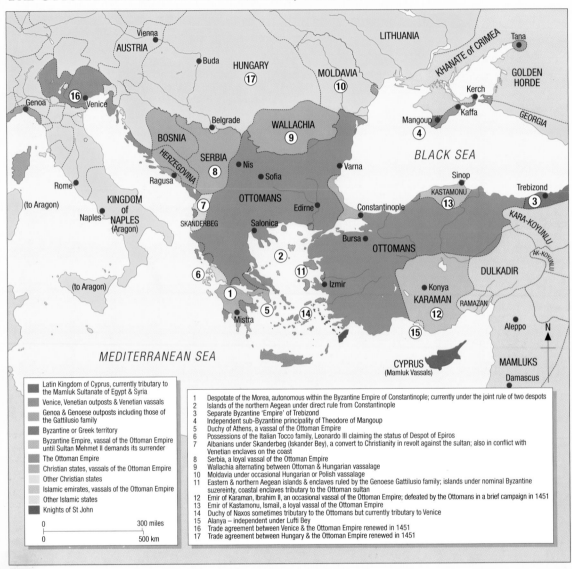

Legend:

- Latin Kingdom of Cyprus, currently tributary to the Mamluk Sultanate of Egypt & Syria
- Venice, Venetian outposts & Venetian vassals
- Genoa & Genoese outposts including those of the Gattilusio family
- Byzantine or Greek territory
- Byzantine Empire, vassal of the Ottoman Empire until Sultan Mehmet II demands its surrender
- The Ottoman Empire
- Christian states, vassals of the Ottoman Empire
- Other Christian states
- Islamic emirates, vassals of the Ottoman Empire
- Other Islamic states
- Knights of St John

0 — 300 miles
0 — 500 km

1 Despotate of the Morea, autonomous within the Byzantine Empire of Constantinople; currently under the joint rule of two despots
2 Islands of the northern Aegean under direct rule from Constantinople
3 Separate Byzantine 'Empire' of Trebizond
4 Independent sub-Byzantine principality of Theodore of Mangoup
5 Duchy of Athens, a vassal of the Ottoman Empire
6 Possessions of the Italian Tocco family, Leonardo III claiming the status of Despot of Epiros
7 Albanians under Skanderbeg (Iskander Bey), a convert to Christianity in revolt against the sultan; also in conflict with Venetian enclaves on the coast
8 Serbia, a loyal vassal of the Ottoman Empire
9 Wallachia alternating between Ottoman & Hungarian vassalage
10 Moldavia under occasional Hungarian or Polish vassalage
11 Eastern & northern Aegean islands & enclaves ruled by the Genoese Gattilusio family; islands under nominal Byzantine suzerainty, coastal enclaves tributary to the Ottoman sultan
12 Emir of Karaman, Ibrahim II, an occasional vassal of the Ottoman Empire; defeated by the Ottomans in a brief campaign in 1451
13 Emir of Kastamonu, Ismail, a loyal vassal of the Ottoman Empire
14 Duchy of Naxos sometimes tributary to the Ottomans but currently tributary to Venice
15 Alanya – independent under Lufti Bey
16 Trade agreement between Venice & the Ottoman Empire renewed in 1451
17 Trade agreement between Hungary & the Ottoman Empire renewed in 1451

To the north, some Albanian clans recognized the leadership of George Kastriotes, better known as Skanderbeg, but he spent as much effort quarrelling with the Venetians as resisting the Ottomans.

To the east, Ottoman domination of what is now Turkey was far from complete. In northern Anatolia the Candar Oghullari of Sinop were loyal vassals of the Ottoman sultan, but to the south the Karamanids only accepted Ottoman overlordship unwillingly. Beyond the Black Sea, part of the immense Mongol Golden Horde had broken away when Hajji Girei created what became the vigorous Khanate of Krim (Crimea). The Catholic kingdom of Poland-Lithuania had also taken control of vast regions of Orthodox Christian Russia, including part of the Black Sea coast. Russia had little real interest in the affairs of Orthodox Constantinople and recently the Metropolitan of Moscow had declared the Church of Russia to be autonomous, effectively turning its back upon Byzantium.

While most Christian countries were concerned with their own affairs, Mehmet II's determination to conquer Constantinople became clear as soon as he returned to the throne in 1451. Though not yet strong enough to remove the cautious old Grand Vizier Çandarli Halil, the young sultan promoted his own closest advisers Zaganos Pasha and Shihab al-Din Pasha as the Second and Third Viziers respectively. He also showed a streak of ruthlessness by having his younger brother Küçük Ahmet killed, thus removing a potential focus of discontent. This still left another claimant to the Ottoman throne, Prince Orhan, who lived in Constantinople like a political refugee.

These carved figures are above the door of a late medieval house in what was Venetian-ruled Dalmatia. Carved between 1441 and 1473, they represent the fully armoured infantrymen or marines who defended Italian colonial outposts around the Balkans. (Photo David Nicolle, No.18, Ulica Juja Barakovica, Sibenik)

The Byzantine emperor and the ruler of Karaman both regarded Sultan Mehmet II as an inexperienced youth. But Mehmet and his warlike advisers had already decided that a great victory was needed to secure their position. The conquest of Constantinople would also stop any Crusade from using the city as a base and would prevent Constantinople being handed over to a dangerous western European rival. Mehmet II summed up the situation simply and succinctly:

The *ghaza* [Holy War] is our basic duty as it was in the case of our fathers. Constantinople, situated in the middle of our domains, protects our enemies and incites them against us. The conquest of this city is, therefore, essential to the future and the safety of the Ottoman state.

Shortly after Mehmet II came to the throne for the second time, Ibrahim Bey of Karaman invaded the disputed Hamid-ili region, but it took only a brief campaign to teach Ibrahim that the young sultan was not to be trifled with. The

The old centre of Istanbul is now so built up that few pictures can suggest its open and almost agricultural state in the mid-15th century. This view from near the Aya Sofia Mosque towards what was the Prosphorianus Harbour does, however, hint at the verdant character of medieval Constantinople. (Frederick Nicolle)

A depiction of the Resurrection on a Transylvanian painted altarback dating from 1480–90. The soldiers reflect Balkan troops such as those who fought both for and against the Ottomans during the siege of Constantinople. (Photo David Nicolle, Lutheran Church, Medias)

Byzantine emperor Constantine XI also thought Mehmet ineffective and tried to extract concessions by threatening to let Prince Orhan stir up an Ottoman civil war. Instead, Mehmet married Ibrahim Bey's daughter and returned home more determined to crush Constantinople. Even Çandarli Halil's impatience boiled over:

> You stupid Greeks … I have known your cunning ways long enough. The late Sultan (Murad) was a tolerant and conscientious friend of yours. The present Sultan Mehmet is not of the same mind. If Constantinople eludes his bold and impetuous grasp it will only be because God continues to overlook your devious and wicked schemes.

On his way back to Edirne, the sultan's passage across the Dardanelles was blocked by Christian ships so he crossed via the Bosphorus, and it was this journey

OPPOSITE

The frontispiece of the fine 15th-century Ottoman manuscript Sulayman-Name. At the top sits Prophet Sulayman, known as King Solomon to Christians. Around and below him are attendants, soldiers, and even monsters. Sulayman wears the costume of an Ottoman sultan. The fourth row down from the top depicts the Prophet-King's army. Two officers carry maces, one flanged, the other a transitional Turkish animal-headed style. T. 406, f.1b. (© The Trustees of the Chester Beatty Library, Dublin)

that apparently prompted Mehmet to built a massive fortress on the European shore. Once back in Edirne, the sultan took control of the Janissary infantry away from Çandarli Halil and placed his own *devsirme*, 'slave recruited', officers in command of other infantry units. Çandarli Halil even feared for his life since many in court referred to him as a friend of the infidels, but Mehmet could not afford to oust the powerful old politician. Sultan Mehmet and his closest advisers also walked around Edirne at night dressed as common soldiers and listened to talk in the taverns to assess the popularity of his proposed attack upon Constantinople.

Meanwhile, Emperor Constantine sent out urgent pleas for assistance. On 14 February 1452 the Venetian Senate answered with excuses and a promise to send military supplies. Many Venetian senators already regarded Byzantium as a lost cause and favoured improving relations with the Ottomans. Aware of such mixed feelings, Çandarli Halil blunted Constantine's appeals for aid by renewing various agreements with Venice, Hungary and the vassal states of Serbia and Wallachia.

Orders had already been despatched in 1451 to collect materials and craftsmen for the building of Rumeli Hisar, while in Constantinople people cried: 'These are the days of the Anti-Christ. This is the end of the city.' The emperor Constantine complained that the sultan had not asked permission to build his castle within Byzantine territory, but Mehmet merely replied that the area was uninhabited and that Constantine owned nothing outside the walls of Constantinople.

In order to build Rumeli Hisar, Mehmet II needed a fleet powerful enough to stop outside interference. The sudden appearance of an Ottoman fleet of six war galleys, 18 smaller galliots and 16 supply ships from Gallipoli took the Christians by surprise. Work began in April 1452 where the Bosphorus was at its narrowest, about 88m across; 500 workmen completed the great triangular fortress by 31 August 1452. The work was not without incident, however. There were brawls between Ottoman soldiers and local Byzantine peasants, mostly over grain supplies as the emperor Constantine wanted all available food to be stockpiled inside Constantinople. Some eunuchs who worked in the sultan's harem strayed too close to Constantinople and were arrested, but begged to be released because their heads would be forfeit if they failed to turn up for duty on time.

The Turks called Rumeli Hisar 'Bogaz kesen', the Greeks, 'Laimokopia'; both phrases meant 'cutter of the Straits' or 'of the throat'. It was immediately garrisoned by 400 men under Firuz Bey, whose duty it was to impose a toll on all passing ships. Those which refused would be fired upon and if possible sunk by cannon along the shore. The biggest gun reportedly fired a ball weighting 600lb (272kg) and surviving cannonballs at Rumeli Hisar certainly weigh 450lb (204kg).

Sultan Mehmet now returned to Edirne and the Ottoman fleet under Baltaoglu Sulayman Bey left a week later. During the autumn of 1452 troops from the Rumelian provinces set up camp next to the élite palace regiments around Edirne.

Armourers were hard at work throughout the state, while the sultan studied the latest military ideas from east and west. One of his advisers appears to have been a famous Italian scholar, traveller and collector of ancient antiquities, Ciriaco de Pizzicolli, better known as 'Ciriaco of Ancona'. Among other experts attracted to Mehmet II's court was a Hungarian gunfounder named Urban, who had left Byzantine employment because the emperor could not or would not supply him with the necessary funds and materials. When asked if he could make cannon to break the walls of Constantinople, Urban replied yes, although he admitted that as a gunmaker rather than artilleryman he was not qualified to work out ranges for the cannon at Rumeli Hisar. Mehmet II offered whatever Urban needed and said that ranges could be sorted out later.

It took two months to make the guns for Rumeli Hisar, but on 10 November they opened fire on a pair of Venetian ships returning from the Black Sea. The Italian crews had a fright but reached Constantinople safely. The Ottoman gunners adjusted their ranges and on 25 November sunk a Venetian ship commanded by Antonio Erizzo. When Sultan Mehmet heard the news he ordered Urban to make a cannon twice the size of the first and capable of shooting a ball weighing over 1,000lb (450kg). This was eventually tested outside the sultan's new palace and duly shot a massive stone cannonball over a mile.

In the face of these overt preparations, Emperor Constantine brought food supplies, wine and even winnowing fans into Constantinople, along with people from outlying villages. During the winter of 1452–53 he also sent ships to the Aegean to purchase food and military equipment. One particularly large ship was trapped by contrary winds at Chios and could not sail homeward until after the siege began. Throughout the winter the defences of Constantinople were improved and silver was taken from churches and monasteries to pay the troops.

Many in the city maintained that only God and the Virgin could now save Constantinople, and that it was folly for the emperor to flirt with the schismatic Catholic western Europeans. Little more than warm words had been supplied by the West so far. The separate Byzantine Empire of Trebizond was preoccupied with its own problems, while in Morea the co-despots Demetrios and Thomas faced a substantial raid by Ottoman troops in October 1452. During this operation, Byzantine troops under Matthew Asanes captured a senior Ottoman leader, Ahmad Bey, but this could not alter the fact that no help for Constantinople would come from this area. The remaining Latin enclaves in Greece were too weak to do anything, and it was the same in the Balkans, where the Despot George of Serbia would support his Ottoman overlord. According to the Byzantine chronicler George Sphrantzes, the great Hungarian military leader Janos Hunyadi had demanded Mesembria or Selymbria in return for helping Constantinople. Sphrantzes also claimed that the Aegean island of Lemnos was given to King

Alfonso V of Aragon to use as a naval base from which to help Constantinople. Nothing came from either of these remarkable proposals. Turkish rulers in Anatolia were either friendly towards the Ottomans or were frightened of them.

Following the sinking of their ship in the Bosphorus, the Venetians were concerned how to protect their merchant convoys to the Black Sea. Gabriele Trevisan, the Vice-Captain of the Gulf, was sent back to Constantinople, where his ships and crews were to help defend the city if necessary. The Senate also decided to arm two transports, each carrying 400 soldiers and accompanied by 15 galleys to sail for Constantinople on 8 April. The Venetian authorities in Crete would similarly send two warships to Negroponte to be placed under the command of Zaccaria Grioni, recently arrived from the Byzantine capital. The command structure was then changed and the fleet for Constantinople was put under Giacomo Loredan, the Captain-General of the Sea, who was already on his way east and was now ordered to wait at Modon for the galleys commanded by Alvise Longo. Further delays followed, and Longo was told to take his fleet to Constantinople and place himself under the Venetian *baillie* (local consul), Minotto, until Loredan arrived. In the event Alvise Longo set sail from Venice on 19 April with only one warship, while the main Venetian fleet, which eventually assembled in the Aegean, was too late to help Constantinople. It is important to remember that it took at least a month for a message to travel between Constantinople and Venice via Negroponte and Corfu.

Meanwhile, the Venetians in Constantinople had to decide what to do. Girolomo Minotto, the baillie, persuaded Trevisan to remain under his command. Other Venetian merchants, captains, crews and soldiers were in the city, including

The Dardanelles, looking from Çanakkale to the Gallipoli Peninsula. In the mid-15th century both banks were firmly under Ottoman control but the waterway itself, unlike the Bosphorus to the north, was too wide to be closed by the guns available to Sultan Mehmet II. (David Nicolle)

The Rumeli Hisar fortress was built for Sultan Mehmet II in 1452 on the European shore of the Bosphorus. With its big cannon it could close the straits to ships sailing between the Black Sea and Constantinople. (Topfoto)

Giacomo Coco, who captained one of the ships which had run the gauntlet past Rumeli Hisar. In December Minotto summoned a meeting of his council with the Emperor Constantine present, and the leading Venetians voted to stay. No ship would be allowed to leave without the baillie's permission, but on 26 February 1453 six ships defied Minotto's orders and fled, carrying 700 people.

In Rome the Pope saw Constantinople's predicament as an opportunity to persuade the Greek Orthodox Church to accept union with the Roman Catholic Church. So Cardinal Isidore was sent to the Byzantine capital in a Venetian galley, arriving in November 1452. He brought some archers and hand-gunners from Naples and enlisted more troops at Chios, where he was joined by Archbishop Leonard. In Constantinople Cardinal Isidore's 200 soldiers were regarded as the advance guard of a great army which would save the city. On 12 December a Unionate service was held in the ancient church of Hagia Sophia and the leaders of the Orthodox Church agreed to a Decree of Union. Unfortunately, most of the

ordinary Orthodox clergy and large numbers of the common people disagreed, and there was widespread rioting led by a monk named Gennadius. He subsequently become the first Orthodox Patriarch appointed by Sultan Mehmet.

In November 1452 Venice's great rival, Genoa, decided to send help and in January 1453 Giovanni Giustiniani Longo arrived in the Golden Horn with 700 troops. The Byzantine chronicler Doukas described them as 'two huge ships which were carrying a large supply of excellent military equipment and well-armed youthful Genoese soldiers full of martial passion'. Longo's reputation was such that Constantine put him in charge of all land forces with the rank of *protostrator* (marshal) and gave him the island of Lemnos as a reward for his services.

During the 15th century a remarkable series of tombs was carved in Bosnia, perhaps reflecting the influence of the country's Bogomil (Manichaean) minority. Two panels on this tomb illustrate the light cavalry and infantry archers who formed a major part of Balkan armies. (Photo David Nicolle, Historical Museum, Sarajevo)

OPPOSING COMMANDERS

OTTOMAN LEADERS

Sultan Mehmet II was the fourth son of Murad II, and was born at Edirne on 30 March 1432. His mother was Murad's first wife, a Turkish woman possibly named Huma Hatun. At the age of 11 Mehmet was sent with his two *lalas* or advisers to govern the province of Amasya. As a young man he had full pink cheeks, a firm red mouth, a blond moustache and a hooked nose. Around 1450 he married Sitt Khatun, daughter of the Dulkadir ruler and a traditional ally of the Ottomans in eastern Anatolia.

Mehmet also had a strong interest in ancient Greek and medieval Byzantine civilization. His heroes were Achilles and Alexander the Great and he could discuss the Christian religion with some authority. As sultan, Mehmet II became a leading patron of Ottoman literature and built many *madrasa*, schools. In addition to his nickname of Fathi, 'the Conqueror', he was also known as Abu'l-Khayrat or 'Father of Good Works', providing pensions for no less than 30 Ottoman poets as well as others abroad. He was a poet himself, writing under the pseudonym of Avni and showing a romantic streak in such *gazals* (verses) as:

> I asked her, why across your cheeks,
> So disordered roam your tresses?
> It is Rum-eli, she replied,
> Why high starred heroes gallop.

The senior figures who supported Mehmet II during the Constantinople campaign included men of very differing characters and backgrounds. Çandarli Halil came from a Turkish family, probably based in Iznik, which provided five Grand Viziers to several early Ottoman rulers. The close but ultimately fatal links between the Çandarlis and the Byzantine court began under Çandarli Halil's father, Ibrahim, himself the son of Ali Pasha Çandarli, who served Bayezid I so well. Çandarli Ibrahim Pasha was also the first to follow the cautious military policy which characterized the reign of Murad II. Ibrahim's eldest son, Çandarli Halil, became Grand Vizier in 1443, continuing his father's cautious line and serving both Murad II and Mehmet II until his execution after the fall of Constantinople.

Though he came from a legal and religious background, Çandarli Halil enjoyed the support of the Janissary corps and probably deserved most of the credit for defeating the Hungarians at the close-run battle of Varna in 1444. Although many in the Byzantine governing élite regarded Çandarli Halil as a friend, stories of his collaboration with the Byzantines during the Constantinople campaign were probably spread by the rival war-faction led by Zaganos Pasha. In fact Çandarli Halil fell from favour immediately after Constantinople fell and was executed soon afterwards. One of his sons, Ibrahim Pasha, became *qadi* or judge of Edirne in 1453 and remained in office despite his father's disgrace, being appointed *Qadi'askar* or chief judge of the army in 1465 and subsequently a *lala* or tutor-adviser to Prince Bayezid. When Prince Bayezid became sultan, Çandarli Ibrahim Pasha steady rose in rank to become Grand Vizier in 1498. Unfortunately there seems to be no information about Çandarli Halil's grave, though his father and grandfather are buried in a fine tomb at Iznik; Çandarli Ibrahim is also buried in that town. Sadly, these fine Ottoman monuments were damaged by Greek invaders in 1921.

Zaganos Pasha was a very different man, in both background and character. He is believed to have been of 'Illyrian' or Albanian origin, recruited into the Ottoman military establishment through the devsirme as a young slave or prisoner-of-war. A committed convert to Islam, Zaganos was above all a soldier who believed that the Ottoman state must continually expand to keep its enemies off balance. He was absolutely loyal to Mehmet, both as prince and later as sultan, knowing that his own prospects depended upon his patron's success. Zaganos accompanied the young Sultan Mehmet into effective exile in 1446 and when Mehmet II returned to the throne, Zaganos Pasha was rewarded with the rank of Second Vizier, and eventually replaced Çandarli Halil as Grand Vizier. In 1456, however, Zaganos Pasha was made the scapegoat following an unsuccessful expedition against Hungarian-held Belgrade. His daughter was expelled from the sultan's harem and both were banished to Balikesir, where Zaganos probably owned property. In 1459 Zaganos Pasha returned to become *Kapudan Pasha* or admiral of the fast-expanding Ottoman navy, then governor of Thessaly and Macedonia the following year. A mosque in the town of Balikesir was endowed by Zaganos Pasha around 1454 and now contains his tomb as well as those of other members of his family.

As leader of the relatively new Ottoman navy, Baltaoglu Suleyman Bey ranked lower than many other commanders and little is known about him. He was the son of a Bulgarian *boyar* or aristocrat, and was almost certainly recruited into the Ottoman kapi kulu as a prisoner-of-war. Baltaoglu first caught Mehmet II's attention in 1444 when the young sultan made him part of an embassy to the Hungarian capital. Five years later, as an officer in the Ottoman fleet, Baltaoglu led a successful attack on the Genoese-ruled island of Lesbos. Baltaoglu may also have been governor of Gallipoli. According to the Byzantine chronicler Doukas:

A portrait of Mehmet II from 1585. (akg-images)

When he was enslaved by Mehmet's father he renounced the religion of his fathers. He had come to Lesbos four years earlier [than the siege of Constantinople] and taken many captives. He was not a good friend of those brigands the Janissaries because he often seized their spoils.

By the siege of Constantinople Baltaoglu was Kapudan Pasha, Commander of the Fleet; the first man to hold this rank. Baltaoglu Suleyman Bey was undoubtedly stripped of his rank following his fleet's failure to stop Christian supply ships breaking through to Constantinople and he then seems to have disappeared from history. One source, however, mentions Baltaoglu commanding a Janissary unit during the final Ottoman assault. Perhaps Sultan Mehmet offered him the chance to redeem his reputation at the head of a forlorn hope. A village just north of Rumeli Hisar on the Bosphorus is called Balta Limani, or Balta's Harbour. Perhaps Baltaoglu retired there after the siege, though it is more likely that the name reflects the fact that the Ottoman fleet moored there whilst protecting the construction of Rumeli Hisar.

CHRISTIAN LEADERS

The command structure in Constantinople was less clear cut than on the Ottoman side though Emperor Constantine XI Palaiologos was, of course, in overall authority. He was born into the ruling imperial family in Constantinople on 8 February 1405, the fourth son of Emperor Manuel II and his wife Helena Dragas. As a younger son he was sent to Morea in southern Greece in 1428, to share the role of Despot with his brothers Theodore II and Thomas Palaiologos. As Despot the brave, energetic, but generally cautious Constantine strengthened local defences and even briefly reconquered Patras, Athens and Thebes.

Following the death of his childless elder brother, John VIII, Despot Constantine became Emperor Constantine XI on 12 March 1449, but was less effective as emperor than he had been as Despot. Flexible in religious matters and willing to accept Church Union, Constantine badly misjudged the domestic opposition within Byzantium and the unity of purpose within the Ottoman camp. Nevertheless, Constantine Palaiologos became a heroic figure in Greek legend, and following the fall of Constantinople many Greeks believed that their last emperor was not dead but had been turned to marble, ready to be awakened by an angel to drive out Turks. In its modernized version, as the *Megali Idea* ('Great Idea'), this legend would lead Greece to catastrophe in Turkey in the 1920s.

Like the emperor himself, Loukas Notaras was born in Constantinople. He was the son of a wealthy courtier who served as an interpreter for the Emperor Manuel and had been part of an embassy to France in 1398. Loukas' brother was also a courtier but had been killed during an earlier Ottoman attack upon Constantinople. As an important landowner in Morea, Loukas had friends and contacts among the wealthy Italian merchants. So in addition to becoming a leading member of the emperor's government and a commander of troops, he was involved in trade and entrusted his own money to Italian bankers. Furthermore, Loukas Notaras became a citizen of both Venice and Genoa and married into the ruling Palaiologos family.

With such wealth and connections, Loukas Notaras served three Byzantine emperors and shared the role of *Mesazon* or Chief Minister. From 1449 to the fall of Constantinople he was also *Megas Doux*, titular commander of the once mighty Byzantine navy. Pragmatic and flexible, but firmly opposed to a union of the Orthodox and Latin churches, Loukas Notaras had rivals, and one of them seems to have been the Byzantine politician Sphrantzes. He wrote that even Emperor Constantine XI once said: 'Notaras publicly and secretly maintains that no other affairs matter except his own and leaves no stone unturned, as the saying goes.' A eulogy written in 1470 sought to clear Loukas Notaras of the charges of treason against Constantinople in its final hours, and there is no evidence that this experienced and realistic political and military leader was in any real sense a traitor.

Wall painting of Manuel Hadzikis above his tomb, 15th century. This nobleman wears typical Byzantine costume, including a tall hat with an upturned brim. (David Nicolle, Pantanassa Church, Mistra)

*Statue of Constantine XI.
(C. Hellier/The Ancient Art
and Architecture Collection)*

THE GATHERING OF FORCES, 1452

The Ottoman Empire
Byzantine or Greek territory
Christian states, vassals of the Ottoman Empire
Other Christian states
Islamic emirates, vassals of the Ottoman Empire
Other Islamic states
Knights of St John (Hospitallers)
Latin (Crusader) Kingdom of Cyprus, currently tributary to the Mamluk Sultanate of Egypt & Syria
Venice, Venetian outposts & Venetian vassals
Genoa & Genoese outposts including those of the Gattilusio family

→ Ottoman movements
→ Christian movements

0   200 miles
0   300 km

1 Ishak Pasha remains in Anatolian provinces as *beylerbeyi*, to suppress revolts & to keep a watch on Karaman
2 Ibrahim Bey, emir of Karaman, remains quiet following his defeat by Sultan Mehmet II in 1451
3 Sultan Mehmet II may have examined the defences of Constantinople on his way to Gallipoli or while sailing past to the site of Rumeli Hisar (26 March 1452)
4 Sultan Mehmet II goes from Edirne to Gallipoli (early March 1452)
5 Sultan Mehmet II accompanies the Ottoman fleet from Gallipoli to anchor at Balta Limani
6 Construction of the new fortress of Rumeli Hisar on the nominally Byzantine shore of the Bosphorus (12 April to 31 August 1452)
7 Sultan Mehmet II looks at Constantinople (28 August 1452)
8 Sultan Mehmet II demands the surrender of Constantinople & returns to Edirne (1 September 1452)
9 Ottoman fleet returns to Gallipoli (6 September 1452)
10 Venetian Senate alerts outposts & warships in the Aegean to Mehmet II to discover his intentions (summer 1452) and sends an embassy to the construction of Rumeli Hisar
11 Emperor Constantine XI gathers grain & people from outlying towns and villages into Constantinople; many of these are probably abandoned (autumn 1452)
12 Mehmet II orders the construction of giant guns in Edirne, supervised by Urban & begins to assemble troops from the Balkan & Anatolian provinces; Mehmet also in Didimotihon, perhaps to decide the fate of the Venetian crew captured when their ship was sunk on 25 November (autumn 1452)
13 Ottoman troops in Macedonia & Thessaly raid the Byzantine Despotate of the Morea, storming the Isthmus of Corinth, ravaging Arcadia & Tripolitza, overrunning Venetian Navarino

& unsuccessfully attack Byzantine Siderokastron (October 1452)
14 Ottoman column from Siderokastron to Leondarion is ambushed by Byzantine forces; Ahmad Bey the son of *Uç Beyi* Turahan of Macedonia is captured & sent to Mistra
15 Cardinal Isidore sails to Constantinople with 200 troops from Naples, also accompanied by Archbishop Leonardo of Chios (October 1452)
16 Two Venetian ships from the Black Sea sail past Rumeli Hisar under fire & reach Constantinople safely (10 November 1452); a third Venetian ship is sunk by gunfire (25 November 1452)
17 Venetian trading galley from Trebizond sails past Rumeli Hisar under fire & reaches Constantinople safely (December 1452); Venetian council in Constantinople agrees that no Venetian ship should leave harbour without permission
18 Joint religious service in Hagia Sophia Cathedral & an agreement to the Union of the Latin & Orthodox Churches leads to rioting in the city (12 December 1452)
19 Byzantine requests for help from Russia are rebuffed
20 Quarrelling princes Peter III & Alexander II of Moldavia unable to help Byzantium
21 Skanderbeg of Albania unable to help Byzantium
22 Regent Janos Hunyadi of Hungary reportedly obtains Mesembria or Selymbria in return for promising to help Constantinople
23 Lemnos reportedly given to the King of Aragon in return for promising to help Constantinople
24 The Voyvode of Wallachia refuses to turn against the Ottoman sultan without direct Hungarian support
25 Tenedos is demilitarized but used as a naval harbour by the Venetians

---

Apart from the tragic Emperor Constantine himself, the greatest Christian hero of the siege is probably Giovanni Giustiniani Longo. Unfortunately very little is known about him before he arrived in Constantinople. The noble Giustiniani family was found in Genoa, Venice and many other parts of Italy but its most famous members are those of Genoa, where the Giustinianis provided soldiers, clerics, writers and political leaders from the 14th century onwards.

The statue of Orlando, made by Bonino of Milan in 1413, was a symbol of the strength and independence of the merchant republic of Dubrovnik. It is also a fine illustration of the Italian-style armour worn by the military élite of the eastern Balkans. (© 2006 TopFoto/ Longhurst)

The superb carvings on the Triumphal Arch of Alfonso V of Aragon in Naples, made between 1455 and 1458 by Francesco Laurana, illustrate the sort of arms and armour that would have been used by many of the defenders of Constantinople, Italians and Byzantine. (akg-images/ Tristan Lafranchis)

Giovanni Giustiniani Longo was himself a professional soldier who had earlier served as *podesta* or military commander in the vital Genoese colony of Kaffa. By the time he arrived in Constantinople in January 1453 at the head of 700 troops he was considered an expert in siege warfare. Consequently, he was put in command of the city's land defences. Mortally wounded in the final Ottoman assault, Giovanni died on his way home. The Giustiniani family continued to play a prominent role in Italian affairs into the 19th and 20th centuries.

Cardinal Isidore was born at Monemvasia in southern Greece around 1385, was educated in Constantinople, became a monk in Morea, then returned to Constantinople in 1417 as *begoumenos* or abbot of the important St Demetrios Monastery. Isidore was also a noted humanist, a friend and follower of the famous Neoplatonist scholar Georgios Gemisthos Plethon. None of this seemed to prepare him for his warlike role in defence of Constantinople, but perhaps Isidore's open-mindedness enabled him to accept that the only real hope for Byzantium's survival lay in western Europe.

In 1434 Isidore was sent by the emperor as an Orthodox Church representative to the Council of Basle. Isidore was next sent to Russia as Metropolitan or supreme figure in the Russian Church, subsequently leading a Russian delegation to the next church council in Ferrara and Florence. Here Isidore signed the Decree of Union, but this was a step too far for the Russians, and in 1441 Isidore, by now a cardinal in the Roman Church, was imprisoned by the Russian Grand Duke Basil II. He soon escaped back to Italy and spent the rest of his life working for a union of the Latin and Orthodox churches.

This little-known wall painting in the last large church to be built in Mistra, capital of the Byzantine Despotate of Morea, shows an infantry archer with a recurved eastern-style composite bow, and a quiver on his hip. On his head however, the artist has given him a somewhat confused visored bascinet. (Photo David Nicolle, Pantanassa Church, Mistra)

It was during one of these efforts that Cardinal Isidore found himself caught up in the final siege of Constantinople, where he had been sent as a Papal Legate at the head of a small military contingent. When the city fell this remarkable churchman escaped once again, to be made Latin Patriarch of Constantinople by Pope Pius II. It was, however, a meaningless title and the unfortunate Cardinal Isidore is said to have suffered senile dementia in his final years, dying in Rome in 1463.

OPPOSING FORCES

OTTOMAN ARMIES

By the mid-15th century the majority of the Ottoman professional soldiers consisted of contractual *sipahi* cavalry or kapi kulu troops of slave or prisoner-of-war origin. The former were greater in number and in some parts of mid-15th-century Rumelia at least half of the *timariots*, or fief-holding sipahis, were still local Christians. The kapi kulu, especially those of the sultan's own household or palace regiments, were fewer and formed an élite which was expensive both to recruit and to train. The famous Janissary infantry were simply one part of the kapi kulu palace regiments.

The bulk of Ottoman infantry were not Janissaries but the azaps who had replaced the earlier *piyade* and *yaya* levy of Turkish foot soldiers. The azaps were irregular light infantry, mostly archers with minimal training, enlisted from the Muslim peasantry and summoned for a single campaign. The majority of irregular cavalry now seem to have been *akinci* frontier light horsemen, who were similarly summoned rather than being volunteers.

At the time of Sultan Mehmet II the largely Christian *voynuq* auxiliaries from Rumelia included Slavs and Romanian-speaking Vlachs. An élite heavily armoured

A late 15th-century cannon made of wrought iron staves surround by wrought iron hoops, Mamluk or Ottoman. (Photo David Nicolle, Askeri Müze, Istanbul)

Helmets of the type worn by the soldiers during the siege of Constantinople. Left, 15th-century bascinet found in Halkis. It has a rigid neckguard, a hinged part of which is missing. Centre, 15th-century bascinet helmet also found in Halkis. It has a rigid neckguard and an unusually small visor. Right, 15th-century Italian salet with a hinged nasal. (Photos David Nicolle, Historical Museum, Athens)

Christian cavalryman was sometimes called a *lagator* and was often accompanied by a more lightly armoured *gebelü*, or squire. Ottoman forces also included Turcoman Muslim auxiliaries from Anatolia, but they do not seem to have played a significant role during the siege of Constantinople.

Even though the majority of Janissaries at the siege of Constantinople were probably recruited as prisoners-of-war, it was kapi kulu recruited through the devsirme system who were now coming to dominate the Ottoman army. They had been forcibly, though not always reluctantly, enlisted as boys or youths from the Christian peasant population of the Balkans, most being Slav and Albanian since Greeks tended to live on islands or in cities which were exempt from devsirme conscription. Not all such conscripts entered the Janissary corps as the best were creamed off for government service or the kapi kulu cavalry. Most of the palace cavalry regiments except for the *gureba* (see below) were increasingly recruited through the devsirme. Under Sultan Mehmet II the ranks of timariot provincial cavalry were also gradually filled with kapi kulu men.

This small bronze cannon was almost certainly made in Venice then sold to the Ottoman sultan's eastern neighbour and rival, the emir of Karaman in the 15th century. (David Nicolle, Historical Museum, Karaman)

The organization and command structure of the Ottoman army was the same in peace as in war. The hierarchy of command was unambiguous and military units were permanent formations, provincial contingents under the *Beylerbeyis* of Rumelia and Anatolia being as fully under the sultan's command as his own palace regiments. As a result the Ottoman army was probably the best disciplined and trained force of its day. The classic Ottoman military structure probably existed by the time of the siege of Constantinople with the Rumelian and Anatolian provincial forces consisting of three elements: the *toprakli süvarisi* fief-holding cavalry, the *serbadkulu süvarisi* frontier cavalry and the *yerlikulu piyâdesi* local infantry. The *Beylerbeyis* of Rumelia or Anatolia were in command of local *sancak beyis*, each of whom commanded up to 50 *subasis* in an *ocak*, or regiment. The auxiliary and largely Christian voynuqs were commanded by *Çeri-basi* officers under the overall command of the *Voynuq Beyi*.

The structure of the sultan's own palace or household regiments was similar, consisting of six regiments of prestigious *Kapikulu Süvarisi* cavalry, plus the *Kapikulu Piyadesi* infantry, who included the Janissaries, the *Bostancis*, the *Segmen* 'dog handlers' and *Doganci* 'falconers' from the Sultan's militarized hunting establishment, various small guard units, youngsters under training, artillery, armourers and support formations. The size of the Ottoman army was, in fact, consistently exaggerated by its foes. In reality each *sancak* (province) supported around 400 cavalry, while the Janissary corps grew from around 5,000 to 8,000 men under Mehmet II, but only after the fall of Constantinople.

Ottoman tactics were sophisticated, but during the siege of Constantinople it was their skill with artillery which brought them success, as well as an ability to combine

their efforts on land and sea. Some tactics and capabilities were, of course, applicable in both open battle and siege warfare. The supposed Serbian Janissary Konstantin Mihailovic made it clear that the initial phases of an Ottoman attack were primarily psychological, making great use of noise and military music. A particular rank of lower officers, the *çavuses*, also had an important role to play as they reported directly to the sultan, not only on the behaviour of the men but also of their officers.

Ottoman cavalry traditions and tactics had virtually nothing in common with the Turks' nomadic Central Asian past. Armoured cavalry made little use of bows and were quite as skilled fighting on foot (as they did in the siege of Constantinople) as on horseback. Less is known about infantry training in the 15th-century Ottoman army, but it clearly emphasized archery in the disciplined Byzantine and Arab manner, rather than the earlier skirmishing and harassment tradition of Turks. Other evidence shows that Ottoman foot soldiers were skilled in the construction and use of siege works and, most notable of all, they were far better able to cope with reverses than were their Christian opponents.

Firearms had been spreading across the Balkans and into Ottoman territory since the 1370s. While it might be an exaggeration to say that artillery conquered Constantinople, the Ottoman army was now the most advanced in the Islamic world when it came to the use of firearms. The *Topcu* gunners corps and the *Top Arabaci* gun carriage drivers had both been created by Sultan Mehmet II's father, whereas the *Cebeci* armourers were established by Mehmet himself. All formed part of the kapi kulu palace army, and the sultan also recruited gunmakers and engineers from abroad. An illegal export of arms, including guns, continued from Italy to the Ottomans, and Anconan merchants were selling gun barrels in Constantinople a decade or so after the city fell to Sultan Mehmet. Ottoman gunfounders were not, however, able to make large

A bronze Ottoman cannon with the narrower powder chamber shown in many 15th-century pictures. (Photo David Nicolle, Askeri Müze, Istanbul)

15th-century Ottoman army. Left, an Ottoman-Balkan yaya, early 15th century. Many Ottoman infantrymen were of Christian origin and this seems to have been reflected in their equipment. This man wears an Italian-style reinforced jacket over eastern dress. In the centre is a Turkish sipahi, c.1400. Feudal cavalry were the backbone of medieval Ottoman armies. This man wears a 'turban' helmet and wields the mace favoured by many Muslim warriors. This Ottoman infantryman is one of the sultan's élite. He wears full infantry armour of mail-and-splints, probably designed for siege warfare. (Angus McBride © Osprey Publishing Ltd)

cast-iron cannon for many decades, their larger guns being either made of bronze or built up of iron hoops and staves. Though Ottoman cannon may have been old-fashioned, Ottoman artillerymen were at the forefront of their art and no other ruler, except Duke Philip of Burgundy, rivalled Sultan Mehmet II in promoting firearms. Mehmet's own knowledge of ballistics was ahead of his time and he was even credited with inventing a new form of long-range mortar during the siege of Constantinople.

Ottoman military engineers are said to have learned much from their Hungarian foes during the early 15th century, but in fact the heritage of Islamic siege engineering was longer and more sophisticated than that of Europe. Wooden siege towers and rams had been largely abandoned since the late 12th century as a result of the Muslims' highly developed incendiary weapons. Stone-throwing mangonels continued to be used, but these, and some briefly revived wooden siege towers, proved ineffective against the walls of Constantinople in 1453.

The Ottoman fleet was a separate arm by the mid-15th century and probably had its own dockyard and arsenal organization. With its main base at Gallipoli, its initial role was to ensure that Ottoman armies could cross between Anatolia and Rumelia without hindrance. Nevertheless, this Ottoman fleet was virtually destroyed by the Venetians outside Gallipoli in 1416. By 1442 the Ottomans reportedly had 60 ships with a squadron based at the Byzantine vassal island of Lemnos and six years later at least 65 vessels supported a demonstration against Constantinople. Despite this, the size of the fleet that appeared outside Constantinople in 1453 came as a shock to the Byzantines and Italians alike.

The Venetians constantly underestimated the skill and initiative of the Ottoman navy but the Ottomans had several highly developed nautical traditions to draw upon: those of Byzantium itself, the Turkish beyliks into which Byzantium fragmented in the 13th and 14th centuries, and the nautical practices of the Islamic Middle East. Since the Ottomans learned so much about land warfare from the Mamluks of Egypt and Syria, they probably also had access to the Mamluks' nautical knowledge. If so, then the Ottomans made considerably more successful use of it than did the Mamluks.

The men who manned the new Ottoman navy were clearly not all Muslims and not all Turks. There was still a substantial Greek population in Gallipoli, only part of which seems to have converted to Islam, while other non-Muslims in Gallipoli may have included Italians and Catalans, or at least the descendants of such settlers. Ottoman ships were essentially the same as those of other

Turban helmet dating from around 1500 with the St. Eirene armoury mark showing that it was once in the Ottoman Sultan's Topkapi Palace armoury in Istanbul. It is now in the Victoria & Albert Museum. (David Nicolle)

Mediterranean fleets, a very common fighting vessel being a fast, light and manoeuvrable galley with a boarding beak and stern rudder. The Ottoman *mavna* was a larger vessel like the Italian galeazza or Great Galley, but this may not have appeared in any numbers until later in the 15th century.

Sultan Mehmet II's plans for the conquest of Constantinople depended upon diplomatic as much as military considerations. Above all, he had to strike quickly before western European powers like Venice and Hungary could react. On the other hand, the sultan also intended to be patient, expending gunpowder and money rather than blood. Finally, he would use new technology including heavy artillery to breach the massive walls of Constantinople, and the newly powerful Ottoman fleet to deny the city food, military supplies and moral encouragement from the outside world. At the same time Sultan Mehmet II wanted to take Constantinople with as little damage as possible and with minimal loss of life to his future Greek subjects. His generally anti-Latin policy reflected the importance he attached to winning over the Orthodox Christian Church.

CHRISTIAN FORCES

The overall population of Constantinople, excluding Galata, was probably now between 40,000 and 50,000 people, with a regular garrison of a few hundred. A list of defenders made for the emperor by the government official Sphrantzes gave a total of 4,973 Greeks, both professional soldiers and militiamen, plus 200 resident foreigners. The number of foreigners is, however, clearly misleading as it only included permanent residents. Most estimates of the number of men who defended the walls in 1453 range from 6,000 to 8,500, most of whom were barely trained local militias. However, Archbishop Leonard of Chios, who took part in the siege, puts the number of active defenders at around 6,000 Greeks and 3,000 foreigners. Giacomo Tedaldi was also there and subsequently wrote a concise report for the Cardinal of Avignon in January 1454. It is perhaps the calmest and most objective account of all, reporting that: 'In the city there were altogether 30,000 to 35,000 men under arms and six to seven thousand real soldiers, making 42,000 at the most.'

By the 15th century the remnants of the Byzantine Empire were too poor to hire many mercenaries. Defence therefore fell to local troops, local militias and foreign volunteers including European soldiers and sailors who, for whatever reason, found themselves at the emperor's gate. The soldiers who accompanied Emperor John VIII to Italy in 1437 included two distinct types of cavalry: armoured *stradioti*, who would probably have rated as light cavalry in western Europe, and even more lightly equipped *gianitzaroi*. Powerful Byzantine noblemen also had their own military followings and Byzantine

soldiers who held land as *pronoia* fiefs were not militarized peasants but still formed a local élite. Many of them, particularly within the Despotate of Morea, which was the only substantial bloc of territory still in Byzantine hands, were of non-Greek origin including Slavs, Albanians and descendants of Latin Crusader or Italian colonial feudal élites.

In the 15th century Constantinople consisted of separated village-sized settlements within the vast ancient walls; there was a more substantial urban area at the easternmost end, parts of which were allocated to foreign merchants such as the Venetians. This probably provided a framework for a structured militia within each quarter or 'urban village' organized under a *demarchos* and supervised by imperial officials. Since Greek monasteries in rural areas employed armed guards, and monks did duty in their monastery's *vigla* observation towers, references to monks patrolling the ramparts of Constantinople should not come as much of a

The European shore of the Bosphorus near Tarabya. All vestiges of the late Byzantine outpost of Therapia seem to have disappeared. During the Byzantine era the area was largely neglected, only becoming fashionable after the Ottoman conquest. (David Nicolle)

These Ottoman artillerymen are putting a huge cannon into position under the supervision of Urban the Hungarian gun master in March 1453. Ottoman artillery at the siege of Constantinople was essentially the same as that seen elsewhere in Europe, and Urban's biggest cannon was probably built of wrought iron staves and hoops. In the 15th century large guns were placed in sloping trenches with massive wooden blocks as shock absorbers. Altering the aim of such weapons was slow and difficult. Ottoman 'giant' guns also formed part of batteries which include smaller cannon. Between these and the walls of Constantinople lay the Ottoman front line consisting of a trench with an earth embankment topped by a wooden palisade. (Christa Hook © Osprey Publishing Ltd)

surprise. Constantinople also had a substantial Turkish Muslim population by this time, though whether any of them chose to support the Ottoman pretender, Prince Orhan, in the final siege is unclear.

Otherwise the military organization of the remaining Byzantine forces is very unclear. The little army in Constantinople itself may still have been known as the *politicon* army, but whether it was still divided into *allagia* (regiments) is unknown. Infantry archers and crossbowmen certainly played a major role. In fact Byzantine crossbowmen were something of an élite, forming themselves into 'brotherhoods' rather like those seen in medieval Italy.

Written sources are clearer when it comes to descriptions of Byzantine troops. They wore western European-style armour, probably of western origin.

OPPOSITE
Venetian artist Vittore Carpaccio was influenced by later 15th-century Balkan costume, arms and armour. This painting, Saint Ursula, the Pope and the pilgrims arrive at the besieged Cologne, shows ships like those which traded with Constantinople, while the soldiers in the foreground are typical of Venetian colonial garrisons. (akg-images/Erich Lessing)

The defenders of Constantinople clearly had firearms, but they were considerably smaller than the Ottoman 'great guns'. Most came from Italy, Hungary or the Balkans along with a larger number of smaller handguns. In 1453 the Byzantines also used Greek fire under supervision of Johannes Grant.

Most of the remaining Byzantine coastal towns in Thrace were abandoned without a fight when the Ottomans advanced in 1453, though some put up a fierce resistance. The reasons for this are not known, but it may be significant that Therapia was on the Bosphorus, north of the Ottoman blockade at Rumeli Hisar, while Selymbria and Epibatos were behind the Ottoman siege lines on the Marmara coast. Perhaps they were intended to provide outlets to the outside world while Constantinople was besieged. The lack of a proper navy was, however, a fatal handicap for the defenders of Constantinople, the last real Byzantine fleet having been destroyed by the Genoese in the 14th century.

Western Europeans helped defend Constantinople, manning the walls and fighting as sailors or marines. In many cases these were one and the same people, though the great majority of them came from Italy. A population explosion in many Italian cities had led to an excess of young men, unemployed, unable to marry, available for adventure and often from the better-off families. In addition to the professional soldier Giovanni Giustiniani Longo, the Venetian baillie Girolomo Minotto and the captain of the Venetian trading fleet at Tana, Alvise Diedo, there were members from the Venetian Dolfin, Gritti, Loredano, Cornaro, Mocenigo, Trevisan and Venier families. Then there were the Genoese Girolomo and Leonardo di Langasco, Maurizio Cattaneo, the Bocchiardi brothers and others, while the Catalans were led by Père Julia. But the bulk of those who served under these men remain unnamed. In fact everyone aboard an Italian ship in eastern waters was expected to be armed, the only exceptions being clergy and pilgrims. The Italian ships that got caught up in the siege ranged from lumbering merchant vessels dependent upon sail alone, through merchant galleys using oars and sails, to lighter war-galleys.

The emperor Constantine XI and his advisers knew that the outcome of the siege of Constantinople would depend on the time factor. If the defenders could endure long enough, help would eventually come from outside, if not as a Hungarian invasion, then by sea from Italy. Constantine was absolutely correct, but unfortunately for the remnants of the Byzantine Empire, the Ottomans' cannon intensified the siege, and the Ottoman fleet brought the attack to bear on every side of Constantinople, even the Golden Horn.

More immediately, Giustiniani Longo believed that the outermost rampart of Constantinople's land-walls should be defended. This tactic had succeeded in 1422 and would, he thought, make the best use of the city's outnumbered defenders while the high inner walls were manned by archers, crossbowmen

All that remains of Galata's medieval fortifications is the Galata Tower, which originally formed a strongpoint at the uppermost part of the town. In later centuries it served as a watch tower for the Ottoman fire brigade. Today the Galata Tower still looks down over a thriving commercial centre which appropriately includes the glass-covered Turkish offices of the Italian Banca di Roma. (David Nicolle)

A highly decorated ceremonial sword found among other Venetian and Ottoman military equipment in the castle of Halkis. (Photo by David Nicolle, Historical Museum, Athens)

and gunners. In fact Constantinople's walls were still so strong that, even in the context of mid-15th century warfare, the Ottoman numerical advantage at first had little impact. Even though the Byzantines and Italians did not expect such aggressive action from the Ottoman fleet, there was little danger of the walls along the Marmara coast being breached, and with adequate ships in the Golden Horn the defenders felt confident of protecting the floating boom. Again they were correct – until the Ottomans seized the Golden Horn behind them. Clearly the idea that Constantinople was inevitably doomed is wrong, and the overall situation was not as one-sided as a simple glance at a map might suggest.

THE CAMPAIGN

CLOSING THE NOOSE

In January 1453 Sultan Mehmet II returned to Edirne, where large numbers of volunteers were mustering for the campaign. In addition to the Rumelian and palace contingents the troops were augmented by camp-followers including merchants to supply Ottoman troops with food and necessities. Early in 1453 a Serbian vassal contingent also arrived, reportedly consisting of 1,500 Christian cavalry and auxiliaries under the voyvode of Jaksa; Serbian miners arrived from Novo Brdo considerably later. According to the Italian Giacomo Tedaldi, Christians in the Ottoman ranks were allowed to worship as they wished.

Karaca, the Beylerbeyi of Rumelia, sent men to prepare the roads from Edirne to Constantinople so that the bridges could cope with massive cannon. Fifty carpenters and 200 assistants also strengthened the roads where necessary. There was no reported resistance and Karaca Bey's pioneers went on to cut down vines and orchards outside the walls of Constantinople to provide a clear field of fire for the Ottoman artillery. In February Karaca Bey's troops also began to take the remaining Byzantine towns along the Marmara and Black Sea coasts. Again, there was minimal resistance and consequently no removal of the Christian population. Only those places which defied the Ottomans were sacked. Silivri, Epibatos and Therapia opposed the invaders and were therefore bypassed, although some troops probably stayed to observe them. Bursa was the main assembly area for Anatolian units and three regiments crossed the Bosphorus to help the Rumelians watch Constantinople. During March larger numbers of azaps and sipahis crossed via Rumeli Hisar, followed by their commander, Ishak Pasha the Beylerbeyi of Anatolia.

Next, the Ottomans brought their massive guns to the walls of Constantinople, the biggest of the three 'giant' guns requiring 60 oxen to pull it. The artillery then assembled 5 miles (8km) from the walls, guarded by Karaca Bey's troops. Meanwhile, the Ottoman fleet under Baltaoglu had gathered outside Gallipoli. In March it sailed for Constantinople and established a base at Diplokionion Bay on the Bosphorus just north of Galata.

The Byzantines still had access to the sea and during the winter of 1452–53 their remaining galleys raided Turkish villages as far as the Cyzikos peninsula on the southern side of the Sea of Marmara. On 26 February Pietro Davanzo's ship

The medieval Byzantine sea-walls still stand along the shore of what is now called Sarayburnu. The biggest dome is that of the Aya Sofia Mosque, while the small dome to the right is that of the St Eirene Church. The Byzantine Old Palace ran from just left of Aya Sofia, through the trees towards the sea-walls on the far left. (David Nicolle)

slipped out, followed by six Cretan vessels with 700 people aboard. They reached Tenedos safely, but the arrival of the Ottoman fleet off Constantinople in March meant that future ships maintaining communication with the outside world had to slip out quietly at night.

Most of the Ottoman ships were newly built, but some were old and had needed repair; estimates of the size of Baltaoglu's fleet vary wildly. According to the Ottoman *Asiqpasazade* there were 400 of all sizes. Kritovoulos put the Ottoman fleet at 350 ships plus transports. A remarkably specific report by Jehan de Wavrin, probably taken from an official Burgundian document, states that there were 18 war galleys, 60 to 70 smaller galliots, and 16 to 20 small craft, while Giacomo Tedaldi specifies that these were 16 to 20 horse-transports. Another realistic report puts the total at six large galleys, ten ordinary galleys, 15 small galliots, 75 *fustae* (which were hardly more than large rowing boats), 20 horse-transports and numerous small boats.

The Byzantines were now confined within the walls of Constantinople, and the Greek courtier Sphrantzes described how the emperor sought to maximize the city's defences:

The Emperor ordered the tribunes to take a census of their communities and record the exact numbers of men, laity and clergy, able to defend the walls and what

THE OTTOMAN ADVANCE ON CONSTANTINOPLE, JANUARY–MARCH 1453

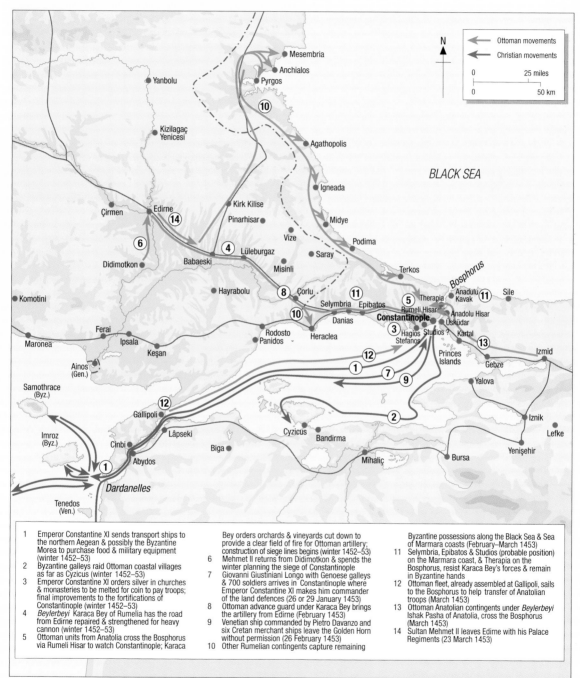

1. Emperor Constantine XI sends transport ships to the northern Aegean & possibly the Byzantine Morea to purchase food & military equipment (winter 1452–53)
2. Byzantine galleys raid Ottoman coastal villages as far as Cyzicus (winter 1452–53)
3. Emperor Constantine XI orders silver in churches & monasteries to be melted for coin to pay troops; final improvements to the fortifications of Constantinople (winter 1452–53)
4. *Beylerbeyi* Karaca Bey of Rumelia has the road from Edirne repaired & strengthened for heavy cannon (winter 1452–53)
5. Ottoman units from Anatolia cross the Bosphorus via Rumeli Hisar to watch Constantinople; Karaca

Bey orders orchards & vineyards cut down to provide a clear field of fire for Ottoman artillery; construction of siege lines begins (winter 1452–53)
6. Mehmet II returns from Didimotkon & spends the winter planning the siege of Constantinople
7. Giovanni Giustiniani Longo with Genoese galleys & 700 soldiers arrives in Constantinople where Emperor Constantine XI makes him commander of the land defences (26 or 29 January 1453)
8. Ottoman advance guard under Karaca Bey brings the artillery from Edirne (February 1453)
9. Venetian ship commanded by Pietro Davanzo and six Cretan merchant ships leave the Golden Horn without permission (26 February 1453)
10. Other Rumelian contingents capture remaining

Byzantine possessions along the Black Sea & Sea of Marmara coasts (February–March 1453)
11. Selymbria, Epibatos & Studios (probable position) on the Marmara coast, & Therapia on the Bosphorus, resist Karaca Bey's forces & remain in Byzantine hands
12. Ottoman fleet, already assembled at Gallipoli, sails to the Bosphorus to help transfer of Anatolian troops (March 1453)
13. Ottoman Anatolian contingents under *Beylerbeyi* Ishak Pasha of Anatolia, cross the Bosphorus (March 1453)
14. Sultan Mehmet II leaves Edirne with his Palace Regiments (23 March 1453)

San Liberale on the Pala di Santa Cristina by Lorenzo Lotto. Not only is the warrior-saint wearing typical late 15th-century armour, but the Virgin and Child are seated above a typical Ottoman Turkish carpet of the same period. (David Nicolle, Church of Santa Cristina, Quinto di Treviso)

weapons each man had for the defence. All tribunes completed this task and brought the lists of their communities to the Emperor. The Emperor said to me, 'The task is for you and no one else, as you are skilled in arithmetic, and also know how to guard and keep secrets.'

The result was, however, so low that Constantine told Sphrantzes to keep it quiet. Archbishop Leonard of Chios added that:

> The greater part of the Greeks were men of peace, using their shields and spears, their bows and swords, according to the light of nature rather than with any skill. The majority had helmets and body armour of metal or leather, and fought with swords and spears. Those who were skilled in the use of the bow or the crossbow were not enough to man all the ramparts.

Around 1,000 Byzantine troops were also kept back as a reserve within the city.

> The defenders' position appeared better in naval terms, and the assorted vessels in the Golden Horn expected to hold their own, including powerful Italian ships with experienced crews which had sought refuge in Constantinople on their way home from the Black Sea. Twenty-six could be rated as fighting ships: five from Genoa, five from Venice, three from Venetian Crete, one each from Ancona, Spain and France, and about ten Byzantines.

On 2 April 1453 the floating chain or boom was drawn across the Golden Horn, supervised by the Genoese engineer Bartolomeo Soligo. The Genoese authorities in Galata decided to remain neutral, but some men and ships slipped across the Golden Horn to help defend Constantinople. The Venetians who lived in the city had no choice but to fight under the command of the Venetian baillie, Girolomo Minotto. In fact Emperor Constantine XI asked Minotto's men to parade their banners along the wall to show the Ottomans they would soon be fighting Venetians. The keys of four vital gates were similarly entrusted to the Venetians, while defence of the emperor's own Blachernae Palace was entrusted to the baillie. Filippo Contarini commanded the wall between the Pege and Golden gates, Jacopo Contarini the Studion quarter, and Venetian and Genoese sailors under Gabriele Trevisan much of the walls along the Golden Horn. Alvise Diedo commanded ships in the Golden Horn, while those protecting the boom were under Zuan Venier. Giustiniani Longo commanded at many as 2,000 Greeks and Italians on the central section of the land-walls which was correctly seen as the most threatened sector.

A hurried attempt to excavate a fosse around the exposed Blachernae walls was left to men from the Venetian great galley from Tana, among others. But the bales of wool and leather sheets hung outside the walls to absorb the shock of cannonballs proved useless against Sultan Mehmet's modern artillery. Each tower between the Golden and Horaia gates was manned by an archer supported by a crossbowman or a hand-gunner, and Loukas Notaras placed some mobile cannon as a reserve in the Petrion quarter.

Sultan Mehmet and the main Ottoman force left Edirne on 23 March 1453 and assembled about 2 miles (4km) from Constantinople. A later source maintains that the main Ottoman encampment was on the other side of the Golden Horn, this perhaps being the site of the pioneers', labourers' and non-combatants' camp. The artillery was already in position close to the walls in 14 or 15 batteries spread along the land-walls. Three such batteries faced Blachernae and included one of Urban's giant guns, probably the second largest named Basiliske. Two batteries faced the Gate of Charisius, four the St Romanos Gate, three the Pege Gate, with two otherwise unaccounted batteries perhaps facing the Golden Gate. Additional batteries of smaller cannon were alongside or between those of the big guns since there are said to have been a total of 69 Ottoman cannon in 15 batteries: five of four small guns, nine of four small guns plus one large, and one of four large guns facing the St Romanos Gate. The largest gun fired a ball reportedly weighing about 1,212lb (550kg), the second largest over 793lb (360kg), the others from 507–198lb (230–90kg). They were supported by a dozen or so sturdy stone-throwing trebuchets which had almost certainly been erected by 11 April.

Back in Europe, in late March or early April, the Pope finally sent three large Genoese ships full of arms and provisions, but they were soon storm-bound at Chios. The Venetians reacted even more slowly and it was not until 11 May that Loredan set out for Constantinople. A few days later news that the siege was under way caused near panic and three more warships were ordered to join Loredan at Tenedos. During the siege of Constantinople János Hunyadi, the Captain-General of Hungary, reportedly proposed a seaborne campaign to outflank the Ottomans, but this came to nothing.

THE SIEGE BEGINS

On 2 April, the day the boom was drawn across the Golden Horn, Sultan Mehmet II's entourage established their tents on Maltepe Hill facing the St Romanos Gate. On the 6th the bulk of the Ottoman army moved forward from its assembly positions, paused for prayers about a mile (1.5km) from Constantinople, then moved up to the siege lines.

The Rumelians were now on the left, the sultan in the centre and the Anatolians the right. Part of the army was kept in reserve, perhaps including much of the palace regiments with the auxiliaries or volunteers. Zaganos Pasha and Karaca Bey also took a few thousand men to occupy the other side of the Golden Horn, while a small unit under Kasim Pasha was sent to watch Galata.

Archbishop Leonard stated that as the Ottoman army moved forward, its troops carried 'pieces of lattice-work made out of branches and slips of trees to protect his soldiers'. He also maintained that they could have been attacked at this point, before they occupied their siege fortifications. The fortifications were

Four terracotta hand grenades, such as those which would have been used by the Byzantines against the Turks during the defence of Constantinople in 1453. Heeresgeschichtliches Museum, Vienna. (akg-images/ Erich Lessing)

over 2 miles (4km) long, stretching from the Marmara coast to the Golden Horn, and consisting of a trench fronted by an earth rampart, with a wooden palisade with posterns and wooden turrets. The two sides were now so close that the Turks mocked the Greeks' long beards, threatening to make them into dog-leashes.

The size of the Ottoman army facing Constantinople has been wildly exaggerated and can have included at most 80,000 fighting soldiers. The majority were cavalry, although they now fought on foot. Again Giacomo Tedaldi may be closest to the truth. 'At the siege,' he wrote, 'were altogether 200,000 men of whom perhaps 60,000 were soldiers (the rest being labourers or non-combatants), 30 to 40,000 of them cavalry.'

On the morning of 6 April Emperor Constantine XI joined Giustiniani Longo at the St Romanos Gate. The Ottoman artillery bombardment also began that day and was continued on the 7th, bringing down part of a wall near the Gate of Charisius. On the second day Urban's big gun facing Blachernae started to overheat. This was temporarily solved by sponging the interior with oil after every shot, but on 11 April the gun either cracked or started to leak. A more widespread problem for the Ottoman artillerymen, however, was the slippage of their guns in the April mud.

217

An isolated tower and the ruined defences of Vize, a small town to the west of Istanbul. Its fortifications would have been typical of those Thracian towns remaining in Byzantine hands at the start of the 15th century. (David Nicolle)

The first Ottoman assault was probably launched on 7 April against the centre of the land-walls. Ill-equipped irregulars and volunteers advanced with great enthusiasm, supported by archers and handgunners, but were met by the defenders at the outermost rampart and were driven back with relative ease. The damaged sections of wall were also repaired the following night. Meanwhile, Byzantine guns commanded by the Bocchiardi brothers were notably effective, until the largest cannon burst. Thereafter the Byzantine cannon were largely limited to the anti-personnel role, each gun shooting from five to ten walnut-sized bullets.

During the first days of the siege the defenders made several sorties but Giustiniani decided they were losing more than they gained and so withdrew his men from the outer rampart to the first main wall. There was now a short pause during which Sultan Mehmet ordered several artillery batteries to be repositioned. On 11 or 12 April the Ottomans reopened their artillery bombardment, after which it remained almost continuous, despite problems with the elevation and aiming of the Ottoman guns. A Hungarian ambassador arrived in the Ottoman camp as an observer around this time, and according to Doukas, advised the Ottoman gunners on how best to lay their guns. Previously they had fired at one point, but the ambassador taught them to fire three shots to form a triangle followed by a shot from one of the 'giant' guns which would bring down the weakened structure. Giacomo Tedaldi reported that the sultan's cannon fired between 100 and 150 times a day, consuming 1,100lb (500kg) of powder. The size of the cannonballs appalled those on the receiving end, and the ammunition was

The Garamszenthenedeki Altar was painted by Koloszvári Tamas in 1427. The Crucifixion scene includes a clear representation of Hungarian arms and armour of the mid-15th century. Although it was similar to the military equipment of Germany, it tended to be more old-fashioned, and the same was true of Serbian and Wallachian equipment. (Kereszteny Museum, Esztergom)

The soldier to the right of the Resurrection scene from the Garamszentbenedeki Altar holds a small Lithuanian pavise-style shield, a characteristically eastern European piece of equipment. (Kereszteny Museum, Esztergom)

sufficiently valuable for Ottoman troops to risk using nets to drag them from the fosse to be used again.

Mehmet sent troops with lighter artillery to take the outlying Byzantine forts at Therapia and Studios. The Ottoman fleet's first attack upon the floating boom across the mouth of the Golden Horn was, however, a failure and Baltaoglu decided to await the arrival of additional ships from the Black Sea. On the 12th the Ottoman fleet was again driven off because the taller ships of the smaller Christian fleet tried to encircle some Ottoman vessels.

On the night of 17–18 April the Ottomans launched a surprise night attack on the mesoteichion sector of the land-walls, but after a four-hour battle the defenders drove them back. It was probably on the following day, perhaps to maintain Ottoman morale, that the fleet was sent to seize the Princes Islands. Two days later the Ottoman fleet suffered a serious reverse when three large Genoese-Papal transports carrying weapons, troops and food suddenly appeared off Constantinople accompanied by a large Byzantine ship carrying wheat from Sicily. They had sailed through the Dardanelles unreported and the furious sultan ordered Baltaoglu to capture them or not return alive. The Christians' sails apparently looked like islands rising from the sea of smaller Ottoman ships, which closed around them using oars

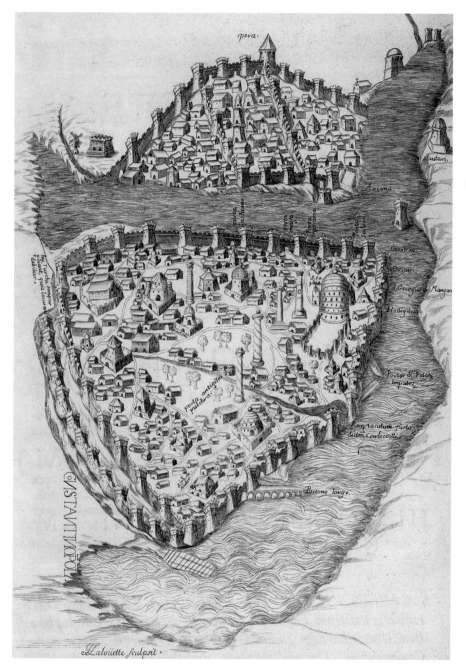

This is a 17th-century engraving of one of the earliest maps of Byzantine Constantinople, which appeared in the Liber Insularium by Cristofori Buondelmonti in 1422. Though schematic, it is remarkably accurate. The Golden Horn is at the top, the doubled land walls with a moat on the left. (akg-images/The British Library)

alone because of a contrary wind. But their oars became entangled and the height of the Christian sailing ships gave their defenders a huge advantage. Baltaoglu's men could only try to board or burn the ships, and they failed on both counts. During the afternoon, however, the wind dropped and the battle drifted towards the shore, where the excited young sultan urged his horse into the sea as he shouted unhelpful, non-nautical orders to Baltaoglu. The latter pretended not to hear and drew back his smaller ships while the larger vessels with guns attacked the Christians. But their elevation was too low to hit the men on deck and their bore too small to seriously damage the hulls, so Baltaoglu reverted to boarding. The Ottoman admiral was wounded in the eye while Sultan Mehmet became ever angrier. Finally, as the sun set, the wind suddenly returned, the Christian ships pushed the smaller Ottoman craft aside and ran for the boom while three Venetian ships sailed out to cover the opening of the boom. Dusk was falling and, unable to reassemble his ships, Baltaoglu ordered them back to Diplokionion.

This highly visible defeat clearly had a serious impact on Ottoman morale while that of the defenders was raised. Turkish sources also refer to competing factions appearing within the Ottoman camp. So next day Baltaoglu was brought before the sultan and publicly threatened with execution. It is unlikely that Mehmet intended to kill such a brave and skilful commander and the testimony of fellow officers as to Baltaoglu's courage may have been prearranged. Nevertheless, heads had to roll and Baltaoglu was stripped of his rank, flogged, and replaced as

The Arrest of Jesus on a wall painting made in 1483. Since Constantinople had now fallen, this should be called post-Byzantine style. Nevertheless, the style, costume, arms and armour reflect the last armies that fought for Byzantium. (Old Katholikon of the Great Meteoreon, Meteora)

commander of the fleet by Hamza Bey. Mehmet now summoned his commanders to Diplokionion to discuss the situation. Çandarli Halil advocated an offer to lift the siege in return for political rights over Constantinople and an annual tribute of 70,000 gold pieces. Zaganos Pasha, the other viziers and the sultan's spiritual adviser Shaykh Aq Shams al-Din, argued to continue the siege, with which the sultan agreed.

THE OTTOMANS TAKE THE GOLDEN HORN

The sultan had most of the cannon taken off the Ottoman ships and mounted ashore to bombard the Italians and Byzantines defending the boom. But most were shielded by the suburb of Galata. This was when Mehmet was credited with devising a new form of long-range mortar. An ordinary cannon was mounted at a very high angle and, according to Mehmet II's Greek biographer Kritovoulos, the sultan told them to 'get the measure by mathematical calculations' in an early example of the new science of ballistics.

Work was also started, or more probably speeded up, on the construction of a wooden slipway from the Bosphorus, across the hills behind Galata down to the Golden Horn. Since the Ottoman fleet had failed to force the boom, their smaller warships would be taken overland. Sultan Mehmet is generally assumed to have been copying what the Venetians had done some years earlier when they portaged a few galleys from the River Adige to the northern end of Lake Garda, but Muslim commanders had done something similar long before. Saladin transported warships in sections from the Nile to the Red Sea in the 12th century, and the Mamluks had taken disassembled galleys from Cairo to Suez as recently as 1424.

The lowest point behind Galata was almost 230ft (70m) above sea level and the route taken by the Ottoman slipway was from present-day Tophane, up a steep valley to what is now Taksim Square, then down a valley to the Valley of the Springs, now called Kasimpasa. The slipway consisted of a planked wooden roadway in a shallow trench, greased like a ship-launching ramp. By 22 April it was complete and under cover of an artillery bombardment the ships were hauled across the hills on rollers then launched into the Golden Horn with their sails ready and skeleton crews aboard. Eventually, 72 of the Ottoman fleet's smaller craft, including 30 galleys, were lowered carefully down to the Valley of the Springs, thus leaving only the largest Ottoman ships in the Bosphorus. The defenders had lost control of the Golden Horn, and men had to be withdrawn from other sectors to defend the threatened walls facing the inlet; the investment of Constantinople was complete.

Presumably believing that the Ottoman fleet in the Bosphorus was now seriously weakened, the defenders attacked it with fire-ships. Two hours before dawn on 28 April a raiding party set out under the command of Giacomo Coco.

The Ottomans launch galleys into the Golden Horn on 22 April 1453. People in Constantinople were horrified to see a long line of Ottoman warships sliding down a long wooden slipway from the hill behind Galata. They had been hauled from the Bosphorus by teams of men and bullocks to a spot known as the Valley of the Springs, apparently ready for immediate action. As a result the defenders lost control of the Golden Horn and the Ottoman galleys were able to threaten the northern walls of Constantinople. (Christa Hook © Osprey Publishing Ltd)

His fleet consisted of two large transports packed with sacks of cotton and wool, accompanied by the galleys of Gabriele Trevisan and Zaccaria Grioni and three smaller ships. Coco then supposedly spoiled the plan by sailing impatiently ahead. The Ottoman ships opened fire and sank Coco's vessel with all hands. Trevisan's galley was also hit but limped back to the Golden Horn. A violent naval battle lasted an hour and a half, with the Ottomans emerging victorious despite the loss of one ship.

Alvise Longo had set out from Venice on 19 April but only with one galley, not the 16 ships first envisaged. Even so he was ordered to wait in the Aegean until Loredan arrived. Meanwhile, Emperor Constantine sent a scout ship to look for this relief fleet; a small vessel with a crew of 12 volunteers dressed as Turks and flying an Ottoman flag slipping out of Constantinople on 3 April. They saw no sign of help outside the Dardanelles and their report on 23 May threw Constantine into despair. For his part, Sultan Mehmet was worried that a fleet would, indeed, arrive from the west, and according to Giacomo Tedaldi, the nine galleys and 20 other ships which eventually assembled at Negroponte would have been enough to save Constantinople even if it had arrived a day before the city fell – but it did not.

THE OTTOMAN BLOCKADE AND SIEGE OF CONSTANTINOPLE, 2 APRIL–29 MAY 1453

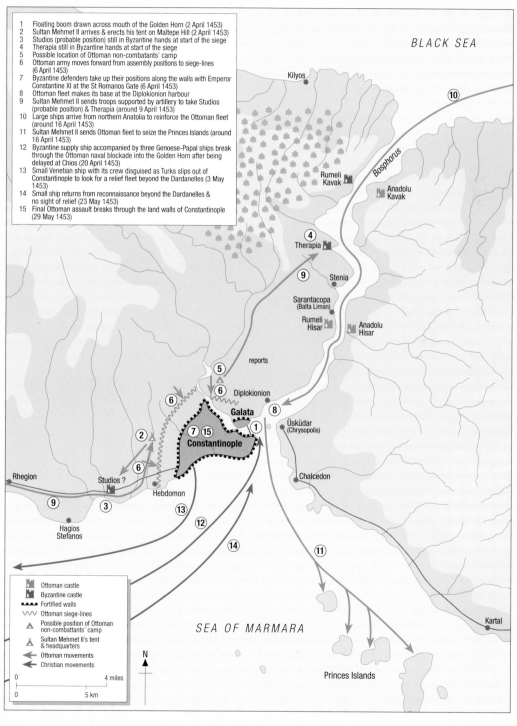

1   Floating boom drawn across mouth of the Golden Horn (2 April 1453)
2   Sultan Mehmet II arrives & erects his tent on Maltepe Hill (2 April 1453)
3   Studios (probable position) still in Byzantine hands at start of the siege
4   Therapia still in Byzantine hands at start of the siege
5   Possible location of Ottoman non-combatants' camp
6   Ottoman army moves forward from assembly positions to siege-lines
     (6 April 1453)
7   Byzantine defenders take up their positions along the walls with Emperor
     Constantine XI at the St Romanos Gate (6 April 1453)
8   Ottoman fleet makes its base at the Diplokionion harbour
9   Sultan Mehmet II sends troops supported by artillery to take Studios
     (probable position) & Therapia (around 9 April 1453)
10   Large ships arrive from northern Anatolia to reinforce the Ottoman fleet
     (around 16 April 1453)
11   Sultan Mehmet II sends Ottoman fleet to seize the Princes Islands (around
     16 April 1453)
12   Byzantine supply ship accompanied by three Genoese-Papal ships break
     through the Ottoman naval blockade into the Golden Horn after being
     delayed at Chios (20 April 1453)
13   Small Venetian ship with its crew disguised as Turks slips out of
     Constantinople to look for a relief fleet beyond the Dardanelles (3 May
     1453)
14   Small ship returns from reconnaissance beyond the Dardanelles &
     no sight of relief (23 May 1453)
15   Final Ottoman assault breaks through the land walls of Constantinople
     (29 May 1453)

BLACK SEA

Kilyos

Bosphorus

Rumeli Kavak

Anadolu Kavak

Therapia

Stenia

Sarantacopa
(Balta Liman)

Rumeli Hisar

Anadolu Hisar

reports

Diplokionion

Galata

Üsküdar
(Chrysopolis)

Constantinople

Rhegion

Studios ?

Hebdomon

Chalcedon

Hagios Stefanos

Kartal

SEA OF MARMARA

Princes Islands

Ottoman castle
Byzantine castle
Fortified walls
Ottoman siege-lines
Possible position of Ottoman
non-combatants' camp
Sultan Mehmet II's tent
& headquarters
Ottoman movements
Christian movements

N

0   4 miles
0   5 km

On 3 May the defenders placed guns on the Golden Horn walls, hoping to drive back the Ottoman ships. More dramatic was the impact of Sultan Mehmet's newly devised long-range mortar, which opened fire on 5 May. At first its aim was inaccurate, but according to Kritivoulos: 'They fired again and this stone went to an immense height and came down with a tremendous crash and velocity, striking the galley in the centre...' The victim was an apparently neutral Genoese merchant ship moored close to Galata. It sank immediately.

Continued skirmishing in the Golden Horn eventually forced all the Christian ships except those guarding the boom to withdraw into the small Prosphorianus harbour, while their crews were sent to defend the Blachernae area. The boom itself remained a problem for the Ottoman fleet, which made unsuccessful attacks on 16–17 and 21 May. At the same time Ottoman engineers constructed a pontoon bridge further up the Golden Horn substantial enough to carry wagons and artillery. A Byzantine attempt to destroy this bridge with Greek fire failed, and this new link between Ottoman forces on each side of the Horn proved very useful.

The bombardment of the land-walls continued, and on 2 May the mighty Basiliske was returned to its original position. On the 6th additional guns concentrated in batteries facing the St Romanos Gate sector made another breach. This was enlarged on the 7th, but was still only 10ft (3m) wide and an Ottoman assault the following night failed. This seems to have been the occasion when, according to Alexander Ypsilanti using Balkan and Turkish sources, Ottoman soldiers under Murad Pasha seemed likely to break through until a Greek nobleman named Rhangabe cut off Murad's leg before himself falling. A general rout of the Byzantine defenders seemed possible until Giustiniani and the voyvode Theodore joined in, followed by Emperor Constantine, Loukas Notaras and the Eparch Nicholas.

Between 8 and 11 May a new breach was made near the Kaligaria Gate, followed by an evening assault on the 12th which penetrated the Blachernae Palace before being driven back. The Ottoman artillery was moved again, many pieces going to the St Romanos Gate sector, which looked the most promising. Nothing is heard of the stone-throwing mangonels, which were probably ineffective, but the Ottoman army did start to undermine the land-walls. Most of the miners were Serbians sent by the Serbian Despot and placed under Zaganos Pasha. Their first mine was towards the Charisian Gate, but this was in the Lycus Valley and the ground proved unsuitable, so the miners tried again, this time aiming for the Blachernae wall near the Kaligarian Gate. A Byzantine countermine, excavated under the direction of Johannes Grant broke into the Serbian shaft on 16 May and further Ottoman mining efforts were defeated on 21 May, some flooded, some smoked out. On 23 May several miners and an Ottoman officer were captured underground. Under torture the officer revealed the location of the remaining mines and by 25 May all had been destroyed. Zaganos Pasha also had some large wooden siege towers constructed. They were not mobile, but served as strongpoints and cover. One was blown up with barrels of gunpowder during a sudden sortie on the night of 18/19 May, and after others were destroyed by various means the rest were dismantled.

For their part, the defenders found it increasingly difficult to plug breaches in the Lycus Valley sector once the fosse had been largely filled. Instead, they erected stockades of rubble, earth and timber within the gaps. It was also increasingly difficult to launch sorties because the shattered gates made the defenders too visible. The Kerkoporta Postern was reopened, however, and used in successful flank attacks, mostly by cavalry under the Bocchiardi brothers, when Ottoman infantry attacked the northern sector.

Nevertheless, morale was declining inside Constantinople with increasing tension between Italian and Greek defenders. Worse still, the Hodegetria, the holiest icon in Constantinople, slipped from its platform while being carried in procession around the city. Next day, probably 12 May, an unseasonable fog shrouded the city and a strange effect of light hovered around the cathedral of Hagia Sophia, causing concern in both camps. Muslim leaders declared that it was the Light of the True Faith which would soon shine within the ancient building. Some of the emperor's advisers suggested he leave and continue the struggle

The road from Edirne to Constantinople (Istanbul) ran along the Marmara coast after reaching the shore west of Selymbria (Silivri). It then had to cross two inlets which reached deep inland: this one at Büyükçekmece, and a second at Küç Çekmece. Another inland route via Vize was probably unsuitable for the Ottoman army's great cannon. (David Nicolle)

DEFEAT OF THE OTTOMAN-SERBIAN MINERS UNDERGROUND, 16 MAY

The underground struggle between Serbian miners and Byzantine miners is one of the least-known aspects of the siege of Constantinople. The Serbs and their Ottoman officers had been trying to undermine the single 12th-century wall around Blachernae, but the defenders broke into all their mines, smoking or flooding out the enemy. On at least one occasion the opposing miners fought hand-to-hand beneath the earth. (Christa Hook © Osprey Publishing Ltd)

elsewhere. Mehmet II now sent a final embassy into Constantinople, led by his brother-in-law Isfendiyaroglu Ismail Bey, the vassal ruler of Kastamonu and Sinop who had friends amongst the Byzantine ruling élite. He presented the Ottoman terms: the emperor must retire to Morea in southern Greece and the city must be handed over to Ottoman rule. But Constantine XI, according to later chroniclers, replied: 'God forbid that I should live as an Emperor without an Empire. As my city falls, I will fall with it. Whosoever wishes to escape, let him save himself if he can, and whoever is ready to face death, let him follow me.' In fact the Venetian fleet had left port and there were rumours that the Hungarians were preparing to march, which may have been why the emperor refused the sultan's terms.

Battle between Byzantines and Turks on the so-called Trebizond Cassone, made in Florence in the mid-15th century. The two sides are almost identical except for the tall caps and flat-topped heraldic shields of the Byzantines. (Metropolitan Museum, New York)

THE FALL OF THE CITY

On 26 May Sultan Mehmet called a council of war. Çandarli Halil still argued in favour of a compromise and emphasized the continuing danger from the West, but Zaganos Pasha insisted that this time the Ottomans' western foes would not unite. He also pointed out that Mehmet's hero, Alexander the Great, had conquered half the world when still a young man. So Mehmet sent Zaganos Pasha to sound out the opinions of the men, perhaps knowing full well what answer he would bring. The following day Mehmet toured the army, while heralds announced a final assault by land and sea on 29 May. Celebration bonfires were lit and from 26 May there was continuous feasting in the Ottoman camp. Criers announced that the first man on to the wall of Constantinople would be rewarded with high rank, and religious leaders told the soldiers about the famous Companion of the Prophet Mohammed, Abu Ayyub (Eyüp in Turkish), who had died during the first Arab-Islamic attack upon Constantinople in 672. In fact, the defenders saw so many torches that some thought the enemy were burning their tents before retreating. At midnight all lights were extinguished and work ceased. The defenders, however, spent the night repairing and strengthening breaches in the wall. Giustiniani Longo also sent a message to Loukas Notaras, requesting his reserve of artillery. Notaras refused, Longo accused him of treachery and they almost came to blows until the emperor intervened.

The following day was dedicated to rest in the siege lines while Sultan Mehmet visited every unit including the fleet. Final orders were sent to the Ottoman

The interior of one of the few relatively accessible original chambers in a tower of the inner wall. These structures were, however, frequently repaired and in many cases modernized during their long history. (David Nicolle)

commanders. Admiral Hamza Bey was to spread his ships around the sea-walls and erect scaling ladders where possible. Zaganos Pasha was to send men to help the ships in the Golden Horn while the rest crossed the pontoon bridge to assist the attack upon Blachernae. Karaca Pasha and the Rumelians would be on their right as far as the Gate of Charisius. Ishak Pasha and Mahmud Pasha with the Anatolians would attack between the Gate of St Romanos and the Marmara shore, massing around the Third Military Gate. Sultan Mehmet, Çandarli Halil and Saruja Pasha would direct the main attack in the Lycus Valley.

Late that afternoon as the setting sun shone in the defenders' eyes, the Ottomans began to fill the fosse while the artillery was brought as close as possible. The Ottoman ships in the Golden Horn spaced themselves between the Xyloporta and Horaia Gate, while those outside the boom spread more widely as far as the Langa harbour. It began to rain but work continued until around 1.30 in the morning of 29 May.

The defenders had also been rearranged to some extent. Manuel of Genoa, with 200 archers and crossbowmen, guarded districts around the Golden Gate and Studion; the scholar Theophilos Palaiologos commanded forces south of the Pege

Gate, while Giovanni Giustiniani Longo with 400 Italians and the bulk of the Byzantine troops was responsible for the most threatened sector around the Gate of St Romanos. The Myriandrion area went to the brothers Antonio, Paolo and Troilo Bocchiardi. Girolamo Minotto was placed in command of the Blachernae Palace area where Theodorus from Karyston, described in Greek sources as 'the best archer on earth', and Johannes Grant, 'an able military engineer', defended the Kaligaria Gate. Archbishop Leonard of Chios and a certain Hieronymus guarded the Xyloporta. Cardinal Isidore's men probably defended the walls to the right of the Xyloporta. Loukas Notaras took charge of the Petrion district as far as the Gate of St Theodosia, while 500 archers and hand-gunners manned walls facing the Golden Horn. Gabriele Trevisan commanded 50 soldiers who guarded the central section of Golden Horn walls, while the crews of Cretan ships manned those around the Horaia Gate, probably under Trevisan's command. Antonio Diedo retained command of the ships. The Catalan consul, Père Julia, defended the Bucoleon district as far as the Contoscalion. Prince Orhan was still stationed near the Langa harbour, while Jacopo Contarini's men defended the sea-walls of the Langa harbour and Psamathia.

Demetrios Kantakouzenos, with his son-in-law Nikephoros Palaiologos and others, took up position at the Church of the Holy Apostles with reinforcements, while the emperor made tours of inspection to boost morale. Monks and clergy conducted constant religious services, and led processions within Constantinople and around its walls, quarrels apparently being forgotten as Orthodox and Latin Christians joined in prayer in Hagia Sophia.

About three hours before dawn on 29 May there was a ripple of fire from the Ottoman artillery, and Ottoman irregulars swept forward led, according to Alexander Ypsilanti, by Mustafa Pasha. The main attack focused around the battered Gate of St Romanos, where Giustiniani Longo had taken 3,000 troops to the outer wall. Despite terrible casualties, few Ottoman volunteers retreated until, after two hours of fighting, Sultan Mehmet ordered a withdrawal. Ottoman ships similarly attempted to get close enough to erect scaling ladders, but generally failed.

After another artillery bombardment it was the turn of the provincial troops. They included Anatolian troops in fine armour who attacked the St Romanos Gate area at the centre. They marched forward carrying torches in the pre-dawn gloom, but were hampered by the narrowness of the breaches in Constantinople's walls. More disciplined than the irregulars, they occasionally pulled back to allow their artillery to fire, and during one such bombardment a section of defensive stockade was brought down. Three hundred Anatolians immediately charged through the gap but were driven off. Elsewhere fighting was particularly intense at the Blachernae walls. Alexander Ypsilanti again adds colourful details, stating that the Beylerbeyi of Anatolia sent five of his tallest soldiers against the breaches where they were met by the protostrator Giustiniani Longo and his 'sons' or the 'three

One of the earliest paintings of the Ottoman conquest of Constantinople is on the outside of a monastery church in Moldavia, in northern Rumania. It was made in the early 16th century. In the foreground a Christian horseman, perhaps representing King Stephen the Great of Moldavia, symbolically knocks a Turk from his horse. (Photo David Nicolle, monastery of Moldavita)

brother-sons of boyars', probably meaning the Bocchiardi brothers. This second assault continued until an hour before dawn when it was called off.

Sultan Mehmet now had only one fresh corps – his own palace regiments including the Janissaries. According to Ypsilanti, uncorroborated by any other known source, the 3,000 Janissaries were led by Baltaoglu as they attacked the main breach near the St Romanos Gate. All sources agree that these Janissaries advanced with terrifying discipline, moving slowly and without noise or music, while Sultan Mehmet accompanied them as far as the edge of the fosse. This third phase of fighting lasted an hour before some Janissaries on the left found that the Porta Xylokerkou had not been properly closed after the last sortie. About 50 soldiers broke in, rushed up the internal stairs and raised their banner on the battlements. They were nevertheless cut off and were in danger of extermination when the Ottomans had a stroke of luck which their discipline and command structure enabled them to exploit fully.

Giovanni Giustiniani Longo was on one of the wooden ramparts in the breach when he was struck by a bullet. This went through the back of his arm into his cuirass, probably through the arm-hole – a mortal wound though none yet realized it – and he withdrew to the rear. The Emperor Constantine was nearby and called out: 'My brother, fight bravely. Do not forsake us in our distress. The salvation of the City depends on you. Return to your post. Where are you going?' Giustiniani simply replied: 'Where God himself will lead these Turks.' When Giustiniani's men saw him leave, they thought he was running away. Panic spread, spurred on by the sight of an Ottoman banner on the wall to the north; and those outside the main walls rushed back in an attempt to retreat through the breaches.

Grand Duke Demetrios and St Nestor on a wall painting made in 1483. The Grand Duke, on the right, is dressed as a member of the last Byzantine military aristocracy. (Old Katholikon of the Great Meteoreon, Meteora)

Precisely what happened next is obscured by legend. Sultan Mehmet and Zaganos Pasha are both credited with seeing the confusion and sending a unit of Janissaries, led by another man of giant stature named Hasan of Ulubad, to seize the wall. Hasan reached the top of the breach but was felled by a stone. Seventeen of his 30 comrades were also slain but the remainder stood firm until other soldiers joined them.

Janissaries now took the inner wall near the St Romanos Gate and by appearing behind the defenders added still further to their panic. Word now spread that the Ottomans had broken in via the harbour, which may or may not have been true. The time was about four o'clock in the morning and dawn was breaking as yet more Ottoman banners appeared on the Blachernae walls. The Bocchiardi brothers cut their way back to their ships but Minotto and most of the Venetians were captured. According to Doukas, the defenders of the Golden Horn wall escaped over the wall while Ottoman sailors swarmed in the opposite direction.

The defence now collapsed. Foreigners tried to reach their ships in the Golden Horn while local Greek militiamen hurried to defend their own homes. Many defenders in the Lycus Valley were captured. The Studion and Psamathia quarters surrendered to the first proper Ottoman troops who appeared, and so retained their churches undamaged. The Catalans below the Old Palace were all killed or captured, which suggests they were cut off when Ottoman sailors broke through the Plataea and Horaia gates. Prince Orhan tried to escape disguised as a monk but was captured, pushed into the hold of a ship with other prisoners, and was later recognized and executed. Loukas Notaras was apparently a prisoner in the same ship, but was taken to Mehmet alive.

Giustiniani Longo was having his wounds dressed when news of the collapse arrived, so he recalled his men by trumpet. Cardinal Isidore disguised himself as a slave and escaped to Galata. Alvise Diedo crossed to Galata to discuss the situation and the Genoese authorities tried to arrest him, but so many Genoese sailors wanted to escape home that they forced their leaders to reopen the gates. Two sailors cut the floating boom and many Christian ships escaped under the command of Diedo. Others sailed out later in the day, including one carrying Giustiniani Longo, who died on his way home. Those ships which remained were captured by Hamza Bey, who with the crews still under his command led some galleys through the now broken boom into the Golden Horn. Cretan sailors manning three towers near the Horaia Gate held out until the early afternoon, refusing to surrender until the ships had escaped. Sultan Mehmet was so impressed by their dedication that he allowed them to return to their own ships and to sail away unhindered. Their captains were Sguros, Antonios Hyalinas and Philomates.

There are two basic versions of the death of the Emperor Constantine XI. One maintains that he and his companions charged into the fray as Ottoman soldiers poured through the main breach near the St Romanos Gate. Constantine supposedly shouted: 'Is there no Christian here who will take my head?' before being struck in the face and back. A different version is recounted by Tursun Bey and Ibn Kemal. This suggests that a band of naval azaps had dressed themselves as Janissaries so that they could enter the city after Mehmet issued his order preventing any but authorized units going beyond the main wall. They then came across the emperor near the Golden Gate and killed him before realising who he was. Perhaps Constantine was heading towards a tiny harbour just inside the point where the Sea of Marmara walls joined the land-walls, looking for a boat to take him to the Despotate of Morea.

A militia formed from the ordinary citizens of Constantinople and perhaps peasants who had fled from the surrounding countryside fought alongside professional soldiers in the final defence of the city. Such armed peasants and shepherds are shown in late 15th-century wall paintings in northern Greece. (Old Katholikon of the Great Meteoreon, Meteora)

THE DEATH OF EMPEROR CONSTANTINE XI

The final moments of the last Emperor of Byzantium are shrouded in legend. The most 'heroic' version has him charging bare-headed into the breach, seeking death once he knew that Constantinople was lost and calling out: 'Is there no Christian here who will take my head?' Another version maintains that he was cut down while trying to escape, perhaps to a tiny harbour in the south-western corner of the city. He is shown here to the left of the picture, raising his sword in defiance as a Turk prepares to strike him from behind. (Christa Hook © Osprey Publishing Ltd)

It is clear that some areas inside Constantinople resisted the first looters before surrendering to regular troops who were sent into the city while the bulk of the army remained outside. Mehmet's soldiers now advanced methodically, taking control and protecting each quarter from looters. Nevertheless, sailors or marines did enter via the other walls, looting Constantinople on a massive scale before regular troops forcibly stopped them. The rich Orthodox churches and monasteries suffered worst, but the survival of the Church of the Holy Apostles, despite being on the main road to the centre of the city, suggests that the sultan intended to keep it as the main Orthodox church while converting Hagia Sophia into Constantinople's greatest mosque. In fact the ordinary people were treated better by their Ottoman conquerors than their ancestors had been by Crusaders back in 1204; only about 4,000 Greeks died in the siege. Many members of the élite fled into Hagia Sophia, apparently believing an ancient prophecy that the infidels would turn tail at the last minute and be pursued back beyond Persia. Instead, Ottoman looters broke down the doors and dragged the people off for ransom.

The lower part of this fresco covering the exterior of the church of Humor Monastery in Romania includes a depiction of the fall of Constantinople in 1453. (©2003 Topham Picturepoint)

The Gate of Charisius, now called the Edirne Gate, has been accurately restored. This was where Sultan Mehmet II made his ceremonial entry into Constantinople, and it is still of great significance to the Turks. (David Nicolle)

The sultan himself remained outside the land-walls until about noon on 29 May, when he finally rode to Hagia Sophia. There he stopped further damage, had the venerable building converted into a mosque, then joined other worshippers in afternoon prayers. According to Tursun Bey, Mehmet went outside the dome to survey the decrepit state of Constantinople and quote a verse by the Persian poet Firdawsi: 'The spider serves as gate-keeper in Khusrau's hall, the owl plays his music in the palace of Afrasiyab.' Later that afternoon Loukas Notaras was brought before the sultan and apparently reported that the Grand Vizier, Çandarli Halil, had been encouraging the defenders to resist during the course of the siege. In return Mehmet promised to place the old man at the head of the city's civil administration. Mehmet also had a list of captured officials drawn up and personally paid their ransoms.

On 30 May Sultan Mehmet took the opportunity of removing his independent-minded Grand Vizier, Çandarli Halil. He was replaced by the ultra-loyal Zaganos Pasha, who next day negotiated the surrender of Galata. On 1 June the outlying castles of Silivri and Epibatos surrendered peacefully. Mehmet also ordered all looting to stop and sent his troops back outside the walls. The siege was concluded.

AFTERMATH AND RECKONING

ESCAPE, RANSOM OR EXECUTION

On 5 June, long before he heard the dreadful news, the Pope finally agreed to pay the Venetian Senate 14,000 ducats to hire and crew five galleys for four months. The Venetian galleys, already on their way to Constantinople, were waiting at Chios for a suitable wind. There they heard of the fall of Constantinople from some Genoese ships which had escaped. The Venetian fleet under Loredan similarly stopped at Negroponte when it heard the news. In Constantinople itself, Girolomo Minotto and his sons were executed for fighting on after the city had surrendered. Loukas Notaras was also executed five days after the fall, largely because the Ottoman ruling élite distrusted all Byzantine officials and wanted them removed.

Mehmet probably left Constantinople on 18 June, arriving back in Edirne on the 21st. Çandarli Halil was now imprisoned, perhaps as the result of rumours about his loyalty, and was executed 40 days after the submission of the Gattilusi-ruled coastal enclave of Ainos (now Enez), in late August or early September. Senior Byzantine and Italian captives were similarly taken back to Edirne, though Loukas Notaras' younger son soon escaped to join his sisters in Italy. Zaganos Pasha had meanwhile cultivated good relations with the Italians by paying the ransoms of 47 senior captives at 1,000 to 2,000 ducats each. Jacopo Contarini cost him 7,000 but all 29 Venetian noblemen were ransomed within the year. According to a Senate report, 40 noblemen and over 500 other Venetian citizens died during the siege. Venice looked after its own and, as was normal, the Senate voted pensions for the families of those killed and damages for those who had lost property. It cost the massive sum of 200,000 ducats. At the same time the Senate was informed that the Emperor Constantine owed Venice 17,163 *hyperpyra* when he died.

A MULTI-CULTURAL EMPIRE

The impact of the conquest upon the Ottoman Empire was profound and affected almost every area of life, from culture to politics, economics to military affairs. The ghaza, or war, with neighbouring Christian states soon focused more upon the Ottoman sultan's actions rather than upon the autonomous, often unorthodox frontier heroes of earlier days. Sultan Mehmet II concentrated his attention upon the reconstruction of his new capital. The walls were repaired and Constantinople

was repopulated with Christian Greeks, Muslim Turks and others. Some were encouraged by tax privileges, but many were forced to settle in the largely empty city. This rapid population growth led to food shortages, which in turn led first to the conquest of grain-producing regions north of the Black Sea.

Naturally, the conquest of the city was followed by a substantial building programme, which produced a new palace, a remarkable hospital with students and medical staff, a large cultural complex, two sets of barracks for the Janissaries, and a Tophane gun foundry outside Galata. Sultan Mehmet wanted to make Constantinople a multi-faith centre for all 'peoples of the Book', Muslims, Christians and Jews alike. This grand imperial statement created a crossroads where the cultures of East and West, Europe and Asia, met and mingled. A new Ottoman Constantinople, or Istanbul as it was named by the Turks, flourished until the tragic nationalism of the 19th century culminated in a massive separation of populations in the early 20th century. Galata, on the other side of the Golden Horn, remained western European in population and culture. Only a few years after the conquest, the Turkish historian, Tursun Bey, could write: 'How curious is this city of Istanbul. For one copper coin one can be rowed from Rum-eli into Frankistan,' meaning that a cheap ferry ride could take a person from cosmopolitan Istanbul to still largely Italian Galata.

Furthermore, Sultan Mehmet II declared himself to be the new Qaysar or Caesar, the legitimate heir to the Roman and Byzantine empires with a claim to territory far beyond the Ottoman Empire's existing frontier. This was widely accepted, not only by the sultan's Turkish and Muslim subjects, but also by Greek scholars such as George of Trebizond, who wrote to Mehmet in 1466: 'No one doubts that you are the Emperor of the Romans. Whoever is legally master of the capital of the Empire is the Emperor and Constantinople is the capital of the Roman Empire.'

A SHOCK FOR CHRISTENDOM

The conquest of Constantinople cut Italian trade through the Dardanelles and Bosphorus to the Crimea. As early as 28 November 1453, the Genoese consul in Kaffa reported that extreme measures would be needed if his outpost was not to be entirely deserted, and there was soon a substantial emigration from all the Genoese Black Sea colonies. Many Armenians moved to the Ukraine or Poland, some Italian craftsmen went as far as Moscow, and within 20 or so years, all Genoa's possessions beyond the Bosphorus had been lost to the Ottomans.

The impact of the fall of Constantinople on the Byzantine world was, of course, catastrophic and many Orthodox Christians blamed it on the disloyalty of the Byzantine military élite. Conversion to Islam was never as widespread in Greek-speaking communities as among Slavs and Albanians, but it became quite

OPPOSITE
The cathedral of Hagia Sophia, now the Aya Sofia Mosque, was in many ways the symbol of Byzantine Constantinople. Not surprisingly Mehmet came here immediately after ceremonially entering the city. (akg-images/Erich Lessing)

The narrow and twisting Golden Horn seen from the Mosque of Eyüp. The northern end of the land-walls, around the Blachernae Palace, would have come down to the water next to the second spit of land protruding from the right. (David Nicolle)

common in what had been the Byzantine aristocracy. Conversion was even commonplace among the clergy, whose faith may have been shaken by what many saw as 'divine punishment'. In the immediate aftermath of the fall of Constantinople, however, much of the Byzantine élite fled; some to the tiny principality of Theodore Mangoup in the Crimea, some to Byzantine Trebizond, others to Morea. Morea, however, was torn apart by internal dissension and rebellion between and against the co-despots, and between Greeks and Albanians.

In October 1454 Mehmet II sent Turahan Bey to help the despots Thomas and Demetrios, but as soon as they left, civil war flared up. In 1460 the Despotate of Morea was finally incorporated directly into the Ottoman Empire, the capital, Mistra, falling exactly seven years after Constantinople, on 29 May 1460.

With the exception of Venetian enclaves that the Ottomans were not yet strong enough to take, the Latin possessions in Greece also fell, Athens being given special privileges because of Mehmet II's interest in ancient Greek civilization. Some of the Genoese outposts in the Aegean lasted longer, Ainos remaining under Gattilusi rule. Palamedes Gattilusi was also entrusted with the island of Imroz, while the island of Lemnos was allocated to Dorino I Gattilusi, the lord of Mytilini, who ruled under Ottoman suzerainty and paid an annual tribute. In 1460 Ainos was given to the deposed co-Despot of Morea, Demetrios. Elsewhere, the Gattilusio family retained Lesbos, under Ottoman suzerainty, until 1462, while a Genoese Maona or 'merchant commune' held the island of Chios until 1566, when the sultan handed it over to the Jewish Duke Joseph Nasi of Naxos.

The siege of Constantinople, as painted on the outside of the church in the Moldavian monastery of Moldovita. Made over half a century after the events, it includes many of the facts and legends associated with the fall of the Byzantine capital. (Photo David Nicolle, monastery church, Moldovita)

Following the fall of Constantinople a series of campaigns confirmed Ottoman domination of the Balkans, although a clash with Hungary led to an Ottoman reverse outside Belgrade in 1456. Elsewhere, George Kastriotes (Iskander Beg or Skanderbeg) continued to resist the Ottomans in Albania until 1468. Wallachia moved more firmly beneath Ottoman suzerainty and even Moldavia was theoretically a tributary of the sultan after 1456. The following year Stefan the Great came to the throne of Moldavia, and spent much of his reign competing with the Ottomans for domination over Wallachia.

Further west the Ottoman conquest of Constantinople caused deep shock. Renaissance humanists were appalled that Greece now lay under Turkish domination, as the scholar Aeneas Sylvius Piccolomini (the future Pope Pius II) wrote: 'Here is a second death for Homer and for Plato too … Now Mohammed reigns amongst us. Now the Turk hangs over our very heads.' Even though some writers pointed out that the Ottomans were good and honest people, horrendous propaganda soon led to the popular image of 'the Terrible Turk'. Ottoman victories were seen as unnatural, along with the Turks' supposedly blind obedience to their officers. Nevertheless, most Europeans still felt secure behind the powerful Catholic kingdom of Hungary, and the fate of the Orthodox Christians was regarded as God's punishment for their weakness and sin. Only when Hungary collapsed in the early 16th century did the rest of Europe fully awake to the danger from the East.

APPENDIX: THE BATTLEFIELD TODAY

Most of the action during the siege of Constantinople took place in one of today's leading tourist destinations, Istanbul. This superb city has abundant hotels in all categories, though camping facilities are distant from the centre. Transport in the form of Istanbul's efficient water buses is something not to be missed. Boats also link Istanbul with the Asiatic shore, practically every village along the Bosphorus and various places on the Sea of Marmara. Many of the buildings which existed in 1453 still survive, including most of the land-walls, the Marmara walls and some fragments of the Golden Horn walls. But the area within these defences is now almost filled with bustling residential and business quarters. Only in a few areas, inside the southern part of the land-walls is there still open land. Suburbs extend far beyond the medieval walls, while Galata has been swallowed by an urban sprawl which stretches far up the Bosphorus. Fortunately, a large part of the area where the Ottoman army established its siege lines remains open, except for the pleasant suburb of Eyüp outside the Blachernae walls.

In contrast to the tourist magnet of Istanbul, eastern Thrace is strangely neglected. The previous Ottoman capital of Edirne, where Sultan Mehmet II prepared his campaign, lies close to the Bulgarian and Greek frontiers. It has adequate hotels and retains the quiet charm which overcrowded Istanbul has largely lost. The Marmara coast, which was still in Byzantine hands at the start of the campaign, includes several seaside resorts, whereas the Black Sea coast of Thrace is virtually undeveloped, lacking even a coastal road. This area was, of course, a vulnerable frontier zone in Cold War days, but north of the border the Bulgarians have exploited the tourist potential of their coast, including towns that were Byzantine in 1453.

VISITING THE WALLS

The entire length of the walls of Constantinople is readily and freely accessible to any visitor to modern Istanbul, yet few people exercise the option, which is a great pity. The walls receive cursory mention in most guidebooks, and no tour operator in Istanbul appears to offer a visit as part of their wares. There are several reasons for this. First, the major parts of the lengths of the walls are nowhere near the other main tourist sights of Istanbul. The Yedikule fortress, which incorporates the Golden Gate, is the one exception. Second, they are difficult to get to by public transport except for the Topkapi Gate area, which can be reached by the modern tramway from Eminonu. Unfortunately this is one of the least attractive parts of the wall in either direction. To the south of the Topkapi Gate the successive

underpasses of the motorway render the area adjacent to the wall remote, lonely and somewhat threatening. To the north lies the mesoteichion section, where the siege damage is most extensive and there is probably less to see than anywhere else. It also involves a walk beside the motorway. The third consideration militating against a visit is security. In spite of the attentions of the Istanbul government long stretches of the wall do not appear to provide personal safety. In some places they provide locations for itinerants, and no tourist would wish to venture near. In other places the walls pass through very unpleasant-looking areas of the city, where a visitor is regarded with suspicion. This unfortunately includes some of the best-restored sections of the wall.

The prospect of walking the entire length of the walls is therefore one that should not be undertaken lightly. However, it is possible to make select visits that should be sufficient to provide a flavour of the whole. For example, picnicking families frequent the area immediately adjacent to the Sea of Marmara on summer weekends. Here are the Marble Tower and the Gate of Christ, and although the walls end at the railway line it is perfectly possible to examine and enjoy this short stretch. Beyond the railway line lies the Yedikule fortress, which is open to the

Few tourists venture into the run-down region around Gül Camii, Mosque of the Rose, which incorporates an earlier Byzantine church. The steep slopes leading down to the Golden Horn were still densely populated in the mid-15th century. (David Nicolle)

public and well worth visiting for its own sake. As noted earlier, it incorporates the Golden Gate. From the Golden Gate the walls may be climbed, and one can walk along and around them for some considerable distance. A short walk along the walls to the north from the Golden Gate is very rewarding. Here the moat area is occupied by gardens growing vegetables, and there are several fine restored sections of wall. It also appears to be the safest area. There is a main road here, not a motorway. The visitor can easily examine the walls from all directions, and enjoy various shaped towers, interesting restored sections and some fine battle-damaged towers and walls. The area becomes less pleasant as one approaches the Topkapi Gate, and the damage to the mesoteichion section caused by the 1453 siege is quite striking. Unfortunately there is a motorway on one side of the walls and squalor on the other. The views get better beyond the Edirne Gate. The area of the Palace of the Porphyrogenitus, where the Theodosian walls end, is very interesting, and one may round off one's walk by making a rewarding visit to the recently landscaped area in the furthest northern point that incorporates the Blachernae Palace. It is easy to walk to the gate where the last emperor was seen alive for the last time in 1453, and to enjoy the new garden laid out in front of the corner of the wall.

The best view of the sea walls on the shore of the Sea of Marmara may be obtained below the Topkapi Palace. The distant view can only be seen from a ferry or a cruise ship. This sight of Constantinople, with its graceful towers and dramatic overall position, is one that has enchanted visitors for centuries, and sums up for anyone the reasons why such a precious jewel had to be defended by the finest walls in the world.

OPPOSITE
The Aya Sofia Mosque at sunset. (© 2005 Charles Walker/Topfoto)

SELECT BIBLIOGRAPHY

Angold, M., *The Byzantine Empire 1025–1204. A Political History* (London: Longman, 1984)

Babingen, F., *Mehmet the Conqueror and his Time* (Princeton, 1978)

Bakapoulos, A., 'Les Limites de l'Empire Byzantin depuis la fin du XIVe siècles jusqu'à sa chute (1453),' *Byzantinische Zeitschrift* (1962, vol.LV) pp.56–65

Barbaro, Nicolo (trs. J. R. Melville Jones), *Diary of the Siege of Constantinople* (New York, 1969)

Bartusis, M. C., *The Late Byzantine Army. Arms and Society, 1204–1453* (Philadelphia, 1992)

Browning, R., 'A Note on the Capture of Constantinople in 1453,' *Byzantion* (1952, vol.XXII) pp.379–387

Concasty, M.-L., 'Les Informations de Jacques Tedaldi sur le siège et la prise de Constaninople,' *Byzantion* (1954, vol.XXIV) pp.95–110

De Vries, K., 'Gunpowder Weapons at the Siege of Constantinople, 1453,' in Y. Lev (ed.), *War and Society in the Eastern Mediterranean, 7th–15th Centuries* (Leiden, 1996) pp.343–362

Dixon, Karen R. and Southern, Pat, *The Late Roman Army* (London, 1996)

Doukas (trs. H. J. Magoulias), *Decline and Fall of Byzantium to the Ottoman Turks* (Detroit, 1975).

Dujcev, I., 'La conquête turque et la prise de Constantinople dans la literature slave contemporaine,' *Byzantinoslavica* (1956, vol.XVII) pp.278–340

Dutu, A., and Cernovodeanu, C. (eds), *Dimitrie Cantemir, Historian of south-east European and Oriental civilizations* (Bucharest, 1973)

Elton, H., *Warfare in Roman Europe, A.D. 350–425* (Oxford, 1996)

Farmer, H. G., 'Turkish Artillery at the Fall of Constantinople,' *Transactions of the Glasgow University Oriental Society* (1929–33, vol.VI) pp.9–14

Foss, C., and Winfield, D., *Byzantine Fortifications; an Introduction* (Pretoria, 1986)

Geanakoplos, Deno John, *Byzantium: Church Society and Civilisation seen through contemporary eyes* (Chicago, 1984)

Haldon, J. F., *State, Army and Society in Byzantium. Approaches to Military, Social and Administrative History* (Aldershot, 1995)

Haldon, J., *Warfare, State and Society in the Byzantine World, 565–1204* (London, 1999)

Haldon, J. F., *Byzantium. A History* (Stroud, 2000)

Haldon, J., *The Byzantine Wars* (Stroud, 2001)

Harris, Jonathan, *Byzantium and the Crusades* (London, 2002)

Hearsey, John E. N., *City of Constantine 324–1453* (London, 1963)

Hess, A. C., 'The Evolution of the Ottoman Seaborne Empire in the Age of Oceanic Discoveries, 1453–1525,' *American Historical Review* (1969–70, vol.LXXV) pp.1892–1919

Housley, N. J., *The Later Crusades: from Lyons to Alcazar 1274–1580* (Oxford, 1992)

Inalcik, H., 'Mehmed the Conqueror (1432–1481) and his Time,' *Speculum* (1960, vol.XXXV) pp.408–427

Inalcik, H., *An Economic and Social History of the Ottoman Empire 1300–1914*, vol. I, 1300–1600 (London, 1996)

Inalcik, H., *The Ottoman Empire: The Classical Age 1300–1600* (London, 1973)

Iorga, N., 'Une source negligée de la prise Constantinople,' *Bulletin de la Section Historique* (Acad. Roumaine) (1927, vol.XIII) pp.59–68

Kaegi, W. E., Jr., *Byzantine Military Unrest 471–843. An Interpretation* (Amsterdam, 1981)

Kaegi, Walter, *Army, Society and Religion in Byzantium* (London, 1982)

Kaegi, Walter, *Heraclius Emperor of Byzantium* (Cambridge, 2002)

Káldy-Nagy, G., 'The First Centuries of the Ottoman Military Organization,' *Acta Orientalia Academiae Scientiarum Hungaricae* (1977, vol.XXX) pp.147–183

Kiel, M., 'A Note on the History of the Frontiers of the Byzantine Empire in the 15th century,' *Byzantinische Zeitschrift* (1973, vol.LXVI) pp.351–353

Langlois, V., 'Notice sur le sabre de Constantin XI, dernier empereur de Constantinople conservé à l'Armeria Reale de Turin,' *Revue Archeologique* (1857, vol.XUV/I) pp.292–294

Mango, Cyril, *Byzantine Architecture* (London, 1978)

Mango, Cyril, and Dagron, Gilbert, *Constantinople and its hinterland: Papers from the Twenty-seventh Spring Symposium of Byzantine Studies, Oxford April 1993* (Aldershot, 1995)

Mango, Cyril, *The Oxford History of Byzantium* (Oxford, 2002)

McGeer, Eric, *Sowing the Dragon's Teeth. Byzantine Warfare in the Tenth Century*, Dumbarton Oaks Studies XXXIII, (Washington DC, 1995)

Melville Jones, J. R. (trs.), *The Siege of Constantinople 1453: Seven Contemporary Accounts* (Amsterdam, 1972)

Mihailovic, K. (ed. and trs. B. Stolz), *Memoires of a Janissary* (Ann Arbor, 1975)

Mijatovich, C., *Constantine Palaeologus, The Last Emperor of the Greeks: 1448–1453: The Conquest of Constantinople by the Turks* (London, 1892)

Miller, T. S. and Nesbitt, J. S. (eds.), *Peace and War in Byzantium*, (Washington DC, 1995)

Needham, Joseph, *Science and Civilisation in China Volume 5 Chemistry and Chemical Technology Part 7: Military Technology; The Gunpowder Epic* (Cambridge, 1986)

Nicol, Donald, *The Last Centuries of Byzantium 1261–1453* (Cambridge, 1993)

Nicol, D. M., *The End of the Byzantine Empire* (London, 1979)

Nicol, D. M., *The Immortal Emperor* (London, 1992)

Nicolle, David, *Romano-Byzantine Armies 4th–9th Centuries* (Oxford, 1992)

Nicolle, D., *Medieval Warfare Source Book, 2. Christian Europe and its Neighbours* (London, 1996)

Norwich, John Julius, *Byzantium: The Apogee* (Harmondsworth, 1991)

Oikonomidès, N. (ed.), *Byzantium at War* (Athens, 1997)

Ostrogorsky, George, *History of the Byzantine State* (Oxford, 1980)

Ousterhout, Robert, *Master Builders of Byzantium* (New Jersey, 1999)

Paviot, J., *Genoa and the Turks: 1444 and 1453* (Genoa, 1988)

Pertusi, A., 'Le notizie sulla organizazione administrativa e militare dei Turchi nello 'strategicon adversum Turcos' di Lampo Birago (c.1453–1455),' in *Studi sul medioevo cristiano offerti a R. Morghen*, vol. II (Rome, 1974) pp.669–700

Philippides, M. (trs.), *Byzantium, Europe and the Early Ottoman Sultans, 1373–1513: An Anonymous Greek Chronicle of the Seventeenth Century* (Codex Barberinus Graecus 111) (New York, 1990)

Philippides, M. (trs.), *The Fall of the Byzantine Empire: A Chronicle by George Sphrantzes 1401–1477* (Amherst, 1980)

Pitcher, D. E., *An Historical Geography of the Ottoman Empire* (Leiden, 1972)

Rolland, M., *Le siège de Constantinople 1453* (1989)

Runciman, S., *The Fall of Constantinople 1453* (Cambridge, 1965)

Shaw, S., *History of the Ottoman Empire and Modern Turkey, vol. 1, 1280–1808* (Cambridge, 1976)

Stacton, D., *The World on the Last Day* (London, 1965)

Treadgold, Warren, *Byzantium and its army 284–1081* (California, 1995)

Tsangadas, B. C. P., *The Fortifications and Defence of Constantinople* (New York, 1980)

Turkova, H., 'Le Siège de Constantinople d'après le Seyahatname d'Evliya Celebi,' *Byzantinoslavica* (1953, vol.XIV) pp.1–13

Turnbull, Stephen, *The Ottoman Empire 1326–1699* (Oxford, 2003)

Turtledove, Harry, *The Chronicle of Theophanes* (Philadelphia, 1982)

Van Millingen, Alexander, *Byzantine Constantinople: The walls of the city and adjoining historical sites* (London, 1899)

Whitby, Michael, and Whitby, Mary, *Chronicon Paschale 284–628 AD* (Liverpool, 1989)

Whittow, Mark, *The Making of Orthodox Byzantium 600–1025* (London, 1996)

Wiliamson G. A. (trs.), *Procopius: The Secret History* (Harmondsworth, 1966)

INDEX